Invitation to
Dogmatic
Theology

A Canonical Approach

Paul C. McGlasson

Brazos Press
Grand Rapids, Michigan

Published by Brazos Press
a division of Baker Publishing Group
P.O. Box 6287, Grand Rapids, MI 49516-6287
www.brazospress.com

Printed in the United States of America

Scripture is taken from the New Revised Standard Version of the Bible, copyright 1989 by the Division of Christian Education of the National Council of the Churches of Christ in the USA. Used by permission.

Library of Congress Cataloging-in-Publication Data
McGlasson, Paul
    Invitation to dogmatic theology : a canonical approach / Paul C. McGlasson.
        p.   cm.
    Includes bibliographical references.
    ISBN 10: 1-58743-174-2 (pbk.)
    ISBN 978-1-58743-174-6 (pbk.)
    1. Theology, doctrinal. 2. Bible—Canonical criticism. I. Title.
    BT75.3.M33 2006
    230—dc22   2005037356

To my mother,
and to the memory of my father,
with gratitude.

Contents

Foreword

From the perspective of biblical studies, the last forty years have rightly been characterized as the "era of the canon." This is to say that from the 1960s to the end of the twentieth century and beyond, large sections of the biblical discipline in North America, Britain, and Europe have focused on issues related either directly or indirectly to the subject of canon. A variety of different reasons have evoked this interest (cf. *Pro Ecclesia*, XIV, 2005, 26–46). Moreover, it is impressive to see that both Catholic and Protestant scholars have been involved in intensive dialogue (cf. the massive volume of essays from the *Coloquium Biblicum* held in Leuven, Belgium, in 2001 entitled *The Biblical Canons*).

What is disappointing, however, is that in spite of the enormous learning reflected and the genuine advances achieved in the areas of philology, history-of-religions, text criticism, and sociology, the theological task of relating the biblical canon to Christian dogmatic theology has been virtually ignored. The irony of this omission lies in the fact that the very category of canon is a theological one. To pursue this critical dimension requires not only a rigorous and learned analysis of its subject matter, but also the central role in establishing a foundation from which to pursue the inner-logical coherence of the theological substance of the biblical witnesses in every aspect of the Christian faith. In the light of this present situation, it is a remarkable and joyful event that the Rev. Dr. Paul C. McGlasson has stepped into the breach and provided a masterful *Invitation to Dogmatic Theology* from a canonical perspective.

Even from a cursory perusal, the reader is made aware immediately that this volume reflects decades of disciplined scholarly research. Equally important is that the context for shaping his reflections has been his active pastoral ministry within a local congregation. The seamless merger between his rigorous academic analysis and his passionate proclamation of the gospel to a concrete audience characterizes this outstanding volume.

There are so many exciting features of McGlasson's book that only a brief selection can be highlighted. First, in his introduction he seeks immediately to define and carefully describe the discipline of dogmatic theology. "It is an intellectual discipline of the church of Jesus Christ, whose necessity is grounded in his call to preach the gospel to the world and to test the content of that preaching by his absolute authority." The guiding rule for critical reflection is that of faith seeking understanding, which is an enterprise aided by careful attention to the great theologians of the church extending from the church fathers, Schoolmen, and Reformers through the twentieth century. But the task is not a retrieval of the past since Christian orthodoxy is never a static substance, but a living challenge for each new generation of the church. "We in our time must turn directly to scripture itself, seeking to hear the living voice of Christ through the guidance of the Holy Spirit."

Second, when McGlasson next turns to his chapter on the authority of scripture, he states unequivocally that the community of faith in Jesus Christ is governed by the norm of Holy Scripture. Scripture is the source for our proclamation of the gospel since it is grounded in the sovereign rule of Christ over all creation and through its witness God's people are guided by the presence of the Spirit. Yet at this point McGlasson is not content merely to repeat the traditional formulations of the past, but in a highly sophisticated manner, fully conversant with all the current debates among biblical and historical scholars concerning the canon, he seeks to break out of the sterile controversies of the past. The pursuit of the continuing authority of the biblical text is not to deny the legitimate role of historical, critical tools that are necessary in the service of canonical analysis, but to make clear that the biblical witness is not locked in ancient history. Rather, the same God still speaks. McGlasson then reflects theologically on the shape and function of a written corpus that developed over a period of time as the tradents of the canon sought to chart the areas within which the church heard the living Word of God. Often decisions were made during times of greatest crises such as that evoked by the Gnostics, whose mythological speculations sought to distort the true image of Christ (cf. Irenaeus). In these chapters of his book biblical scholars should recognize the enormous contribution of the well-trained dogmatician who is able to bring a new measure of conceptual clarity to the subject of canon.

Third, there is another feature of this volume that extends through all of the chapters and serves as an illuminating road map to the history of theology, especially for those readers seeking guidance in the present struggles facing the church today. By using a device by which to delineate with great force the confessions of the church's faith in accordance with patterns of apostolic orthodoxy, McGlasson seeks to sketch the threats that continue to emerge throughout the church's history, both on the left and right of the theological spectrum. Thus, in the modern period Friedrich Schleiermacher and Paul Tillich often serve as representatives of liberalism's turn-to-the-subject that substitutes the individual religious self-consciousness as a medium of universal truth in place of scripture's christological focus. On the right, Charles Hodge and B. B. Warfield frequently illustrate conservative Fundamentalism's rationalistic defense of natural theology that seeks to ground the Christian faith on common, empirically supported "evidences" apart from faith.

Although McGlasson is unequivocal in his rejection of both these positions, his criticisms remain focused on the content of his disagreement and never degenerates into personal attacks or emotional rhetoric. For the modern period, there are cogent assessments of many of the leading contemporary theologians whose works are measured by McGlasson's appeals to the witness of scripture and to the creedal confessions that often constitute a broad consensus among Catholics, Protestants, and Orthodox. Although McGlasson freely recognizes areas of genuine tensions within the various Christian confessions, he attempts to be both fair and generous in his evaluations, often acknowledging a writer's sincere motivations even when judging his position inadequate or erroneous.

Finally, perhaps one of his most powerful sections is that on proclamation. A basic question of dogmatics is how Jesus Christ is known in the world today. The answer lies in the proclamation of the Word of God as the instrument by which the living Lord governs his church in every new age. After stating this conviction, McGlasson then attempts to probe deeply in exploring the full implications of preaching that he feels has been inadequately understood in both liberalism and evangelicalism. The threat of pietism frequently emerges on both the left and right, and McGlasson uses it to illustrate again his repeated comment that liberals and fundamentalists are children of the same Enlightenment father. In contrast, the great promise of true proclamation lies in the transformation of the church and the world when God's living Word fashions a new creation as a gracious divine gift.

To conclude, I can think of no modern volume that will better serve to introduce theological students and hard-pressed pastors into the full range of critical issues involved in serious reflection on Christian faith. Especially attractive is the joyful tone of his radiant confession of faith in a living and loving Lord.

Brevard S. Childs

Preface

The church's confession of the biblical canon is in a unique position with respect to the remaining contents of its confession. On the one hand, canon is the first article of the church's confession, both historically and theologically. Canon provides the comprehensive context for all theology. On the other hand, the church's confession of canon is itself an article of faith. To confess canon is already to take up the theme of dogmatic theology, which is the church's longstanding conversation concerning the substance of its faith. Canon is part of dogmatic theology; yet it is the first part and in some sense guides the whole. To reflect theologically upon canon is thus an introduction, or even better an invitation, to dogmatic theology. The present volume is an attempt to give a fresh assessment of the church's confession of canon and is likewise an invitation to dogmatic theology.

Even as I write these words I am profoundly conscious of the range of overwhelming creativity and devotion that has attended the field of dogmatic theology from the very beginning. Dogmatic theology goes back not a decade, nor a century, but now two millennia. One is astonished to see the stunning quality of reflection that has been produced, often in moments of great peril for the church at large and indeed for the individual theologian. For some theologians, the very act of writing such a work in faithfulness to Christ has brought personal insult and injury of the worst sort. And yet in every age of the church willing hands have undertaken the labor, willing minds have focused intently upon the problems and possibilities, and willing pens have sounded forth the beauty of divine truth in the language of the day. The great names of the discipline of dogmatic theology stand as giants, casting lengthy shadows over the history of the church: Irenaeus, Athanasius, Gregory of

Nazianzus, Augustine, John of Damascus, Anselm of Canterbury, Thomas Aquinas, Martin Luther, John Calvin, Karl Barth. Dogmatic theology is by definition an exercise in the communion of the saints.

The present endeavor brings together several strands of influence in my life. The first is the *Church Dogmatics* of Karl Barth. I discovered Barth while still an undergraduate and at that time began the exciting task of learning from him the rigorous discipline of faith seeking understanding. My doctoral dissertation on Barth expanded my knowledge somewhat, but it was only as I took up the task of writing dogmatics itself that I realized the full weight of debt that I owe. The light of the gospel that shines so brightly in the writings of the Reformers was all too quickly overshadowed by the rationalism and pietism of the modern period; but suddenly at the dawn of the twentieth century, the bright light of the gospel shone once again in all its radiant glory. Barth saw once again the connection between dogmatics and scripture and the relation of dogmatics to preaching. He wrote for the universal church and tested proclamation by the burning question of truth. His work begins a new era, though how that era will play out in the future is too soon to tell.

The second influence is the ethical writing of Dietrich Bonhoeffer, especially *The Cost of Discipleship*. Despite the sheer tragedy of his early martyrdom, there is no doubt that Bonhoeffer pointed the church at large in the right direction for the future of theological ethics. He insisted upon the close connection between ethics and dogmatics, in sharp contrast to the easy cultural Christianity of the social gospel then popular in North America and elsewhere. He likewise saw the connection between theological ethics and scripture, and his own exegesis stands out in the entire modern period for its stunning force of clarity and truth. Yet for all the radical quality of his understanding of obedience, he was also a thoroughly modern human being who loved the world and was deeply engaged in it. He understood the christological basis for ethics and lived his life in conformity to Christ, even unto death. Surely the fads and gimmicks of much contemporary "spirituality" must give way to a new engagement with the obedience of faith.

The third decisive influence is the biblical work of Brevard S. Childs. I attended Yale Divinity School primarily in order to learn directly from Childs, and my eager expectation was met by an even greater reality. It is now clear that the work of Childs on canon amounts to nothing less than a brilliant new vision of scripture without parallel in the history of the church, though deeply rooted in the church's tradition of reading scripture. Every theologian worthy of the name has turned directly to scripture as the one source for the knowledge of God. Where else does the church learn to know Jesus Christ? However, never before has the church been closer to the shape and subject matter of scripture than in Childs's work on canon. The confession of canon was the first and foundational creedal affirmation of the ancient church; yet not until Childs's work have the full implications of that confession been so crystal clear and inviting for reflection. Once again, a new era has begun. Theology can never again go back behind Childs when it wrestles with scripture, nor can it count as genuine Christian theology unless it sees with precision the full force of the vision he articulates. The future of dogmatic theology lies with realizing the connection of the discipline with the Bible, and that connection depends upon a firm theological grasp of the issue of canon. The confession of canon is an ontological necessity for dogmatic inquiry and the proper beginning of all valid theological reflection.

The final influence is my own experience of preaching. After several enjoyable years of teaching, I turned to the practice of parish ministry. Words that I had learned by heart from youth suddenly took on new life for me, as I realized that they form the very existence of ordinary Christians everywhere. I do not believe that fresh work in the field of dogmatic theology requires a sustained practice of preaching in the background. Nevertheless, if one takes the broad view, there seems little doubt that the direct engagement with the witness of scripture that preaching requires on a regular basis surely contributes to the shaping of theological insight. Clearly the divorce of Bible and theology must be overcome; yet can it ever really be overcome apart from the challenge of proclamation? Is it not from orientation to the task of preaching that dogmatic theology derives the energy and concentration of its own proper substance? In the end, is not dogmatic theology itself a guide to proclamation; is it not an introduction to the scriptures for the special task of proclaiming the living Word of God in our contemporary world? It is my fervent hope that the present work will be useful in the training of a new generation of pastors for the Christian church, for without doubt that is the great need of the hour in the church today.

Despite the debt that the contemporary church owes to the church fathers, the Reformers, and the architects of a new theological direction in the twentieth century, dogmatic theology of the present cannot simply retreat into the past. Just as Protestant scholasticism failed, despite its best intentions, to encompass the electrifying power of Luther and Calvin, so too does a theology of retrieval fall short of the needs of proclamation in the contemporary world. We cannot discharge our present responsibility in the church simply by repeating the theology of previous generations. Christian orthodoxy is never a static substance but a living challenge for each new generation of the church. Instructed by the teachers of the church, we in our time must turn directly to scripture, seeking to hear the living voice of Christ through the guidance of the Holy Spirit. Only then is the gospel heard in our world today as the power of God for salvation to the whole creation.

I would like to express my deep gratitude to Brevard Childs and Rodney Clapp for their excellent advice concerning this volume, and to Ruth Goring for her skillful job of editing.

INTRODUCTION

The Discipline of Dogmatic Theology

The church of Jesus Christ lives by his commission to preach the gospel to all the nations of earth. Christ the risen Lord sends forth his disciples to baptize in God's triune name and to teach his commands, and promises his continuing presence. His commission is based upon his own supreme authority over all reality as exalted Lord of creation (Matt. 28:16–20). The very being of the church is grounded in the absolute authority of Christ. Our commission flows from his universal rule over the cosmos. All things in creation now serve his gracious purpose of love for the world. We are sent by him to proclaim the gospel to all corners of the creation. It is an astonishing commission; it is a marvelous task; it is a gleeful and wondrous calling. We are the heralds of his redemptive love to all humankind: to the poor and the brokenhearted, to the lost and afflicted, to the blind and the oppressed. We are responsible to him for the content of our words and deeds; we are accountable to him for our speech and action in the world. This responsibility is true everywhere in Christian witness, whether in care for the poor, the hymns that we sing, the pastoral care that we exercise, or the communal life that we celebrate. As a whole body, the universal church is accountable to its Head, by whom it lives and whom alone it serves. This responsibility is especially true, however, for the Christian ministry. Preaching the gospel is the ultimate fulfillment of the commission of Christ to the church. The ordained ministry of preaching shares therefore a special burden of responsibility for the content of its proclamation.

In his great treatise *On the Priesthood*, John Chrysostom describes with acute observation the existential situation of the preacher. According to

Chrysostom, the genuine preacher must avoid errors on both extremes of the theological spectrum, left and right: "The way of orthodoxy is narrow and hemmed in by threatening crags on either side, and there is no little fear lest when intending to strike at one enemy we should be wounded by the other."[1] The truth can be found only in the middle course that avoids the errors of the extreme on either side. There is need for constant vigilance in the preparation and delivery of truthful sermons. Profound concern is to be exercised in applying the divine Word to the contemporary world. Piety is not enough to ensure authentic fulfillment of obligation to God; true preaching requires hard study in true doctrine. The issue is not a matter of changing styles of sermons, or differences in delivery, or improvement of diction; the issue rather is knowledge and accurate statement of the truth of the gospel. There is no use boasting of lack of skill in interpreting scripture; lack of skill is a sham, a mere pretext for simple laziness. Preachers have the burden not only of right words but also of right deeds. Still, preaching cannot be by example only; the pastor must be able to explain what is required from scripture of the congregation. The preacher must know how to defend the truth against heresy and must be fully engaged in the world without falling into the trap of worldliness. The preacher must understand the human condition in all its hidden depths. Above all else, there is required of the preacher the expenditure of great labor in constructing good sermons. True preaching is thus a trial of faith; even established and practiced preachers never escape the toil of struggle that comes with the calling. True preaching does not come naturally but only through careful study. The ultimate aim of all preaching is to please God, not to stroke the crowd: "For the public are accustomed to listen not for profit, but for pleasure, sitting like critics of tragedies, and of musical entertainments. . . . For a sufficient consolation in his [the preacher's] labors, and one greater than all, is when he is able to be conscious of arranging and ordering his teaching with a view to pleasing God."[2] Yet despite the difficulty of the challenge, the role of the preacher is indispensable: "Priests are the salt of the earth."[3]

Surely the challenge of proclamation today is identical to this remarkably familiar account. In a day of rampant biblical illiteracy, there is enormous need for well-trained preachers who know the content of scripture in the core of their being. In a day of ideological distortion on the religious left and the religious right, there is overwhelming need for proclamation that is true to the subject matter of scripture in living

1. Chrysostom, 66.
2. Ibid., 70, 73.
3. Ibid., 76.

contact with the confessing heritage of the Christian church. In a day of rapid cultural and social change in the global community, there is the greatest possible need for ministers of the Word skillful in bringing home the truth of scripture to the contemporary situation. The church continues desperately to need preachers who are well educated in the duty they perform, for the very future of the church rests upon the energetic and imaginative execution of their task. The contemporary church needs ministers of the Word who are fully involved in the world, fully aware of its profound confusion and marvelous possibility, and yet who preach a message not of the world but of God's redeeming love in Jesus Christ freely given to all humankind. The church needs dedicated ministers obedient to the gracious call of God, who strive not for success but for faithfulness to Christ in all things. There is a crying need for careful and thoughtful practical application of scripture to the living questions of everyday life of ordinary Christians, showing forth to the entire world the inviting and winsome life of Christian discipleship. Above all, there is the gravest need for a virtual renaissance of Christian proclamation carried on by those who are the intellectual and moral leaders of the church. The harvest is indeed plentiful; the laborers are indeed terribly few (Matt. 9:37). Perhaps at no other time in the church's life has the need for faithful preaching of the Word been greater, for leaders in the church to teach the language of faith patiently and lovingly to a new generation of God's people.

Through the miraculous provision of God's blessing, there have always been preachers of the gospel in the Christian community. God does not leave the world without a witness to his good will for humankind. So also, accompanying and aiding this endeavor, has there always been dogmatic theology. Dogmatic theology is an intellectual discipline of the church of Jesus Christ, whose necessity is grounded in his call to preach the gospel to the world and to test the content of that preaching by his absolute authority. Dogmatic theology is of course not the only intellectual discipline of the church; it has, however, been an essential element in theological education since the beginning. The first great treatise of dogmatics is *Against Heresies* by Irenaeus, written sometime in the second century. As the title suggests, the work is a careful and sustained exposure of the errors of Gnosticism, as well as a powerful and illuminating presentation of the content of scripture in both Testaments. It is the concern of Irenaeus throughout his treatise to show that the catholic faith represents the true and genuine teaching of the biblical message, while the heresy of Gnosticism contains only distortions and falsehoods derived from an alien philosophical basis. The most recent grand treatise of dogmatic theology is the *Church Dogmatics* of Karl Barth. Barth's work was written during and after the church's struggle in

Germany against the followers of Adolf Hitler. He argues throughout that the theological errors of those who opposed the Confessing Church were in fact long in the making, being largely derived from nineteenth-century liberalism and earlier. Barth also offers a majestic unfolding of the true content of scripture according to the logic of its own inner order.

In between Irenaeus in the second century and Barth in the twentieth is an established sequence of volumes in dogmatic theology, including the other church fathers, the medieval scholastics, the Protestant Reformers, and church theologians of the modern era. Despite important differences that still need to be addressed, there is a strong family resemblance among these various writers of dogmatics. What is clear immediately from the example of Irenaeus and Barth is that dogmatics always has a twofold task. On the one hand, it is charged with the critical task of exposing heresy on the basis of scripture. On the other hand, it is also charged with the constructive task of teaching the true content of scripture for each new generation of the church. At times the church has remained frozen in time and simply repeated the dogmatics of a previous era. Thus, liberation theology is largely a rehash of classical theological liberalism, while fundamentalism is in many ways a reproduction of Protestant scholasticism. Nevertheless, crisis in the universal church has always shaken the church free from its lethargy, and the genuine theme of dogmatics has been undertaken once again. Dogmatic theology can never be done once for all; every successive generation must come face to face with its responsibility to preach and teach the Word of God in fulfillment of the living commission of Christ. There must always be a fresh attempt to do dogmatic theology, for Christ the risen Lord encounters each new age of the church afresh. In all its various dimensions, the function of dogmatics is to aid the ongoing task of proclamation in the present world. Dogmatic theology exists in order to serve the needs of proclamation in obedience to Christ, whose merciful presence in the church is the only way forward to the future.

To speak of heresy is to raise an issue of life or death for the church. In normal times perhaps accusations of heresy are all too easily flung by one theological party at another. Some disagreements in theological conviction are strong but should not be church dividing; one characteristic of fundamentalism, unfortunately, is to draw lines of church division where no lines exist. Scripture allows for theological variety, and that variety must be respected and preserved in a tolerant and open-minded church. On the other hand, it is one characteristic of liberalism to deny any such lines whatsoever, and that too is a serious mistake. In times of church crisis, sober consideration of the question of heresy is essential, and no dogmatic theology can avoid it. As H. E. W. Turner successfully shows in *The Pattern of Christian Truth*, there is a pattern of orthodoxy governing church speech and action right from the beginning of the church's existence. The pattern of truth is a characteristic theological framework shared by churches in a wide variety of geographical and social contexts. The pattern of orthodoxy is not identical to any one creed or confession, and yet the same pattern—the same inner ordering of basic theological ideas, the same rhythm and flow of fundamental church confession—is present in them all. Of course there was a "gradual growth in precision" in the church's ability to state that pattern with clarity and a gradual increase in the "level of concern" to do so as the church faced new problems and tasks; but the basic pattern of orthodoxy was there from the outset and was consistently referred to in matters of church speech and action.[4] There was always a great deal of fluidity across regional and theological lines; the pattern of truth never meant that a single theology was operative wherever Christian faith was present. Nevertheless, the movement of ideas across the boundaries of independent theological traditions not only did not detract from but profoundly enhanced the articulation of that pattern. The pattern of truth is not independent of scripture but rather derived from the subject matter of the Bible. The church's speech and action have never lacked the radiant pattern of truth, grounded always in the sovereign rule of Christ.

Nor also, unfortunately, has it ever been without the threat of heresy. According to Turner, heresy can come in many forms.[5] It comes in the form of theological trivialization, in which the message of the gospel is so watered down by extraneous philosophical and cultural agenda as to lose all contact with the truth. It can come in the form of willful disseverance of the truth, in which parts of the biblical witness are simply excised and ignored when they do not fit the needs of ideology. Heresy can be a distorting domestication of the truth, in which the full grandeur of the substance of scripture is emptied of its glory. Or it can be stubborn retreat into the past, with a perverse and blind refusal to accept new truth or to face the challenge of new tasks imposed upon the church by the ever-changing conditions of its ongoing life. Some err by adding to the radical claim of biblical truth, others by subtracting from it; some err by failing to discern and express the inner logic of truth manifest in the common faith of the church derived from scripture. Whatever the shortcoming, the essence of heresy is to look to the Bible for illustrations of a theological view essentially derived elsewhere and thus to twist the true subject matter of scripture. The inner harmony of the biblical witness is thrown off center. The classic passage of exposing heresy comes from Irenaeus against the Gnostics: "Their manner of acting is just as if one,

4. Turner, 487.
5. Ibid., lecture 3.

when a beautiful image of a king has been constructed by some skillful artist out of precious jewels, should then take this likeness of the man all to pieces, should re-arrange the gems, and so fit them together as to make them into the form of a dog or of a fox . . . and by thus exhibiting the jewels, should deceive the ignorant."[6] Jesus Christ is the one true subject matter of scripture; the effect of heresy is always to substitute a very different content, producing a very different faith—though of course there is only one faith in the one gospel, because there is one Lord of all creation (cf. Eph. 4:1–6). Heresy shatters the true unity of the church.

The creeds and confessions are the church's answer to heresy, in which the pattern of truth is laid down for faithful Christians everywhere at a given time and place. Their role is largely negative: creeds and confessions chart the area within which the search for truth is profitably undertaken, rather than fully exhibiting that truth. They are not a rival to scripture but a servant of the authority of scripture for the sake of the church. In these documents of theological witness, the church acting with common consent seeks to protect the truth of scripture from heresy. Dogmatic theology by definition must be concerned about the fact of heresy, not only in the church of the past by also in the church of the present; otherwise it is no longer engaged in the special task for which it labors for the common good of the people of God. Guided by the church's creeds and confession under the authority of scripture, dogmatics must help the church ward off heresy in the contemporary church. Dogmatic theology is always undertaken by the confessing church of Jesus Christ in every new age of its unfolding life.

What does that mean for the church today? There remain serious tensions of theological reflection between the historic communions of the Christian church, including Roman Catholic, Eastern Orthodox, and Protestant. Is only one of these historic traditions correct? Are the other viewpoints heresies? In the sixteenth century, as is well known, all sides of the dispute were convinced that the other had crossed the line of Christian truth. Dogmatic theology cannot simply ignore the theological differences that continue to divide the historic Christian communions. Doctrinal indifferentism is not the same as genuine ecumenism. Even today there are vital issues that must be discussed in the ongoing ecumenical dialogue of the church. Tensions must not be covered over but honestly faced. However, surely it is now clear that such differences amount to creative tension within the one family of faith rather than heresy. Dogmatic theology must allow for ample theological flexibility on the basis of scripture, even as it pursues in earnest the question of truth. Scripture sets boundaries of truth outside of which the gospel is

6. Irenaeus, 326.

not rightly preached; however, within those boundaries a rich variety of theological testimony is preserved and protected. Dogmatic theology does not aim for a single, comprehensive system of true propositions but for a living witness of faith that points to the one truth of the gospel alongside other witnesses.

Surely it is time once and for all to recognize that despite the crucial and weighty issues that remain, and that must be taken up by dogmatic theology, Roman Catholic, Eastern Orthodox, and Protestant communions share the same faith in the same Lord. We are all catholic, sharing our life in the unity of faith in the one Lord; we are all orthodox, maintaining a living connection with the consent of the faithful throughout all time; we are all protestant, fearlessly pursuing the question of truth in the service of Christ in confrontation with all centers of influence and power. Indeed, dogmatic theology has the role of helping along the task of mutual theological engagement and interpretation without seeking to conceal the difficult doctrinal differences that remain. Doctrinal disagreement within the historic church is not confrontation with heresy but constructive criticism, given in charity for the purpose of building up the community of faith. Protestant, Roman Catholic, Eastern Orthodox—despite our differences, we are brothers and sisters in one family of faith, in the service together of one Lord. The historic apostolic faith lives on in the mainstream church, despite the poverty of our fragmentation; we live by grace.

Yet is that all that must be said about heresy? If only it were so! For running across the denominational divide in the present-day church is a twofold division of an entirely different order. Here the issue is not theological disputation among longstanding communions of the historic Christian church; here the issue involves factional parties in the church formed along ideological lines. Here the issue is not the remaining challenge of mutual address among the branches of the universal church; here the issue is cultural, political, and personal agendas foisted on the church from outside, polarizing its message on the extreme edges. I refer to the twin movements of theological liberalism on the religious left and conservative evangelicalism or fundamentalism on the religious right. It is the argument of the present volume of dogmatic theology that both liberalism and fundamentalism are heresies, of equally destructive potential for the life of the church. I do not doubt for a moment the good intentions of those who espouse these views; indeed, dogmatic theology never attacks people but only theological positions held in pervasive and destructive error. Nevertheless, it must by its very nature expose and critique heresy, or it has failed to offer the church the aid that it desperately needs. The future of the church rests in guarding its message and order from both of these heretical factions.

Both fundamentalism and liberalism have deep roots in the development of modern religious thought. Both crystallized in the nineteenth century: fundamentalism in the *Systematic Theology* of Charles Hodge, liberalism in Friedrich Schleiermacher's *The Christian Faith*. The twentieth century began and ended as a battleground between these two parties. It is essential for the church in constructing its message for a new era to avoid the pitfalls of both the religious left and the religious right. Despite a rightful desire for a new generation of ecumenical consensus, we cannot build and plant unless we first pluck up and pull down (Jer. 1:10). The answer of the gospel to heresy is not to seek a position midway between two extremes, for that would be to gain our bearings by the standard of error rather than the standard of truth. Nor is truth a simple correspondence between concept and reality. Truth is not a human position, however diplomatically contrived; truth is an overwhelming divine gift. Truth is the effective power of God in accomplishing his living Word in the world: "For as the rain and snow come down from heaven, and do not return there until they have watered the earth . . . so shall my word be that goes out from my mouth; it shall not return empty, but it shall accomplish that which I purpose" (Isa. 55:10–11). The way forward for the church is a fresh hearing of the living voice of Christ through the pages of scripture. Beyond the conflict of liberalism and fundamentalism, the universal church today is, I believe, engaged in a new search for *Christian orthodoxy*, and the present volume aims to join in that search.

One primary issue along which the line of heresy must be observed and traced is in the relationship of Christ and culture. As H. Richard Niebuhr argues in his illuminating mid-twentieth-century essay *Christ and Culture*, there are five different types of answer given in the history of the church to the relation of Christ and culture. On the one extreme is the sheer rejection of culture within anticultural Christianity, including fundamentalism, in which the realm of human culture is considered simply evil. On the other extreme is the easy cultural Christianity of modern Protestant liberalism, typified by Albrecht Ritschl, in which Christ is treated as the symbolic embodiment of human cultural aspiration. Somewhere in the middle is the "central church,"[7] which includes agreement within disagreement between synthesists such as Thomas Aquinas, for whom human culture is provisionally affirmed as a necessary but not sufficient foundation for the study of divine revelation; dialecticians such as Luther, for whom dynamic interaction between the gospel and culture plays itself out in paradox; and transformationists such as Augustine and Calvin, for whom the rule of Christ ultimately

---

7. H. R. Niebuhr, 117.

transforms all human culture. Niebuhr also shrewdly observes that the fundamental theological structures of anticultural and cultural Christians are largely identical: "extremes meet."[8]

It is indeed remarkable how persuasive and helpful Niebuhr's basic classification remains. Moreover, it helps to explain the virtual collapse of dogmatic theology as a discipline of the church over the last half of the twentieth century, which was clearly dominated by the party fighting between the religious left and the religious right, for according to Niebuhr both camps dislike theology.[9] However, the last fifty years have made necessary, I believe, a further clarification of Niebuhr's still sound typology. First of all, the development of the counterculture after Niebuhr's death provided an alternative basis for the high-culture tradition of Protestant liberalism. Marx replaced Kant; the New Left replaced the social gospel; liberation theology replaced liberalism. Since high culture shifted and counterculture became politically correct, Niebuhr's model must now make room for the new "Christ of Counter-Culture"—though it is not really new, for its theological method is identical to that of the older liberalism, which it vainly tries to critique as something outdated, even though it clearly preserves and lives off its legacy. Christ is now the symbolic embodiment of countercultural aspiration, be it radical feminist, Third World, or black consciousness; the theological method of cultural Christianity is the same, only the actors have changed.

Second, in reaction to the religious left, the religious right began aggressively and actively to form the basis for a new "Christian" culture. Evolutionary science is to be replaced by "creationism"; religion is to underscore the role of "moral values"; Christian faith is to become the legally established religion. In other words, in a mirror image of the religious left, which shifted to counterculture, the formerly "anticultural" religious right suddenly vied for the prestige of filling the cultural vacuum left behind. Anticulture became the new culture, though of course what is being conserved, as Niebuhr once again clearly saw, is not the lordship of Jesus Christ but "older cultures."[10] Neither liberation theology nor modern neoevangelicalism significantly alters Niebuhr's brilliant analysis; they do, however, add certain nuances that must be theologically observed (and critiqued), for they now represent the extremes of left and right.

Third, Vatican II reopened a dynamic dialogue among the mainstream traditions of the Christian church, including synthesists, dialecticians, and transformationists, though such dialogue has often enough been

8. Ibid., 110.
9. Ibid.
10. Ibid., 102.

co-opted and even drowned out by the ideological distortions of left and right. Even more than Niebuhr could foresee in the 1950s, the possibility of mutually enhancing interaction among the major communions of historic Christianity is now more potentially fruitful than at any time since the sixteenth century and perhaps even earlier. While it must say no to both liberalism and fundamentalism, the great "church of the center"[11] is perhaps poised to move beyond the simple outlining of its historic differences. Surely a new vision of the relation of Christ and culture remains a decisive issue in the emerging consensus of theology today.

Fourth, the last half of the twentieth century saw the steady emergence of a global church no longer centered in Western Europe and North America. Philip Jenkins, describing the startling growth of the church around the world, speaks of nothing less than "revolutionary times" for world Christianity.[12] The seeds of mission planted in previous generations have now borne fruit; churches have blossomed in the so-called Third World. There is now a global church. It is more essential than ever to observe the firm distinction between the absolute claims of the gospel and the relative cultural mores of Western civilization. The one criterion by which the distinction is drawn is the command of Christ. The universal church needs the voices of all its members to be heard—women and men—including African Americans, Hispanics, and other minority voices in the West, as well as the churches of Asia, Africa, and South America. Liberation theology was not misguided because it sought to make such a witness possible, for that is a worthy and necessary goal; it was misguided because it sought to do so on the model of nineteenth-century theological liberalism, thus unknowingly misdirecting the enterprise from the outset. The profound challenge now facing dogmatic theology is to join with the voices of the global church in a new era of faith seeking understanding, in order that the universal church may bear true witness to the risen Lord. The globalization of the church has not spelled the end of Christian doctrine; on the contrary, we must now speak of the globalization of doctrine, for wherever the gospel goes, concern for doctrine goes with it. The great challenge of our time is the search for a new global orthodoxy: "O sing to the Lord a new song; sing to the Lord, all the earth" (Ps. 96:1).

Last, while I certainly agree with Niebuhr's effective critique of the theological extremes of left and right, I am less convinced by the notion of a church of the center. The gospel has never been found in a middle way of adjusting its message between two poles. The hope of the church does not lie in a diplomatic search for the middle but in the divine gift

11. Ibid., 117.
12. Jenkins, 68.

of reformation of God's beloved people. Christ the risen Lord is the only measure of truth, for whom we must search with our very being in the liberating joy of the gospel.

Dogmatic theology not only has the critical task of confronting heresy in the church; it also has the constructive task of helping the church in its positive mission of proclamation. This constructive dimension is shared with other disciplines of church scholarship, and especially with biblical theology. I share with many the feeling that somehow dogmatic and biblical theology must act in renewed cooperation for the common benefit of the church. The legacy of separation between the disciplines is profound and deep seated: a tradition of theology that is suspicious of the biblical field for its lack of theological grounding, a tradition of biblical studies that is suspicious of dogmatics for its lack of careful precision in handling the witness of scripture. One solution, now common, is clearly a dead end: to leave scripture to biblical studies and pursue more philosophical themes in theology. Both dogmatics and biblical studies lose in this formulation; and above all, the church loses the help it should rightly expect from both fields. So what is the solution?

There remains the need for both fields in church scholarship. Granted the perils of specialization, the church seldom sees the likes of a Luther or Calvin who could command both disciplines. Training for the Christian ministry requires a course of study in biblical theology, taught by biblical scholars, and a course in dogmatic theology, taught by dogmatic theologians. The academic training of both sets of scholars is different, the former concentrating on introduction and the history of exegesis, the latter on systematics and the history of doctrine. Nevertheless, the aim of both fields is to give the highest-quality illumination of scripture possible. Biblical theology and dogmatic theology share the task of expounding scripture for the church, though in different but complementary ways. Biblical theology gathers the results of exegesis and channels them into a unitary interpretation of scripture, moving from the witness of the text to the subject matter of which it speaks, which is Jesus Christ. While biblical theology certainly speaks directly to the concerns of the present-day church, its special responsibility is to insist on the sheer coercive force of the biblical message as a corrective over against the church. Biblical theology protects the authenticity of the gospel from distortion by the church. Dogmatic theology begins with the results of biblical theology. It trusts biblical theology to provide a basic orientation to the true subject matter of scripture. It then returns to the witness of scripture in light of the subject matter, offering the church a presentation of the truth of scripture according to the inner logic of its content. It focuses its reflective capacity on the theological framework that it recognizes in the mirror of the biblical witness. Its special responsibility is to aid the church in applying the biblical message to the issues of contemporary life in accordance with the rule of faith. Biblical theology and dogmatic theology are thus complementary disciplines of scriptural interpretation; both are essential for the health and well-being of the church, and neither can be neglected without terrible loss.

In fact, the relationship between biblical theology and dogmatic theology has recently been given a fresh point of departure, from the side of biblical studies. The unity in difference between the disciplines is not simply a matter of shared aim. Their relationship is grounded at a far more basic, theological level. What ties them together, and ties the theological scholarship of the church to the active ministry, is commitment to canon. Canon is the basic theological context for the life of the church as a whole, including all theological scholarship. Here full credit goes to the work of Brevard Childs, who has brilliantly and convincingly shown that the church's affirmation of canon involves far more than a simple list of approved books in the Bible. The confession of canon is a recognition and description of the shape and function of scripture as the authoritative norm for all church belief and practice. The essence of canon is an authoritative scripture shaped for the very purpose of guiding the church in all future generations to discern the living will of God. Canon provides the context for both biblical theology and dogmatic theology and indeed makes possible their mutual relation, yet with different concentration. Canon likewise provides the context for ongoing proclamation and therefore ensures the mutually interdependent relation of preaching and scholarship. Because of canon, preaching needs scholarship for essential help in its task, while church scholarship is defined in terms of the guidance and support it provides the Christian ministry.

Specifically for dogmatic theology, a part on canon should now replace the older concentration on "prolegomena." It was Schleiermacher's system that solidified the modern tradition of beginning a work of theology with an essentially philosophical introduction. According to Schleiermacher, the language of faith must first be situated in human history and psychology, using the techniques of sociological and philosophical discourse. From this procedure an "essence" of religion is defined, which then becomes the measuring rod for all that follows. Then the language of faith is to be interpreted and corrected from the point of view established prior to the actual consideration of the church's confession. As he candidly stresses in the opening lines of *The Christian Faith*, the prolegomena to theology is not dogmatic in orientation: "Since the preliminary process of defining a science cannot belong to the science itself, it follows that none of the propositions which will appear in this part can themselves have a dogmatic character."[13] Despite many differences with Schleiermacher, there is no doubt that conservative evangelicalism on its side follows the same procedure. The well-known commitment of Charles Hodge to Scottish Common Sense Realism provides just the same formal entry point as Schleiermacher's idealistic romanticism; the difference lies only in Hodge's philosophical base in Baconian inductive reasoning. According to Hodge, every science deals with "facts" and "ideas"; therefore, because theology is a science, it too must deal with the "facts" contained in scripture and their interrelation.[14] Hodge thus begins his theology with a methodological introduction keyed toward his philosophical rationalism. For Hodge, as for Schleiermacher, scripture is locked into a system that is profoundly philosophical—and profoundly suspicious from the point of view of the gospel. The true risk of faith has nothing to do with "facts" and "claims" and "evidence" as Hodge assumes, nor does the inbreaking new world of God have anything to do with Schleiermacher's feeling of piety.

Of course the fundamental approaches of Schleiermacher and Hodge, and the liberal and evangelical traditions that followed them, are well intentioned. Each tried in its own way to appeal to modern unbelief; each attempted to convince the modern skeptic that Christianity offers redemptive truth. Both turned dogmatic theology into a branch of apologetics. However, their serious mistake resulted from the fact that the genuine offense of the gospel was thereby removed. What was offered to modernity was no longer Christian faith but a misguided and misshapen distortion. Well-meaning error became deadly heresy.

It was Karl Barth who saw through this problematic with overwhelming insight. Barth was not the first to raise the issue of philosophical incursion into dogmatics. The Reformers mounted a similar case against the improper use of philosophy by the scholastics. For example, Philipp Melanchthon berated scholasticism for the ill effects of its rationalistic disputation: "Now, if I wanted to be clever in an unnecessary pursuit, I could easily overthrow all their arguments for the doctrines of the faith. Actually, they seem to argue more accurately for certain heresies than they do for the Catholic doctrines."[15] That is, scholastic rationalism, designed to defend, ends up despite itself twisting what it is meant to defend. Even more incisive is the crystal-clear formulation of Martin Luther in the Heidelberg Disputation: "No one can become a theologian unless he becomes one without Aristotle."[16] Scholasticism too, at least

13. Schleiermacher, 2.
14. Hodge, 1:1.
15. Melanchthon, 21.
16. *LW*, 31:11.

according to the Reformers, tried to base theology on philosophy in order to argue for the truth, but ended up distorting the truth itself.

Nevertheless, without doubt Barth saw through the profound error of all apologetics more clearly than any other theologian in the history of the church. Far from being a theologically neutral "orientation" or even a mildly helpful point of contact with the surrounding culture, a prolegomena of the sort common on the religious left and the religious right is highly charged with a theological standpoint full of radical error. Modern theology, left and right, is a house built on sand (Matt. 7:24–27), as shown already in the very shape of its self-presentation. Barth therefore wisely and rightly considered prolegomena as part of dogmatic theology itself and began his presentation with the doctrine of the Word of God.

Barth was absolutely right and persuasively denounced the catastrophic procedure of modern theology, liberal and conservative. Dogmatic theology is now in a position to solidify the gains that Barth made and to push them a step forward. Barth wrote at a time in which the separation between dogmatics and biblical studies was absolute. He was therefore forced to work out his theological commitment to scripture in relative isolation from the biblical field. The results were of permanent help to the church. Still, Barth's basic understanding of scripture was still largely within the orbit of the historical criticism of the nineteenth century. The conditions have now changed. With the work of Childs on canon, the biblical field itself has offered the church a stunning new grasp of its basic point of theological orientation. The present volume argues therefore that dogmatic theology should replace the older tradition of a prolegomena, even in its modified form in Barth, with a first part on canon. Such a move captures the essence of Barth's contribution and yet works it out in a way more promising for the future of the dogmatic discipline. The fundamental agreement with Barth remains secure; in sharpest possible contrast to the "apologetics" of liberalism and evangelicalism, dogmatic theology shares with biblical theology the method of faith seeking understanding. We do not begin outside the church; we begin with the church by confessing canon as the fundamental theological orientation of our entire endeavor. Here we can only proceed dialectically: dogmatic theology must reject absolutely any form of grounding in human reason and experience. On the other hand, as it pursues the task of faith seeking understanding, it is free to use whatever tools of critical rationality truly aid in the search for illumination. The ultimate aim is rightly to discern and express the living substance of which scripture bears truthful witness.

The proposal to make theological reflection on canon the prolegomena to dogmatic theology moves in the exact opposite direction from the proposal by William Abraham in his *Canon and Criterion in Christian Theology*. Abraham's thesis has two primary concerns: to insist that canon should not be limited to Holy Scripture and to remove canon from its status as the epistemological criterion in theology. Abraham's stated reason for resisting the move within traditional theology to treat canon as criterion in theology is its strangeness: "To construe an ecclesial canon, like Holy Scripture, as an epistemic norm is odd in the extreme. It is straightforwardly wrong. A list of religious documents drawn up by a Church is simply not a candidate for a criterion of rationality, justified belief, or knowledge."[17] Against Abraham, we must affirm that scripture as canon is indeed the criterion for the true knowledge of God; and that scripture alone, together with the content to which it bears witness, is canon, not the list of saints, fathers, etc., which Abraham proposes. Canon is not a "heritage," as Abraham proposes[18]; canon is an authoritative text, shaped for the very purpose that it serves. Indeed, the hope for church renewal that Abraham himself evidently shares is possible in the church not when it marginalizes the concept of canon and separates it from the category of epistemological criterion, but only when it takes its own special way of knowledge seriously. Canon is the criterion for Christian theology and the only proper context in which to ask and seek answers to the questions of theological epistemology. The new world of God in scripture is indeed odd, infinitely so: "Strange is his deed! . . . alien is his work . . . !" (cf. Isa. 28:21). How can it be otherwise? For God is *God*.

Another option is given in a book by John Webster, *Holy Scripture: A Dogmatic Sketch*. There is much in Webster's volume with which I fully agree, and in some sense I share his obvious concern to struggle forward to a fresh affirmation of the authority of scripture. Nevertheless, his broad proposal of housing the doctrine of scripture in the doctrine of God[19] strikes me as fundamentally flawed. Webster is certainly right that scripture is the instrument for the self-revelation of the Trinity; for that reason, following Barth, the present proposal treats the doctrine of the Trinity in the part on canon. But Webster's proposal would, I believe, simply eliminate prolegomena altogether, beginning theology with the doctrine of God rather than an opening part on canon. Would not scripture then be locked into a fully self-grounded theological system? Is not the doctrine of scripture then a hermetic theological abstraction, sealed off in every direction from the hard work of direct theological interpretation of the Bible? Would not dogmatic theology in some sense

17. Abraham, 12.
18. Ibid., viii.
19. Webster, 42–43.

be protected, and therefore domesticated, by its careful circumscription of scripture within self-grounded theological argument? Of course, these results are not intended by Webster's proposal, but they seem clearly to follow from it.

While I believe that a first part on canon is now the necessary introduction to dogmatic theology, I affirm the loci method perfected by Barth, in which there is no systematic center or principle but only the unfolding of the inner order of the subject matter of scripture according to its own self-given reality. Dogmatic theology is divided into five broad parts—canon, God, creation, reconciliation, redemption—though there is considerable flexibility concerning the arrangement of the material. In the loci method embraced here, each of the parts stands on its own as a comprehensive avenue to illumination of divine truth, yet each part is also interconnected with the remaining parts into one whole in accordance with the analogy of faith. The aim of dogmatic theology is to understand scripture in the light of its one true content, while at the same time we discern that content only through theological exegesis of the biblical witness.

One final point is in order. It was also Karl Barth who clearly saw through the unfortunate division between systematic theology and ethics. The division was unknown to classical theology and slowly crept into academic work in the post-Reformation period; according to Jaroslav Pelikan, the two branches were permanently separated in the seventeenth century, in the work of the Lutheran theologian George Calixtus.[20] Barth convincingly argued that the division not only is problematic but is in fact theologically unacceptable. What is the meaning of Christian doctrine that has no bearing on the direction of human life? And what is the meaning of a Christian ethic not grounded in the reality of God? Barth therefore began the procedure of including ethics in dogmatic theology, a procedure that is honored in the present volume by a chapter on general ethics. There is a slight difference of approach, however. Barth rightly emphasized the vertical dimension of Christian ethics: Christian life has nothing to do with moral values, ethical principles, noble ideals, in abstraction from the commanding God. Theological ethics must make it clear that all life is lived in obedience to the eternal Now of God's living will. Barth also correctly stressed the horizontal dimension, pointing out that scripture contains several summaries of the obedient life, which serve as guides by which the church seeks and finds the divine will. Once again, the aim of this invitation to dogmatic theology is to solidify and advance the position that Barth staked out. Childs's work on canon has shown more clearly than Barth could see, given the bibli-

20. Pelikan, 1:3.

cal resources of his era, the close connection between the vertical and horizontal dimensions, a connection grounded squarely in Christology. The Decalogue represents the unique and irreplaceable intersection of the vertical and horizontal dimensions of theological ethics. I therefore include a section on the role of the Ten Commandments in the shaping of Christian life under the authority of Christ.

In summary, dogmatic theology is a guide to scripture for the sake of better proclamation in the contemporary world. In dogmatics, the question is pressed: what do we proclaim when we preach Jesus Christ to the nations in our world today? On the one hand, care must be taken to avoid errors in what we proclaim. Precisely because we are all fallible, the church has always insisted on carefully drawn lines outside of which the gospel is not rightly preached. Dogmatic theology seeks to trace the outline of those boundaries on the basis of scripture, in continuity with the historic confession of the church, and in confrontation with the heresies of the present. On the other hand, all creative energy must be expended in hearing the profound joy and liberating energy of the gospel message, in discerning the gospel's illumination of all life, and in applying the gospel to the conditions of the contemporary world. While there is only one gospel, each new generation of the church must learn to sound it forth anew. Drawn from scripture, the language of faith is a living language. As Bernhard Lohse eloquently argues, progress in theology is not measured along a continuous stream but comes only in the existential struggle of the present hour: "It is not enough, therefore, to insist upon the continuity of the history of dogma. . . . In every new day and every new situation everything that was inherited must be won anew."[21] Dogmatic theology is no more than an aid to proclamation. It is not a system of revealed propositions and can never replace scripture itself as the norm of church life. Nevertheless, it is an essential and time-honored aid, which at its best has stimulated the church to a fresh encounter with the living Lord of all creation.

One final point is in order. It is worth remembering that, as important as the task of dogmatic theology surely is, the gospel of Jesus Christ encompasses far more than the limited role of technical theological reflection. These may be terribly confusing times for the witness of faith, as indeed they are; nevertheless, the gospel of Jesus Christ is living and powerful throughout the world. The gospel is on the lips and in the hearts of those who proclaim the Word, whether Catholic, Eastern Orthodox, or Protestant; the gospel is celebrated and enjoyed as the true bread of life in the partaking of the common loaf and cherished as the free gift of eternal life in the savoring of the cup. The gospel is present in the hymns

21. Lohse, *Short History*, 17.

and liturgy of the church universal and cherished by those who faithfully recite the creed from one Sunday to the next. The gospel gathers the community of faith together in the local congregation and is often most clearly manifest where small but active local churches serve Jesus Christ together in the unity of the Spirit and the joy of faith. The gospel is sung by church choirs in numerous languages on every continent and sends its followers on mission to the world in soup kitchens, clothes pantries, famine relief, and other forms of care for the poor and distressed around the world. The gospel is present wherever the new humanity is reflected in the everyday lives of ordinary Christians. Dogmatic theology has a crucial role to play in the service of the gospel; but the gospel is far greater than the discipline of theology: "At that time Jesus said, 'I thank you, Father, Lord of heaven and earth, because you have hidden these things from the wise and the intelligent and have revealed them to infants; yes, Father, for such was your gracious will" (Matt. 11:25–26). In the end is the grandeur of simplicity.

Reading List of Dogmatic Theology

What are the classic works of dogmatic theology, ancient and modern? The following is suggested as a basic working list of the indispensable volumes of dogmatics. These works are highly recommended for the personal library of pastors and teachers. Familiarity with the issues they raise will only aid in the endeavor of proclamation, pastoral care, mission, Christian education, and the like. All are available in a variety of inexpensive formats and can often be found most cheaply on CD-ROM.

Early Church

Irenaeus, *Against Heresies*
Origen, *On First Principles*
Athanasius, *On the Incarnation of the Word*
Gregory of Nyssa, *The Great Catechism*
Gregory Nazianzus, *Five Theological Orations*
Augustine, *Enchiridion*
  On the Trinity
  The City of God
  Confessions
  On Christian Doctrine

Cyril of Alexandria, *On the Unity of Christ*
John of Damascus, *On the Orthodox Faith*

Medieval

Anselm, *Why the God-Man*
Thomas Aquinas, *Summa Theologica*
Bonaventure, *Breviloquium*

Reformation

Martin Luther, *Large Catechism*
   The Freedom of the Christian
   To the Christian Nobility of the German Nation
   The Babylonian Captivity of the Church
   The Bondage of the Will
John Calvin, *Institutes of the Christian Religion*
Martin Bucer, *On the Kingdom of Christ*
Philipp Melanchthon, *Loci Communes*

Modern

Heinrich Heppe, *Reformed Dogmatics*
Heinrich Schmid, *Dogmatic Theology of the Evangelical Lutheran Church*
Catechism of the Catholic Church, 1994
Timothy Ware, *The Orthodox Church*
Karl Barth, *Church Dogmatics*
Dietrich Bonhoeffer, *The Cost of Discipleship*
Reinhold Niebuhr, *The Nature and Destiny of Man*

Part I

The Authority of Scripture

Scripture as Witness to Christ

As we are the community of faith in Jesus Christ, all our words and deeds are governed by the norm of Holy Scripture. Scripture is the source for our proclamation of the gospel to the world, the guide for the difficult decisions of Christian life and mission, the treasure of truth in the midst of uncertainty and confusion, the challenge of faith to single-minded obedience to Christ. Our adherence to scripture is grounded in the sovereign rule of Jesus Christ over all creation. The authority of Christ is the one subject matter of both Testaments of the Bible. Scripture is the instrument through which the risen and exalted Lord continues to manifest himself to the church and the world. It is through the instrument of scripture that Jesus Christ guides his people, by the presence of the Spirit, as they move in eager expectation from the resurrection to the final consummation of all things.

The authority of scripture, both the text itself and the content of which it speaks, is included in the word *canon.** Canon means an authoritative witness shaped for the purpose of addressing every new generation of the church with the living will of God. Canon is thus the first article in our confession of faith. That is true materially, for all dogma is based upon the limits circumscribed by the theological context of canon. It is also true historically, for the church's decision concerning canon was the stimulus and norm for every future decision. As Bernhard Lohse correctly observes: "The establishing of a canon constitutes the first basic doctrinal decision of the church. . . . Its significance is overriding.

. . . [Canon] represents a basic dogma of the church, i.e., it represents a witness to the revelation of God in Jesus Christ, one on which all later doctrinal decisions are based and which, in fact, makes these decisions possible."[1] Faith seeking understanding can begin only in an affirmation of canon. The study of dogmatics begins with theological reflection on canon. We are compelled to begin with canon by the subject matter of scripture, which is Jesus Christ. The confession of canon is grounded in Christology—that is, not in a christological principle but in the risen and exalted Lord.

Before we turn more directly to examine the christological basis of scriptural authority, it is helpful to review briefly the view of Brevard Childs on canon, which the present volume seeks to adapt to the field of dogmatic theology. While a comprehensive overview is beyond the scope of the present study, several central facets of Childs's view are key to the theological concerns that follow. The first point is that scripture as canon constitutes a normative guide for the ongoing community of faith. Canon does not mean a list of books, as is often supposed, or it means so only indirectly. Rather, canon means primarily a normative rule of faith by which the church lives in every new generation: "The fundamental theological issue at stake is not the extent of the canon, which has remained in some flux within Christianity, but the claim for a normative body of tradition contained in a set of books."[2] To speak of canon is therefore always first of all to speak of norm: "To do Biblical Theology within the context of the canon involves acknowledgement of the *normative* quality of the Biblical tradition."[3] Childs stresses that the full force of canon as norm ought not to be missed, for the whole of Christian theology rests upon a genuine grasp of the normative quality of the Bible: "The Bible must function normatively and not merely illustratively for the church."[4] Confession of the normative quality of the Christian canon is not in any way demonstrable by human reason or experience but is in fact a confession of faith.

Second, to speak of scripture as canon means to affirm the function of the biblical texts within the community of faith that treasured them. The function of these texts as scripture is built into the very structure of the texts themselves, not necessarily by individual authorial intention—a modern concept largely foreign to the biblical world—but by the anonymous editors who handed the text along from one generation to the next: "To take the canonical shape of these texts seriously is to do justice to a literature which Israel transmitted as a record of God's

1. Lohse, *Short History*, 23, 29.
2. Childs, 1970, 99.
3. Ibid., 100.
4. Ibid., 101.

revelation to his people along with Israel's response."[5] Therefore, one cannot sever the text from the living reality of God to which they bear witness; a purely history-of-religions approach fails to grapple with the theological dimensions that are built into the very form of the biblical witnesses. The Bible points to a self-revealed reality and cannot only be understood according to its inner scope by reckoning with the function of witness. But nor can one deny in any way the active role of the tra-dents of the biblical witness. Israel and the early church were shaped by God's self-manifestation, but so also did they actively shape the biblical text as a witness to the same God. The process of shaping is now largely unrecoverable historically, but the effect of shaping on the literature is precise and comprehensive.

Third, just as the biblical witness was shaped theologically to function as an authoritative text in the community of faith, so those who now take their stand in the same community by an act of confessing faith are guided by the same witness. The witnesses of the biblical record were all certainly written many generations ago; however, the function of canon is to render these texts in such a way as to make them accessible for every new generation of the church: "The Scriptures of the church are not archives of the past but a channel of life for the continuing church, through which God instructs and admonishes his people."[6] To speak of the continuing authority of the text is not to deny the legitimate role of historical-critical tools, which in fact are necessary precisely in the service of canonical analysis; but it is to make clear that the biblical witness is not somehow locked into the era in which it came into being. The same God who once spoke in the past still speaks: "The appeal to the canon understands Scripture as a vehicle of a divine reality, which indeed en-countered an ancient people in the historical past, but which continues to confront the church through the pages of Scripture."[7] Revelation is not therefore limited to a time-bound era in the past; revelation is also God's continuing act of self-disclosure through the medium of the Bible. Nevertheless, the focus of a canonical reading of scripture is not upon the faith response of the reader but upon the descriptive reality of the text and the content that it renders: "The major task of a canonical analysis . . . is a descriptive one. It seeks to understand the peculiar shape and special function of these texts which comprise the . . . canon."[8]

And fourth, the confession of canon involves taking serious the theo-logical shape of the biblical witness. While the process of handing on the biblical text in the ancient community is largely obscure, the effect

5. Childs, 1979, 73.
6. Childs, 1970, 99.
7. Childs, 1970, 100.
8. Childs, 1979, 72.

on the text is both discernible and profound. The final form of the text is structured in an intentional way to render the material an ongoing authority for the life of the community. Two examples will help, one from the Old Testament, the other from the New. It is well known that the patriarchal narratives come from a variety of sources, written and oral, in a complex history of tradition that is often somewhat opaque. Nevertheless, it is clear that the final form of the book has been canonically shaped into a unified theological witness by the repeated use of the *toledot* formula (Gen. 2:4; 5:1; 6:9; 10:1; 11:10; 11:27; 25:12; 25:19; 36:1(9); 37:2). The canonical shaping does not arbitrarily bring together otherwise disparate narrative material, but it does decisively shape it for a particular theological purpose, involving the divine promise to the patriarchs. Reading the book canonically means therefore following the theological direction laid down by the shaping it has received: "To speak of Genesis as scripture is to acknowledge the authority of this particular viewing of Israel's tradition which in its particular form provided a critical theological standard for future generations of Israel."[9] A second example of theological shaping is the fourfold witness of the Gospels. The titles of the four biblical Gospels are not part of the original composition but were added by canonical editors. Each is entitled "The Gospel according to . . ." The point of the preposition "according to" is not limited to authorship but describes one self-same content (the gospel) that is handled by four different witnesses (according to Matthew, Mark, Luke, John). There are not four gospels; there is only one gospel, which is nevertheless accessible only through the manifold witness of the biblical texts: "The collectors therefore provided this material with a new context which allowed for its diversity, yet laid claim also on its unity."[10] Theological interpretation of the scriptural canon means following the definitive guidelines provided by the theological shape of the Bible.

With this brief outline of Childs's approach to canon in mind, let us return to the basic question that dogmatic theology must first face: where does the Bible get its normative authority in the life of the church? The authority of scripture is itself derived from the authority of Jesus Christ, of whom it bears witness. The one is not to be separated from the other: to acknowledge the authority of scripture is to acknowledge the authority of Christ; contrariwise, there is no true allegiance to Christ without allegiance to scripture. Why is that so? Here at the very outset of our study of dogmatics we probe at the heart of the gospel. We immediately focus our attention upon the central mystery of our faith. In Jesus Christ, the eternal God entered space and time in order to redeem

9. Childs, 1979, 157.
10. Childs, 1984, 152.

the world. This is not a classic myth or a profound image; the incarnation is an affirmation of the entry of God into the real world in order to transform it from the inside. The gospel concerns "what we have looked at and touched with our hands, concerning the word of life" (1 John 1:1). The scandal of particularity means that there and then, in the midst of a short stretch of human history, God revealed himself by becoming a human being, without being any less God. God's time entered directly into human time, in order to reconcile the entire creation to himself.

Now, just as the scandal of particularity governs the subject matter of the gospel, so also does it govern the witnesses of that redemptive event. Not in all times and in all places but at that time and at that place—first in the form of Old Testament promise, then also in the form of New Testament kerygma—a witness to the event of God's self-manifestation was established by the One of whom it speaks. By virtue of the mystery of the incarnation itself, there is only one narrow circle of witnesses, for there is only one Lord Jesus Christ. Only these witnesses were there to see and to hear: "We declare to you what was from the beginning, what we have heard, what we have seen with our eyes . . ." (1 John 1:1). Therefore, at stake in our confession of the authority of scripture is the central confession of the incarnation of Jesus Christ. We cannot retreat from the authority of scripture without abandoning our confession of Christ himself.

Scripture is given to the church and to the world because the redemptive power of God revealed in the life, death, and resurrection of Jesus there and then is here and now the same redemptive power for the reconciliation of the entire cosmos. The power of the gospel for the salvation of the world does not fade or grow old; it is rather the eternally new reality of God's merciful love for his entire creation. Scripture is the means by which the wondrous truth of the gospel is handed on from one generation to the next. Each new generation turns to the same scriptures with fresh eyes and open ears, and there encounters the Lord of all time. There is no hermeneutical key or system by which to make what is true there and then true here and now. The Spirit of God opens our hearts and minds to hear the living voice of Christ through the witness of scripture. Contemporaneity with Christ is not a human possibility but the miraculous gift of Christ's living presence received in faith. But just as the eternal Word of the Father assumed human flesh in Jesus of Nazareth and no other, so the message of Christ the Lord is enfleshed in the human witnesses of the biblical Word. We have a scripture in order that the redeeming love of God in Jesus Christ may be spoken in the world for every new age of human life.

The authority of scripture is ultimately grounded in Christology. Christ the risen Lord chose for himself apostles and prophets to teach the nations the glory of his will. "Whoever listens to you listens to me, and whoever rejects you rejects me, and whoever rejects me rejects the one who sent me" (Luke 10:16). The voice of Christ is heard only through the witnesses whom he chose. There is no discontinuity here between the words of the exalted Christ and commands of the earthly life of Jesus. The entire New Testament assumes at every point the identity of the two. Rather, the disciples are commissioned to teach others "to obey everything that I have commanded you" (Matt. 28:20). The present-day existential encounter of the church with the living Christ—an encounter that can never be denied or set aside—is thus forever tied to the normative words of the apostles and the prophets. We hear the living voice of Jesus Christ, but we hear it through the written words of the biblical text. We live by the rule of Christ, the one Head of the church, but he rules his church through the sacred scriptures we cherish. Through scripture, Christ himself is present to guide and comfort his people, as well as to correct and renew.

Who established the authority of scripture? The question must be addressed on two different levels. On the one hand, canon by its very nature implies a community of faith. Canon describes the relationship which the Christian church has to the Bible it cherishes. There is no canon where there is no community; there is no scripture where there is no living company of the faithful. Scripture, community, and faith all belong together and can never be separated. On the other hand, it is precisely the community of faith that confesses that scripture is a divine gift received and acknowledged in an act of obedient response. The Christian church does not believe that the decision concerning canon confers authority upon a text that in itself is without authority. None of the creeds and confessions of the church have ever spoken in this way. On the contrary, the church has always stressed that the reality of canon shapes the very identity of the church. The authority of scripture can and must be acknowledged and received; there is no sacred scripture without the community of faith to treasure and learn from it. Nevertheless, the authority is not thereby transferred to the community that receives it. Otherwise, scripture is dissolved into a mere extension of the church's act of self-identification, thus throwing open the possibility of ideological self-delusion. When the church receives the authority of scripture, it confesses that scripture has the right to exercise the authority it does.

So from where does scripture receive its authority? From where does it receive the inherent right to command our ultimate allegiance in the confessing church? The authority of scripture, its right to summon our confidence, is established by Christ himself. The prophetic and apostolic testimony is commissioned by Christ himself as the sole authoritative witness of his true and sovereign claim upon all human life. The point is not to separate scripture from the life of the church. Not at all, for by definition *authority* is a "functional" term, describing the relation of inferior to superior. The study of scripture is necessarily an activity of the Christian community. The affirmation of scripture is necessarily an article of faith, which cannot be based on rationalistic and apologetic grounds. Scripture and the church belong together. The point rather is to establish the relation of priority. The authority of scripture secures the absolute precedence of Christology over ecclesiology. Jesus Christ is first, we the church are second; Jesus Christ is Lord, we the church are his servants; Jesus Christ is Master, we the church are his disciples; Jesus Christ is Teacher, we the church are his learners; Jesus Christ is the Word of God, we the church are hearers and doers of the Word. Without the authority of scripture, the relation of priority is disastrously overturned. At best there is misguided effort at cooperative partnership; at worst that "partnership" becomes sheer apostasy. The ultimate issue is simple and direct: we confess that the authority of Holy Scripture is established by Jesus Christ himself. We gratefully receive and acknowledge the scriptures; yet we do not point to ourselves in our love for scripture but to the One who delivers them for the safeguarding of our faith. Canon is not a conferral of authority but a due recognition of it, because the confession of canon as an article of faith is grounded in the authority of the risen Lord.

Thus the debate between Protestants and Roman Catholics in the sixteenth century can now be clarified and overcome. The tendency of Protestants was to argue that the authority of scripture precedes the authority of the church. The tendency of Roman Catholics was to argue that the authority of the church precedes the authority of scripture. The debate was largely conducted along a two-dimensional continuum. What was missing was the decisive third dimension, the christological, which in fact provides the ultimate key. The authority of scripture necessarily includes the role of the church—on that issue Roman Catholicism is right and hyper-Protestantism is wrong. The church was active in shaping canon, not passive; the scriptures were handed along and shaped by the early church for all future generations. On the other hand, the active role of the church in no way confers authority on scripture—on that the Reformers are right and a triumphant ecclesiasticism is wrong. The authority of scripture is not self-grounded, neither is it conferred by the church; it is based solely on the sovereign commission of Christ, who acts according to his own purpose and at his own initiative. The self-grounded majesty of the exalted Christ is the basis of the authority of scripture, as gladly and willingly professed by the confessing church of every age by our adherence to canon.

Here we must guard against two errors, the first on the religious left, the second on the religious right. In his widely influential book *The Uses of Scripture in Recent Theology*, David Kelsey argues for a concept of authority that has clearly guided a whole generation of theology. Despite the inner consistency and wide appeal of his argument, in the end it must be discarded as an apology for liberalism. Kelsey offers his analysis as a theologically neutral description of a variety of recent theological opinions. That is to say, he aims at suggesting no one particular theological position, only at uncovering the general logic of all positions through careful linguistic observation. He samples a variety of nineteenth- and twentieth-century Christian theologians: B. B. Warfield, Hans-Werner Bartsch, G. Ernest Wright, Karl Barth, L. S. Thornton, Paul Tillich, and Rudolf Bultmann. In each case, he asks a series of "diagnostic questions" intended to discover the logic of their position. His conclusion is summarized as follows: "The expression, 'Scripture is authoritative for theology' has self-involving force. When a theologian says it, he does not so much offer a descriptive claim about a set of texts and one of its peculiar *properties*; rather he commits himself to a certain kind of activity in the course of which these texts are going to be *used* in certain ways."[11] Clearly if Kelsey is right, then my initial theological analysis of canon is wrong. Is he right?

In my judgment, Kelsey's analysis suffers from a series of fatal flaws. First of all, Kelsey claims to offer a purely descriptive analysis without a theological agenda. He states categorically: "The essay makes no Christian theological proposals."[12] Yet his claim to theological neutrality is surely spurious in the extreme. He assumes going in to the study the very conclusion he purports to reach by careful analysis (*petitio principii*). Thus at the very beginning he states: "'Scripture is not something objective that different theologians simply use differently. In actual practice it is concretely construed in irreducibly different ways."[13] Needless to say, this is not a "theologically neutral" assumption; on the contrary, it is a flat-out affirmation of the liberal position of theological pluralism. Clearly, he is out to prove this position in the study: why does he not openly admit his theological starting point rather than concealing it behind the facade of detached objectivity? It is one thing for Kelsey to disagree with other theologians, such as the Protestant Reformers, who clearly hold to the authority of scripture as in some sense an objective property (as well as a subjective response); it is quite another for Kelsey

11. Kelsey, *Uses of Scripture*, 89.
12. Ibid., 9.
13. Ibid., 2.

to force all other positions into agreement with his before any meaningful debate can take place.

Second, his selection of theologians is hardly significant enough to
bear the weight of his theological conclusions. After all, he does not argue
for the structure of "contemporary" theology; he argues in part 3 for the
necessary logical structure of *all* theology. Where then is his analysis of
Irenaeus, or Augustine, or Thomas, or Calvin, or Luther, and so on? At
best he offers an apology for the logic of modern theology, conservative and liberal, but of course that is only one era of theology, heavily
disputed at that; yet his claims are couched in universal terms. Surely
theological analysis of such a weighty issue as the authority of the Bible
should go well beyond a handful of contemporary and near contemporary
voices. Kelsey cannot object that his study is a merely historical analysis
of certain interesting theological writers, chosen according to his own
preferences, for he himself continually draws universal, pantheological
conclusions from his analysis. At the very least, an informed theological
analysis should also wrestle with the great voices of the heritage that
have long since proved their worth.

Third, I find Kelsey's defensiveness concerning his interpretation of
other theologians disturbing. Repeatedly, Kelsey claims that "it would
be a sign of misunderstanding to object to any part of the following that
it is historically in error; it makes no historical claims, nor even any
exegetical ones."[14] This strange statement is either disingenuous at best
or simply self-deluding, for Kelsey's book contains several chapters of
"exegesis" of other theologians, as any reader can plainly see. Anyone
who offers an interpretation must be willing to submit the work to correction by other competent scholars. And in at least one case, Kelsey
does make an egregious error of interpretation. He argues that Barth
understands the authority of scripture in functional terms in such a
way as to deny altogether any inherent property.[15] This interpretation
is not true. While Barth was very critical of the orthodox Protestant
understanding of scripture, which severed scripture from church, he
nevertheless unambiguously affirmed the inherent authority of scripture:
"Scripture is holy and the Word of God, because by the Holy Spirit it
became and will become to the Church a witness to divine revelation."[16]
Or again, "the Church does not claim direct and absolute and material
authority for itself but for Holy Scripture as the Word of God."[17] Barth
certainly underscored the relation of scripture to the church, against
any form of unwarranted objectification; nevertheless, he also clearly

14. Ibid., 9.
15. Ibid., 47.
16. Barth, *CD* 1/2, 457.
17. Ibid., 538.

spoke in ways that accorded to scripture an inherent right to command the authority it receives.

Indeed, Kelsey's error in reading Barth points to a fourth serious problem with his approach, and that is his assumption that a relational understanding of authority automatically moves the locus of authority from scripture to the church. Kelsey is certainly right: the authority of scripture is relational. That is why the conservative evangelical view of scripture is wrong, as we shall see. However, he expands this legitimate and important observation to an untested and unwarranted conclusion: that canon is therefore an act of communal self-identification. In contrast to Kelsey, the church has never spoken in this way: "We choose these books because they are a reflection of who we are." There of course remain acute tensions among Roman Catholics, Protestants, and Eastern Orthodox on the issue of scripture and tradition. These tensions must be candidly addressed by any responsible church dogmatics. Nevertheless, all Christian communions are agreed—contra Kelsey—that scripture possesses an inherent authority. From the Roman Catholic communion comes this confession: "For Holy Mother Church, relying on the faith of the apostolic age, accepts as sacred and canonical the books of the Old and the New Testaments, whole and entire, with all their parts, on the grounds that, written under the inspiration of the Holy Spirit, they have God as their author and have been handed on as such to the Church herself."[18] From the Eastern Orthodox tradition, this: "We believe the Divine and Sacred Scriptures to be God-taught; and, therefore, we ought to believe the same without doubting."[19] From the Lutheran, this: "We believe, teach, and confess that the prophetic and apostolic writings of the Old and New Testaments are the only rule and norm according to which all doctrines and teachers alike must be appraised and judged."[20] From the Reformed: "The authority of the holy Scripture, for which it ought to be believed and obeyed, dependeth not upon the testimony of any man or church, but wholly upon God (whose truth it is), the Author thereof; and therefore it is to be received, because it is the Word of God."[21] And from the Anglican: "Holy Scripture containeth all things necessary to salvation: so that whatsoever is not read therein, nor may be proved thereby, is not to be required of any man, that it should be believed as an article of the Faith."[22]

How can Kelsey legislate the logic of the church's position, when the universal church confesses what Kelsey denies? By definition, the con-

---

18. *Cat* 31, quoting from *Verbum Dei*.
19. The Confession of Dositheus, Decree 2, in Leith, 486.
20. Formula of Concord, Epitome 1, in *BC*, 464.
21. Westminster Confession of Faith 1.4, in Leith, 195.
22. The Thirty-nine Articles, art. 6, in Leith, 267.

cept of canon implies an inherently valid norm, a standard, which the church accepts for its life and by which it is judged. Canon is not an act of self-identification but an act of grateful acknowledgement. The issue is profoundly christological, as the Scots Confession, for example, makes clear: "We affirm, therefore, that those who say the Scriptures have no other authority save that which they have received from the Kirk are blasphemous against God and injurious to the true Kirk, which always hears and obeys the voice of her own Spouse and Pastor, but takes not upon her to be mistress over the same."[23] Kelsey's assumption brings with it a massive theological agenda—to prove that the idea of a scriptural norm or standard by which to measure the church's speech and action is "meaningless"[24]—which runs directly counter to the ecumenical mainstream of the historic Christian church.

Finally, Kelsey's view—again masquerading as objective description—that all theology is an act of imagination similar to literary criticism[25] involving a logically prior *discrimen* concerning the essence of Christianity[26] means that the discipline of dogmatic theology would be cut free from accountability to the discipline of biblical theology. Theology for Kelsey is a free-standing enterprise, ultimately based on a self-validating act of autonomous reason. This is surely a supreme act of arrogance, equivalent in fact to a straightforward Pelagianism. It breaks apart the community of scholarship that constitutes the genuine ecology of scholarship in the church. Despite his evident intention to speak for the church, Kelsey in fact emerges as a supreme apologist for the Enlightenment view of autonomous reason. If the field of dogmatics is to recover the health of the discipline and its crucial role in the Christian community, it must move in the exact opposite direction from Kelsey: by beginning precisely with the results of biblical theology and only then moving to a full exercise of creative imagination in the dogmatic theological interpretation of scripture.

In summary, the crucial issue that Kelsey ignores is implied in the very concept of canon. Canon reflects the fact that scripture is *already construed*. The biblical text is already shaped by Israel and the early church to serve as the instrument by which the risen Christ rules his church. The Bible is already shaped theologically for a specific purpose, into which the community of faith enters in each new generation. Here we are merely following the self-presentation of scripture itself: "For we did not follow cleverly devised myths when we made known to you the power and coming of our Lord Jesus Christ, but we had been eye-

23. Scot's Confession 19, in *Conf*, 21.
24. Kelsey, *Uses of Scripture*, 5.
25. Ibid., 9.
26. Ibid., 160.

witnesses of his majesty . . . because no prophecy ever came by human will, but men and women moved by the Holy Spirit spoke from God" (2 Peter 1:16, 21). Or again, "But as for you, continue in what you have learned and firmly believed, knowing from whom you learned it, and how from childhood you have known the sacred writings that are able to instruct you for salvation through faith in Jesus Christ" (2 Tim. 3:14–15). Christ teaches his church through an authoritative collection of sacred scripture. The theologian in the church does not play the role of conducting a logically prior act of construal; rather, he or she receives in the community an authoritatively construed text through a corresponding affirmation of faith. Thomas Aquinas makes the theological point very skillfully and succinctly: "Therefore, we must not attempt to prove what is of faith, except by authority alone, to those who receive the authority."[27] Similarly clear is the summary statement by Ellen Davis: "Reading the Scriptures *as the Word of God* is the basic identifying activity of the Christian community."[28] Only then are human intellect and imagination unleashed—guided by the presence of the Spirit—to search the scriptures for the living voice of Christ in every new age. To base theology on a logically prior determination of the "essence of Christianity"—what is that if not the essence of Protestant liberalism?

We must now, however, just as vigorously reject the conservative evangelical understanding of the authority of scripture. That understanding was clearly mapped out already by Charles Hodge, carried on by B. B. Warfield, and has remained virtually unchanged among evangelicals since their comprehensive presentation. Hodge clearly intends to defend the historic faith of the Christian church in a modern scientific and philosophical climate. He accepts what he considers to be the "rational" conception of human knowledge: "Knowledge is the persuasion of what is true on adequate evidence."[29] He then proceeds to interpret the basic structure and content of Christian doctrine upon this "rational" basis. The Bible is analogous to the natural world, according to Hodge; it contains "facts." Much as the scientist arranges the facts of nature into a system, so must the theologian arrange the facts of scripture into a similar set of true propositions. The reason for this approach is simple: God has made the human mind to work this way. As Hodge asserts, "Such is the constitution of the human mind that it cannot help endeavoring to systematize and reconcile the facts which it admits to be true."[30] But according to Hodge, God never requires human beings to accept as true what cannot be proved. Thus even the "claims" of the

27. *ST*, 1.169.
28. Davis, 1995, 244.
29. Hodge, 1:1.
30. Ibid., 1:2.

Bible must be proved; indeed, even the authority of scripture itself must rest on a rationally valid basis. Reason must always judge the evidence by which a purported instance of revelation is guaranteed. This is so because "as faith involves assent, and assent is conviction produced by evidence, it follows that faith without evidence is either irrational or impossible."[31]

So why assent rationally to the authority of scripture? What "evidences" support its "truth-claims"? There are two main reasons in Hodge, one historical and the other cultural. Historically, apostolic authorship of biblical books guarantees their authenticity. He argues that "it can be historically proved that those books were written by the men whose names they bear; and it can also be proved that those men were the duly authenticated organs of the Holy Ghost."[32] Culturally, the Bible plays an essential role in underlying the various forms of human society, and without it they will collapse. Hodge maintains: "The Bible ever has been and still is, a power in the world. It has determined the course of history. It has overthrown false religions wherever it is known. It is the parent of modern civilization. It is the only guarantee of social order, of virtue, and of human rights and liberty. Its effects cannot be rationally accounted for upon any other hypothesis than that it is what it claims to be, 'The Word of God.'"[33] The cultural influence of the Bible is evidence of its divine status.

It is easy to recognize the good intentions upon which Hodge founds his system and with which his numerous followers continue in the conservative evangelical path. Nevertheless, the theological errors that are made are of such weight that one can only conclude that the teaching he represents is a profoundly misguided corruption of true Christianity, a major departure from the historic confession of faith. First, there is not the slightest indication in Hodge that the authority of scripture rests upon the authority of Jesus Christ, the risen Lord of all reality. In his attempt to ground the faith on rational grounds, Hodge has unwittingly denied the very One in whom Christian faith is centered. We are given the scriptures in order to learn of Jesus Christ, not in order to accumulate and arrange "facts." As Jesus said, "You search the scriptures because you think that in them you have eternal life; and it is they that testify on my behalf. Yet you refuse to come to me to have life" (John 5:39–40). The entire tradition of the church has insisted that scripture is already rendered in order to focus upon a particular *scopus*, or purpose. Calvin, for example, wrote the *Institutes* for this very reason: "For

31. Ibid., 1:53.
32. Ibid., 1:129.
33. Ibid., 1:39.

I believe I have so embraced the sum of religion in all its parts, and have arranged it in such an order, that if anyone rightly grasps it, it will not be difficult for him to determine what he ought especially to seek in Scripture, and to what end [*quem in scopum*] he ought to relate its contents."[34] Hodge's rationalism has blinded him to the genuine chris-

tological basis for scriptural authority. Consequently, his concept of theology as a scientific arrangement of true propositions removes him entirely from the inner logic of the subject matter of scripture, which is based on God's self-manifestation in Christ. His system is constructed on the basis of purported human need for internal logical consistency, not on the basis of the biblical analogy of faith (Rom. 12:6). The church owes nothing whatsoever to the canons of rationality; it owes everything to the Word of God.

Second, whereas the dogmatic tradition of the church has always insisted that canon is an article of confessing faith, Hodge seeks to make it a rationally established fact. In so doing, Hodge seriously distorts the meaning of biblical faith. For Hodge, faith is rational assent based on evidence. Not so for scripture, where faith is absolute adherence to the Word of God, precisely when it *contradicts* the evidences of human reason and experience. Faith does not come from "evidence"; the very idea of evidence is an invention of the Enlightenment, not a teaching of scripture. Rather, faith comes "from what is heard, and what is heard comes through the word of Christ" (Rom. 10:17). Above all, the faith of Father Abraham makes this clear, who believed not because of the evidence but *despite* the evidence of his own senses and rational appraisal: "And he believed the LORD; and the LORD reckoned it to him as righteousness"(Gen. 15:6). In the brilliant formulation of Martin Luther: "The Holy Spirit is no Skeptic, and it is not doubts or mere opinions that he has written on our hearts, but assertions more sure and certain than life itself and all experience."[35] Moreover, Hodge equally distorts the source of faith, which is not in the least the exercise of a natural human capacity, as he clearly asserts: "Revelation is the communication of truth to the mind. But the communication of truth supposes the capacity to receive it."[36] There is no "capacity" for revelation in scripture. Such a "capacity" can be argued only on the Pelagian grounds that Hodge shares unwittingly with liberalism. On the contrary, revelation is always a miraculous gift of the Holy Spirit: "For by grace you have been saved through faith, and this is not your own doing; it is the gift of God" (Eph. 2:8).

34. Calvin, 1.4.
35. *LW,* 33:24.
36. Hodge, 1:49.

Third, the authority of scripture is not at all based on any "evidences," historical, cultural, or otherwise; rather, the authority of scripture is supreme and sovereign in its sheer self-validation. As Calvin states: "Let this point therefore stand: that those whom the Holy Spirit has inwardly taught truly rest upon Scripture, and that Scripture indeed is self-authenticated."[37] Calvin is not trying to separate scripture from the church, which would be a misunderstanding of self-authentication. Rather, he is insisting that the authority of scripture cannot be achieved by its being incorporated into a larger system of rational validation. For then its authority rests on human reason—which is blasphemy—rather than on the authority of Christ. In his effort to find human certainty for biblical authority, Hodge has in fact lowered the scriptures to a human level; he has made them subject to human rational judgment, thus eliminating their divine certainty. Despite his much-avowed Protestantism, how utterly different this is from the Reformers, and the Reformation confessional heritage, for whom the Word of God can in no way whatsoever be subjected to human approval or authorization. Calvin is insistent: "But a most pernicious error widely prevails that Scripture has only so much weight as is conceded to it by the consent of the church. As if the eternal and inviolable truth of God depended upon the decision of men! For they mock the Holy Spirit when they ask: Who can convince us that these writings came from God?"[38] Yet it is precisely the supposedly Reformed theologian Hodge who needs to be convinced, and who would seek to convince others.

Fourth, in seeking historical and cultural proofs for biblical authority, Hodge has slipped over into a historical referential reading of scripture that runs counter to the canonical intentionality of the authoritative text. He has committed himself to a modern conception of authorship that is foreign to scripture itself. Furthermore, he has purchased an established role of the Bible in human culture at the price of a critical appraisal of that culture on the grounds of scriptural authority. The religious right after Hodge unfortunately all too easily evolves into a form of cultural Christianity, upholding the status quo of social moral values; the gospel of Jesus Christ in sacred scripture, on the other hand, overturns all human moral values, left and right, in the light of the rule of the exalted Christ: "Do not be conformed to this world, but be transformed by the renewing of your minds, so that you may discern what is the will of God—what is good and acceptable and perfect" (Rom. 12:2). The role of the gospel is to transform the whole of society, not, as Hodge declares, to underwrite the existing social order.

37. Calvin, 1.80.
38. Ibid., 1.75.

In seeking to establish the authority of scripture on rational grounds, Hodge ignores the church's theological confession of the reality of canon. *Canon* by definition refers to a sacred text treasured in an ongoing community of faith. Hodge unwittingly severs the scriptures from the church that reveres them. Of course his intention is to bring them back together again on rational grounds, but the damage is already done; for now Hodge can join faith to the scriptures only according to the requirements of perverse human will, which is "only evil continually" (Gen. 6:5). He also subjects the living will of God in Christ to human rational judgment and therefore to human manipulation. From a biblical perspective, such grounding of the authority of scripture makes a sheer mockery of the authority of God; it substitutes human piety for authentic faith: "When you come to appear before me, who asked this from your hand? Trample my courts no more; bringing offerings is futile. . . . New moon and sabbath and calling of convocation—I cannot endure solemn assemblies with iniquity. . . . Your new moons and your appointed festivals my soul hates" (Isa. 1:12–14). Hodge is clearly seeking to give the same honor to scripture as was accorded it by Luther and Calvin, yet the logic of his position moves him squarely into the Enlightenment, alongside the liberalism he vainly strives to overcome. Hodge joins Kelsey—extremes meet—as a triumphant assertion of sinful human reason in defiance of the free grace of the gospel.

In contrast to both left and right, the authority of scripture is acknowledged by an act of confession in the community of faith. Only then is due honor brought to the risen Lord of whom scripture bears faithful witness. That act of confession was made long ago in the church, but it is made again and again in each new generation by the eager endeavor to search the scriptures for the living will of God. The same God who once gave the scriptures, the same God who summoned a response of faith from the early church in setting them apart from all other writings on earth—the same God even now actively communicates his living will through these writings. "Authority" is not therefore a burden upon us, as if we must blindly accept what is given without exercise of our intellect and imagination. Rather, authority shows us where to look—where most fruitfully to seek with the mind, to yearn with the heart, to deliberate with the will, to reflect with the imagination. Authority is an invitation to know God where he gives himself to be known, as those who are known by him. In the paradox of faith, the authority of scripture rightly understood is the true guarantee of our freedom to seek the living God.

2

Inspiration and Illumination

The concept of canon includes the inspiration of scripture by the Holy Spirit, as well as the absolute need for illumination by the same Holy Spirit. In confessing canon, the universal church confesses the inspiration of scripture and illumination of the present-day church by the Spirit. We turn to Holy Scripture because it comes from the Holy Spirit; yet we cannot recognize its divine source without the present action of the same Spirit in the church today. The inspiration of scripture is a theological confession, not an apologetic appeal. Through the mysterious work of the Spirit in our lives today, we turn to scripture and there discover the same Spirit shining the light of truth for the entire world.

The issues of inspiration and illumination by the Holy Spirit are embedded deeply within the tradition of the Christian community. The tradition is based upon the self-witness of scripture, in two passages in particular. First, from the Pastorals: "All scripture is inspired by God and is useful for teaching, for reproof, for correction, and for training in righteousness, so that everyone who belongs to God may be proficient, equipped for every good work" (2 Tim. 3:16–17). The emphasis here is upon the source of scripture in God, the fitness of the sacred text for the role that it performs, and the function it serves in training and equipping the community of faith. The relation of scripture to the risen and present Christ provides the broader christological context for the affirmation of inspiration. In the Pastorals, there is no attempt to tear apart the continuing presence of Christ in the ongoing life of the Christian community from the sacred text. Rather, it is precisely the scriptures that serve as the instrument by which the exalted Lord instructs the faithful in the duties of service as well as the perils of error. The inspiration of scripture characterizes the text itself as formed by the Spirit of God for its essential and exclusive role. Second, from the catholic epistles: "First of all you must understand this, that no prophecy of scripture is a matter of one's own interpretation, because no prophecy ever came by human will, but men and women moved by the Holy Spirit spoke from God" (2 Peter 1:20–21). The emphasis here is upon the absolute authority of the written text of scripture as given by the Spirit, an authority that it possesses apart from all human arbitration. No individual can rightly interpret scripture according to personal caprice. The point is not to contrast an institutional, ecclesiastical interpretation with a private, charismatic interpretation. The point rather is to insist that the scriptures must be read according to the intention of the Holy Spirit, who is their author. Scripture is not like every other human word, which can be adapted to fit the ideological agenda of the reader; scripture is the Word of God and must therefore be received and understood as divine authority. In both passages, the focus is on the canonical extension of the authority of Paul and Peter for future generations of the community in the form of the written word. A modern notion of authorship is not implied, and the historical relation of these two apostolic figures to these particular letters is best described as "indirect."[1]

Unquestionably the doctrine of inspiration and illumination of scripture is a prominent feature of the church's historic confession. The Nicene Creed affirms clearly that the Holy Spirit "spoke by the prophets." The church fathers, both East and West, teach both dimensions.[2] In the early church, the entire scriptures are considered of divine origin in every respect and therefore without theological error or unnecessary words. For the most part, the reality of inspiration is declared, but without speculation concerning the mode of inspiration. It is not accurate to say that the fathers use a "mechanical" idea, in which the active personality of the prophets and apostles is denied. Rather, according to J. N. D. Kelly, "the majority were content to accept the fact of the inspiration of the sacred writers, without examining further the manner or the degree of its impact upon them."[3] Especially Origen stresses the origins of scripture in the Holy Spirit, and the need for that same Spirit in order to understand them aright. That is to say, inspiration and illumination must go together and should never be separated. He states categorically: "The

1. Childs, 1984, 386.
2. See the convenient summary in Kelly, 64.
3. Kelly, 64.

Scriptures were composed by the Spirit of God." But then he adds the crucial corresponding clarification: "On this point the entire Church is unanimous, that while the whole law is spiritual, the inspired meaning is not recognized by all, but only by those who are gifted with the grace of the Holy Spirit in the word of wisdom and knowledge."[4] In our language, inspiration by the Spirit is truly understood only through illumination by the Spirit. According to Origin, heresy indeed always results when the Bible is not interpreted according to the gift of the Spirit: "Now the cause . . . of the false opinions . . . about God appears to be nothing else than the not understanding the Scripture according to its spiritual meaning, but the interpretation of it agreeably to the mere letter."[5]

This basic view of the dynamic interrelation of inspiration and illumination in the early church is then shared by the major branches of the mainstream confessing church. According to the *Catechism of the Catholic Church*, "The divinely revealed realities, which are contained and presented in the text of Sacred Scripture, have been written down under the inspiration of the Holy Spirit." Yet the ontic reality of inspiration must be completed by the noetic gift of illumination: "Sacred Scripture must be read and interpreted in the light of the same Spirit by whom it was written."[6] The *Confession of Dositheus* affirms, "We believe the Divine and Sacred Scriptures to be God-taught; and, therefore, we ought to believe the same without doubting."[7] However, a particular reader response is required for appropriate reading: "Nevertheless, [the Scriptures] should not be read by all, but only by those who with fitting research have inquired into the deep things of the Spirit."[8] According to the *Second Helvetic Confession*, "God himself spake to the fathers, prophets, apostles, and still speaks to us through the Holy Scriptures."[9] Similar quotations abound in the confessional and orthodox writers of the Reformation and post-Reformation period, both Lutheran and Reformed.[10] The ecumenical consensus of the church on this issue is clear: it affirms both the ontic inspiration of the biblical text and the noetic need for the Spirit's work of illumination if the church is to understand it aright. Both dimensions are essential for canon, which asserts the divine origin of the biblical witness—scripture is the Word of God—as well as the promised presence of the Spirit for genuine understanding in the community of faith—scripture becomes the Word of God.

4. Quoted in Quasten, 2:92.
5. Origen, 357.
6. *Cat*, 31–32, quoting from *Verbum Dei*.
7. Decree 2, in Leith, 486.
8. Question 1, in Leith, 506.
9. Chapter 1, in Leith, 132.
10. See Schmid, 38–70; Heppe, 12–41.

In modernity. the balanced economy of the ecumenical understanding has been thrown off center in two different directions. The religious right has separated inspiration from illumination by seeking to defend an inspired text on rational grounds. The religious left has separated illumination from inspiration by eliminating the inherent dignity and authority of the scriptural witness. Both movements fall well short of the church's authentic and theologically rich confession of canon. In hindsight, the separation of inspiration from illumination on the religious right begins in an otherwise innocuous section of Calvin's *Institutes* 1.8. The section clearly contradicts Calvin's own insistence on the witness of the Spirit for true recognition of the authority of scripture. Indeed, the section includes a disclaimer that all but invalidates the argument: "For truth is cleared of all doubt when, not sustained by external props, it serves as its own support."[11] Nevertheless, Calvin then continues by offering a series of rational arguments in support of scriptural authority: the antiquity of the Bible, the grandeur of its subject matter, the miracles and prophecies, the authentic transmission of historical tradition, the consent of the church, and the death of the martyrs. He concludes by returning to the Spirit and faith: "But those who wish to prove to unbelievers that Scripture is the Word of God are acting foolishly, for only by faith can this be known."[12] It is not fully clear to whom these defenses of scripture are directed; apparently Calvin felt that feeble faith itself requires aids to support it. Though Calvin himself never meant the chapter to sever the connection between inspiration and illumination, the unintended after-effect was to open a door to reformed rationalism. The effort was quickly made to turn these secondary arguments into primary proofs, as if to establish the inspired authority of scripture on a rationally objective basis. The Hodge-Warfield school of modern evangelicalism is the inheritor of this unfortunate misdirection in Christian doctrine.

No one can deny the enormous learning of Benjamin Breckenridge Warfield, who solidified and defended the position staked out earlier at Princeton Seminary by Charles Hodge. Nevertheless, the modern reader of Warfield is left with the painfully tragic impression of a brilliant mind channeled toward a narrow, defensive position that is already well out of contact with the mainstream of the historic Christian faith. Nowhere is this posture more clear than in his numerous and lengthy writings on "plenary inspiration." In his article "The Real Problem of Inspiration," Warfield sets out to offer a rational proof for the inspiration of the Bible. Warfield asserts the privileged use of reason in theology in a way that Calvin never dreamed and in fact often vehemently denies. He criticizes

11. Calvin, 1.82.
12. Ibid., 1.92.

those, such as Charles Augustus Briggs, who according to Warfield have abandoned the true defense of the doctrine against the onslaught of modern historical criticism. Instead of such liberal waffling, Warfield will offer a rational proof, largely couched in the Baconian empiricism of Princeton scholasticism: "But facts are somewhat stubborn things, and are sometimes found to prove rather the test of theories which seek to make them their sport."[13] Warfield offers a rational proof of the fact of plenary verbal inspiration on the grounds of two kinds of evidence. The first is factual evidence that the biblical writers themselves held the doctrine to be true: "There is the exegetical evidence that the doctrine held and taught by the Church is the doctrine held and taught by the Biblical writers themselves."[14] The second is similarly factual evidence that the biblical writers are trustworthy: "There is the whole mass of evidence—internal and external, objective and subjective, historical and philosophical, human and divine—which goes to show that the Biblical writers are trustworthy as doctrinal guides."[15] These two factual propositions combined yield an airtight logical conclusion: "If they are trustworthy teachers of doctrine and if they hold and taught this doctrine, then this doctrine is true, and is to be accepted and acted upon as true by us all."[16] Warfield, then, would base the church's affirmation of inspiration upon a logical proof related to the evidence of facts.

Warfield further develops his proof for inspiration by a careful description of the correct logical method to be employed. First the biblical doctrine must be found; then the biblical doctrine must be tested by the facts of the Bible as "ascertained by Biblical criticism and exegesis."[17] The incorrect logical method would proceed in the reverse direction, first examining the Bible exegetically, then testing its claim to inspiration. Warfield rests his case for biblical inspiration on the iron logic of induction. His conclusion, of course, upholds the biblical test, and yet the force of his affirmation is by nature of the case limited to the results of induction. The "real problem" of inspiration is therefore not really solved by the proof but instead lingers at the end of his argument: "The real problem brought before the Churches by the present debate ought now to be sufficiently plain. In its deepest essence it is whether we can still trust the Bible as a guide in doctrine, as a teacher of the truth."[18] Indeed, one has to wonder whether Warfield has so much solved the real problem by his proof as he has created it. At any rate, in arriving at what

13. Warfield, 172.
14. Ibid., 174.
15. Ibid., 174.
16. Ibid., 174.
17. Ibid., 223.
18. Ibid., 226.

he considers the "biblical doctrine" of inspiration, Warfield exhaustively studies the phenomena of inspiration in the ancient world, including not only the biblical texts but also Plutarch, Pseudo-Galen, the Sibylline Oracles, Philo, and others. He concludes that biblical usage fully accords with the general usage in the ancient world: "Thus it appears that such a conception as 'God-breathed' lies well within the general circle of ideas of the Hellenistic writers, who certainly most prevailingly use the word."[19] While Warfield denies the so-called dictation theory, he emphasizes the merely passive role of the prophets: "What this language of Peter emphasizes—and what is emphasized in the whole account which the prophets give of their own consciousness—is, to speak plainly, the passivity of the prophets with respect to the revelation given through them."[20] The minds of the prophets were not passive in receiving the divine word but were entirely passive in creating the prophetic message: "It is intended to deny only that their intelligence was . . . creatively as distinguished from receptively active."[21]

However well-meaning his intention may have been, Warfield's rationalistic affirmation of inspiration is a radical departure from the Christian faith. Despite his sincere professions of orthodoxy, his view is in fact false doctrine and must be rightly criticized as such. First of all, the Bible nowhere makes a single rational claim about inspiration, or about anything else for that matter. The Bible makes no rational claims; it makes *assertions*. The Bible is kerygmatic from beginning to end, a faith construal that can be received only in faith. It proclaims its own inspiration and leaves no room whatsoever for any "proofs." "Proofs" are for fools, not for the church of Jesus Christ, "for God's foolishness is wiser than human wisdom, and God's weakness is stronger than human strength" (1 Cor. 1:25). In the words of Luther, "It is not the mark of a Christian mind to take no delight in assertions; on the contrary, a man must delight in assertions or he will be no Christian. And by assertion—in order that we may not be misled by words—I mean a constant adhering, affirming, confessing, maintaining, and an invincible persevering."[22] On the basis of scripture we confess the doctrine of inspiration; we do not, as Warfield does, submit it to rational disputation. Any attempt to prove Christian doctrine on rational grounds will inevitably, despite one's best intentions, utterly distort what is being proved, for human reason is fallen. To approach Christian doctrine through human reason, including inspiration and illumination, is to distort the truth of the gospel. No human being whatsoever is in a position to judge the things of God:

19. Ibid., 286.
20. Ibid., 91.
21. Ibid.
22. *LW,* 33:20.

"For my thoughts are not your thoughts, nor are your ways my ways, says the LORD. For as the heavens are higher than the earth, so are my ways higher than your ways and my thoughts than your thoughts" (Isa. 55:8–9). Warfield's search for a rational proof of inspiration shares all too fully in the spirit of the Enlightenment.

Second, by attempting to construct a rational proof for inspiration, Warfield eliminates the only possible basis upon which the confession of the church stands, and that is the testimony of the Spirit. Paul clearly states that "no one comprehends what is truly God's except the Spirit of God. Now we have received not the spirit of the world, but the Spirit that is from God, so that we may understand the gifts bestowed on us by God" (1 Cor. 2:11–12). Only God can make himself known in his Word, and he submits to no human criterion of rational proof for his self-revelation whatsoever. God's Word is not in the least way beholden to human concepts of logic. In seeking to prove inspiration rationally, Warfield has accredited to human beings a natural capacity for discernment that the Bible straightforwardly and vigorously denies. Without the Spirit, no one can understand the inspired text of scripture: "Those who are unspiritual do not receive the gifts of God's Spirit, for they are foolishness to them, and they are unable to understand them because they are spiritually discerned" (1 Cor. 2:14). Calvin states profoundly and clearly: "The same Spirit, therefore, who has spoken through the mouths of the prophets must penetrate into our hearts to persuade us that they faithfully proclaimed what had been divinely commanded."[23] To be sure, we are to test the spirits, but the only "standard" for revelation is Jesus Christ as he is attested in scripture alone, the one norm of all truth. Despite his short section on "aids to faith," Calvin makes fully clear in his brilliant chapter on faith that there is no room whatsoever for setting rational conditions for divine truth. Against all forms of rationalism, Calvin roundly asserts that faith must "hold to be beyond doubt that whatever proceeds from [God] is sacred and inviolable truth."[24] There are no conditions, no tests, no rational proofs, only utter confidence.

Third, Warfield makes the thoroughly modern movement from the possibility of inspiration as a general human phenomenon to the truth of revelation as a biblical reality. He finds the ultimate content of the biblical doctrine of inspiration embedded within the cultural history of the Hellenistic world. In this context it is worth remembering that both evangelicalism and liberalism are ultimately products of the Enlightenment, even though one considers itself "conservative" and the other "progressive." Of course Warfield's sole interest is in defending

23. Calvin, 1.79.
24. Ibid., 1.549.

inspiration on grounds shared with modern rationalism. The result of his apologetics, however, is subtly but profoundly to alter the inner logic of the doctrinal position he is trying to defend. The true meaning of biblical inspiration is not in the slightest degree one instance of a class of such culturally defined phenomena. From the biblical perspective, God has not spoken his Word to every nation on earth; God has not communicated his will to every people in the world. With absolute astonishment, the biblical witness confesses that God has spoken only to his chosen people: "He sends out his word. . . . He declares his word to Jacob, his statutes and ordinances to Israel. He has not dealt thus with any other nation; they do not know his ordinances. Praise the LORD!" (Ps. 147:18–20). The reality of biblical inspiration is not grounded in a general human possibility but rather in the sheer mystery and wonder of divine election. When Warfield then seeks to define inspiration against the backdrop of general human phenomena (of course in order thus to defend the inspiration of the Bible), he unknowingly directly contradicts the clear teaching of scripture.

Fourth, Warfield in essence sought to build a wall between the church's doctrine of inspiration and the use of historical criticism in the church. In doing so, he wrongly consigned a fine church theologian such as C. A. Briggs to heresy. The wall Warfield sought to erect was a serious theological mistake. Warfield failed to make a distinction between the tools of historical criticism and the theological use to which those tools are put. Theological liberalism wrongly uses the tools of historical criticism; but instead of carefully constructing a better alternative by making a better use of those tools, Warfield defensively rejected historical criticism at large as a threat to faith. His Baconian logic of induction gave him the illusion of standing on defensible ground, when in fact the best he could hope for was one holding action after another. As a result, Warfield entirely underestimated the role of response in ancient Israel and the early church. Inspiration is not a "supernatural phenomenon"; inspiration is a miracle. The miracle of inspiration comprises a process of collecting, sorting, and editing a sacred collection of texts for the ongoing life of the church. The result of that process is the inspired text of the Bible, which is the Word of God, given by the Spirit; but historical critical tools are helpful in showing the depth dimension of the biblical witness, which includes both the active witness of the biblical text and the divine reality of which the text speaks. By eliminating the tools of historical criticism, Warfield inevitably flattened the text of the Bible to its verbal dimension, thus ignoring entirely the true content of which it speaks. Inspiration is not "verbal" merely; inspiration includes both the words and the reality together, and these cannot be separated. Warfield separates inspiration from revelation in a way that orthodox church doctrine of the canon must never do.

Finally, and most important, Warfield has isolated scripture from the present work of the Holy Spirit. Second Peter firmly asserts that no prophecy of scripture "is a matter of one's own interpretation" and that no prophetic text "ever came by human will" (cf. 2 Peter 1:20–21). The issue is not private versus communal interpretation. Appeal is not rightly made to an institutional authority of scriptural interpretation, notwithstanding the continuing claims of the Roman Catholic magisterium to the contrary.[25] The issue is the present work of the Holy Spirit guiding the community of faith and the individual within the community to a true understanding of his purpose for the church and the world through the instrument of scripture. Scripture must be interpreted according to the intention of the Holy Spirit. The Westminster Confession correctly states that the "Supreme Judge, by which all controversies of religion are to be determined, . . . can be no other but the Holy Spirit speaking in the Scripture."[26] By isolating the doctrine of inspiration from the necessary theological correlative of illumination, Warfield in essence separates scripture from the church. But the same Spirit who was active then in the inspiration of the Bible is the very Spirit who is active now, instructing the church in the way of Christ through the witness of scripture. Inspiration cannot be separated from illumination; scripture cannot be separated from the church. Warfield's search for rational proof implies a disembodied individual, cut free from the confessing faith of the community. Despite Warfield's evident love for the church, the logical force of his own theological position sadly separated his theological legacy from the very community of faith he sought to serve.

The legacy of Warfield's position on inspiration is best seen in the figure of J. Gresham Machen. Armed with the Hodge-Warfield doctrine, which cuts the truth of scripture free from the life of the church and from the christological subject matter of which it speaks, Machen undertook to critique liberalism from the vantage point of Christianity. Yet right from the beginning of his infamous book *Christianity and Liberalism*, it is abundantly clear that the vantage point from which he launches his criticism is not the gospel of Jesus Christ but instead the cultural and political agenda of conservatism. Christianity is the old religion, which as a "lost secret" lies forgotten in the mists of the "glories of the past."[27] From Machen's standpoint (the book was published first in 1923), one can only look back upon the "lamentable decline"[28] of the present world,

25. *Cat*, 85.
26. 1.10, in Leith, 196.
27. Machen, 15.
28. Ibid., 10.

which embraces all dimensions of human culture. The "realm of art" is the clearest example of such decline, including poetry, music, sculpture, and painting: "Despite the mighty revolution which has been produced in the external conditions of life, no great poet is now living to celebrate the change. . . . Gone, too, are the great painters and the great musicians and the great sculptors."[29] Similarly, the writing of great treatises of history has disappeared: "Even the appreciation of the glories of the past is gradually being lost."[30] Even further, the loss of the individual in various expressions of "socialism" has degraded human experience at the most basic level: "The result is an unparalleled impoverishment of human life. . . . Personality can only be developed in the realm of individual choice."[31] Finally, the world has lost the sterling quality of leadership: "It cannot be denied that great men are few or non-existent."[32] According to Machen, the world is left with a stark and simple choice between liberalism and conservatism, with the future itself in the balance.

How are we to respond to Machen? Perhaps it should be pointed out that T. S. Eliot published his monumental and epoch-making poem "The Wasteland" in 1922; that Claude Debussy's recent compositions were revolutionizing the world of music in the 1920s, after his death in 1918; that Claude Monet was just finishing a similarly revolutionary body of painting before his death in 1926; that Auguste Rodin had just offered the world of art a magnificent body of sculpture before his death in 1913; that Douglass Southall Freeman had begun his epoch-making historical narrative of the life of Robert E. Lee in 1915, to be published finally in 1934 and given the Pulitzer Prize the next year; that President Woodrow Wilson—a Presbyterian—had just led the world as a champion of democracy through the horrors of world war and would be followed in a few short years by Franklin Roosevelt and Winston Churchill. History has an ironic way of defeating ideology, whether conservative or liberal. But with such a response, the issue would be wrongly placed theologically. For what business has any church theologian placing their confidence in good art, in outstanding history writing, in great leaders, or in individual choice to begin with? Throwing the whole world into distant shadow in both its tragedies and its possibilities is the glorious gift of God's redeeming love in Jesus Christ. Jesus Christ is the gospel, not a cultural and political ideology of conservatism. Those who look back in nostalgia do not see the face of Christ but see rather the reflection of their own inner poverty, for biblical faith is always focused not on the past but on the future: "Come, Lord Jesus!" (Rev. 22:20). Warfield's

29. Ibid.
30. Ibid.
31. Ibid., 11.
32. Ibid., 15.

doctrine of inspiration opened the door for a freelance cultural agenda severed from the gospel; sadly, Machen walked through the door and with him took the religious right.

The error of the religious left is the mirror image of the religious right. If evangelicalism defends the inspiration of scripture on rational grounds and thus effectively eliminates the absolute need for the Spirit in discerning the true subject matter of the text, liberalism collapses inspiration into illumination and thus transfers the theological focus to an autonomous act of creative imagination. Nowhere is this clearer than in the work of David Kelsey. Kelsey offers his work as a theologically neutral descriptive analysis of the inner logic of theological positions. He begins with the assumption that key terms such as *scripture, canon, authority* are used in irreducibly pluralistic ways among the nineteenth- and twentieth-century theologians he considers. He then adds to this the further assumption that there can therefore be nothing objective about scripture which controls the discussion of theology. He states that "'Scripture' is not something objective that different theologians simply use differently."[33] According to Kelsey this is a descriptive statement, not a theological proposal. Because there is no objective authority in scripture that confronts the church as a controlling norm, every theologian must make a set of decisions about how scripture will be used in a particular theology. He repeats several times the point that all decisions about scripture are performative in nature and imply nothing about an actual property of the text.[34] Among these decisions is a position concerning the inspiration of scripture. According to Kelsey, inspiration too necessarily fits into the purely functionalist nature of the Bible, which is logically necessary for all theology. Discussion of inspiration should belong in the section of theology on Christian existence; that is to say, it belongs in ecclesiology. Inspiration is by definition a second-order accounting for the reason that scripture functions authoritatively in the Christian community. Kelsey argues that "a doctrine of 'inspiration' gives a theological explanation of why, when scripture is used that way, certain results sometimes follow."[35] In other words, the results come first, the explanation comes second. But who or what determines what Christian existence means? Or what are genuine results from the reading of scripture? Kelsey is very clear: every theologian must make at the outset an imaginative construal. He states: "But just how a theologian does finally construe and use scripture is decisively determined, not by the texts as texts, nor by the texts as scripture, but by the logically prior

33. Kelsey, *Uses of Scripture*, 2.
34. Ibid., 108, 152, etc.
35. Ibid., 211.

imaginative judgment."[36] Scripture is relevant but not decisive to the
making of that judgment. For Kelsey, then, inspiration is the explanation for a particular theological activity, whose nature is determined by
a logically prior theological judgment. The crucial outcome of this view
is that inspiration is not about the text of scripture as the written Word
of God. Indeed, the very notion of "Word of God" must be discarded:
"Our analysis of how 'scripture' is 'authority' in the context of actual
theological practice suggests that it would be less misleading and more
fruitful of insight . . . if a theologian made it explicitly clear when he uses
'Word of God' in his doctrine about scripture that it is a way of drawing
attention, not to 'what God is using the Bible to *say*,' but to 'what God
is using the Bible *for*,' viz., shaping Christian existence."[37]

Once again, the church's doctrine of inspiration is a direct contradiction of Kelsey's entire program, for it most definitely asserts straightforwardly a divine property of scripture itself: namely, scripture is the
Word of God written. In the logic of the church's confession, this is not
at all a second-order description of Christian activity, though Christian
activity certainly flows from it. This is a description of reality, though
a reality that can be perceived only through the gift of the Spirit in
the community of faith. The logic of church confession of inspiration
and illumination simply does not follow the prescriptions that Kelsey
claims to draw from nineteenth- and twentieth-century theology but
that are in fact derived from his own very clear (but unexpressed and
unexamined) theological commitments. If the logic of church confession
is correct—and I believe it is—then Kelsey's model must be in error on
theological grounds.

First of all, as suggested earlier, Kelsey operates with an aggressive
and partisan theological position; it is troublesome, if not absurd, that
he does so under cover of theological neutrality. Kelsey is doing liberal
theology. Moreover, he is suggesting that liberal theology is logically
necessary for everyone. It is one thing to argue for one's own position;
it is quite another matter to argue that one's own position is the only
logically meaningful position available. I fully concede that Kelsey's position is logical and meaningful; I simply believe that it is wrong, because
it contradicts scripture itself and fails to account for the longstanding
and universally held inner logic of the church's confessional position.
Furthermore, he claims that everyone else is doing liberal theology,
whether they know it or not. Such a claim is arrogant, and historically
false in the extreme, as is clear in the case of inspiration. All of the great
confessional traditions of the church agree that sacred scripture is in-

36. Ibid., 206.
37. Ibid., 213.

spired by God. They do so not because they have reached a logically prior theological judgment but because scripture describes itself this way. We confess that scripture is inspired because it says that it is inspired; we profess no more and no less than the self-witness of the biblical text, as received in faith. This is not a "conclusion" or a "claim" or a second-order evaluative "judgment"; this is a confession of faith, universally shared by all Christians. Surely Kelsey should somehow have come to grips with the broad teaching of the historic church as contained in its creeds and confessions in a proposal so comprehensive in aim.

Second, Kelsey reverses the proper relation of the inspired text of scripture and the shaping of the Christian life that flows from it. Scripture is not simply relevant to the Christian life, as Kelsey suggests. It is in fact profoundly and utterly decisive in every respect. It stands as the critical norm by which every aspect of Christian faith and life is measured. Genuine Christian existence speaks of scripture by using a far different language from Kelsey's. As Thomas Cranmer, for example, declares in the Edwardian homily "A Fruitful Exhortation to the Reading and Knowledge of Holy Scripture,"

> For the scripture of God is the heavenly meat of our souls; the hearing and keeping of it maketh us blessed, sanctifieth us, and maketh us holy; it turneth our souls, it is a light lantern to our feet; it is a sure, steadfast, and everlasting instrument of salvation; it giveth wisdom to the humble and lowly hearts; it comforteth, maketh glad, cheereth, and cherisheth our conscience; it is a more excellent jewel or treasure than any gold or precious stone; it is more sweet than honey or honey-comb; it is called the best part, which Mary did choose, for it hath in it everlasting comfort.[38]

This is the voice of true Christian experience, for which the reading of scripture is an act of profoundly joyous and life-changing discovery, not an act of finding secondary warrants for a logically prior *discrimen*. Kelsey has drastically reversed the logic of interpretation, in which the life of the reader is adjusted to the subject matter of scripture rather than the reverse. As Luther states already in the first Psalms Lectures of 1513–1515: "The strength of Scripture is this, that it is not changed into him who studies it, but that it transforms its lover into itself and its strengths . . . because you will not change me into what you are . . . but you will be changed into what I am."[39] This is not a second-order reflection on Christian activity but a true expression of direct encounter with the living will of God made known through the pages of scripture. If

38. Leith, 233.
39. Quoted in Lohse, *Martin Luther's Theology*, 52.

Kelsey's view is logically necessary, then it must be said that the canons of human logic must give way to the superior force of divine truth.

Third, because he refuses to acknowledge the descriptive force of inspiration as an objective property of the text, Kelsey's understanding of illumination is dramatically altered. In fact, Kelsey's position ends up rather similar to Warfield's; what for Warfield is the individual act of rational proof is for Kelsey a personal act of free imagination. Both are an invitation to ideology, in which scripture is used to support a social and political cause derived elsewhere. What is scripture all about, according to the "imaginative construal" of Kelsey? According to his own constructive statement, it is about "public acts undertaken with other persons and aiming at those deep social changes through which justice and human liberation may be brought about."[40] Surely not; surely it is about God's redemptive and transforming love for the whole creation through Jesus Christ! Kelsey cannot escape captivity to the ideological agenda of the political and cultural left, any more than evangelicalism can escape captivity to the political and cultural right. Kelsey's view is tailor-made to underwrite the many projects of so-called liberation theology, which regularly appeal to his position for support.

Fourth, Kelsey can make no room in his analysis for the verbal nature of inspiration. The overwhelming confession of the entire ecumenical Christian tradition is that scripture is the written Word of God. Inspiration has a verbal component, which has the crucial effect of distinguishing the divine Word from all other human words. According to Jeremiah, God hears the words of the false prophets and denounces them: "How long? Will the hearts of the prophets ever turn back—those who prophesy lies, and who prophesy the deceit of their own heart?" This stands in sharp contrast to the true prophet, who speaks the divine word: "But let the one who has my word speak my word faithfully." Therefore, no human being can lay claim to the divine purpose: "When this people, or a prophet, or a priest asks you, 'What is the burden of the Lord?' you shall say to them, 'You are the burden, and I will cast you off, says the Lord'" (see Jer. 23:23–40). The spoken Word of God is completely different from every other human word. Now, what is true of the prophetic and apostolic testimony is true of the Word of God written, which preserves and transmits that testimony for the ongoing life of the community. Holy scripture is the inspired Word of God. Through the gracious presence of the Spirit, we hear the voice of God in the human voices of scripture. Without the present illumination of the Spirit, we cannot know the inspiration of the text; the biblical text remains lifeless. But through the illumination of the Spirit, we do not bring life to a dead text; rather, we

40. Kelsey, "Bible and Christian Theology," 389.

discover that the living divine Word of Holy Scripture has been waiting for us all along, ready to teach, to challenge, to transform. Of course, the words of scripture can be understood rightly only when the true content of which they speak is properly grasped. However, it is precisely through these words that God's living will is declared to each new generation.

Despite the controversy and misunderstanding that continue to surround the issue, confession of canon involves affirming the inspiration of the Bible. The mechanical notion of inspiration—in which the biblical authors are simply passive channels for direct divine speech—has never been part of the ecumenical mainstream of Christian confession and must certainly be denounced. Israel and the early church were active tradents of the scriptures, shaping their witness even as they were shaped by it. The people of God formed the testimony to the divine will, yet God himself through inspiration gives the true content of that will, which the people of God gratefully receive. Inspiration is not tied to a narrow conception of authorship but leaves ample room for the lengthy process of oral and written transmission and editing of the biblical literature for future generations that is constitutive of canon. The conservative misunderstanding of inspiration turns scripture into an objective system of propositions torn asunder from the use of the Bible in a community of faith. The rationalistic adjustment of propositions to one another without any understanding of the creative tensions within the canon—tensions necessary for the testimony it makes to Jesus Christ—is the price paid for this misunderstanding. However, it is one thing to insist upon the sheer plurality and variety of witnesses within the biblical canon, witnesses often in considerable tension with one another; it is something else altogether different to deny that all these disparate voices are inspired by the same Spirit and indeed bear witness to the selfsame divine reality. On this latter point the church cannot yield a single inch. Inspiration cannot be discarded or collapsed into illumination. We believe in the necessity of the Spirit's work in making alive the biblical witness for our contemporary generation. Scripture does not speak directly to us; scripture does not contain in itself the positive force of truth. Rather, Jesus Christ speaks to us, and to the whole world, through the instrument of scripture through the guidance of his Spirit; the Spirit of Christ alone is the forceful energy of divine truth. But the crucial point here is that the Spirit's presence is tied to the witness of scripture. As Calvin long ago carefully argued against the fanatics, appeals to the Spirit apart from the written testimony of the Bible are null and void.[41] Word and Spirit belong inseparably together. The one divine Spirit uses scripture to shape the one church into the image of its one Lord. Despite creative tensions, the

41. Calvin, 1.9.

variety of biblical witness is not a mass of self-contradictory fragments or images; it is to be rendered holistically because the content of which it speaks is a whole, greater than the sum of its parts. At stake is the unity of Christ, the one Word of the Father.

Because we believe in the inspiration and illumination of scripture, it is also essential to confess our trust in the truthfulness of scripture. Here again, the errors of the right and the left are all too apparent. Both seek to adjudge the truthfulness of the Bible from a neutral standpoint. Evangelicals attempt to prove the truth of scripture from such a standpoint; liberals attempt to dismiss the truth of scripture from the same identical neutral viewpoint. Yet against both it is necessary to assert that there is no valid neutral standpoint in reference to scripture. The biblical words demand faith; all else, including misguided attempts to prove the truth of that faith, comes from unbelief. The truthfulness of scripture is therefore an analytical statement, not a synthetic judgment. However, from the proper theological point of view, the truthfulness of scripture is not only a valid but indeed a crucial point of church doctrine. Through the present action of the Holy Spirit we affirm the absolute reliability of scripture. We trust that in turning to scripture we will not be led astray. We know that in relying on scripture alone for every issue of life and death we will in fact encounter the living divine will, whose truth is perfect because it is the Truth itself by which all else is judged. We share our certain confidence in scripture with the church of all ages, which has never turned away disappointed from a fresh hearing of the sacred message of the Bible. Because of our affirmation of the truthfulness of scriptures, we ourselves can never be indifferent to the concern for truth. As Christians, we do not know the right answer to every question; nevertheless, we offer to the surrounding world nothing less than the one truth by which joyous freedom is given to all humanity, the truth of God's gracious forgiveness of sins through the gospel. Based on the truthfulness of scripture, the church's role in the world is to be the herald of divine truth, making known to the nations of the earth the reality of God's redeeming love for the entire creation. We believe in the truthfulness of scripture, and we are led by the Spirit through the biblical witness to the One who is the absolute Truth for all humankind: Jesus Christ, the risen Lord of all reality. We cannot speak of the inerrancy or infallibility of scripture; even Jesus himself criticizes the Old Testament food laws (Mark 7:19). Similarly, in the New Testament the sheer fallibility of the disciples is regularly portrayed with no attempt to cover it up. There can be no simple identification of scripture with God's living will in the manner of modern biblicism. Even given inspiration, there is still the need for the church's wrestling with the content of scripture. However, it is not only appropriate but necessary to acknowledge that scripture infallibly leads to the true God, who can be known in no other way.

Both inspiration and illumination flow from Christology. Jesus gives his disciples the promise of the Spirit: "And I will ask the Father, and he will give you another Advocate, to be with you forever. This is the Spirit of truth, whom the world cannot receive, because it neither sees him nor knows him. You know him, because he abides with you, and he will be in you" (John 14:16–17). The role of the Spirit is to point to Christ: "When the Spirit of truth comes, he will guide you into all the truth; for he will not speak on his own, but will speak whatever he hears, and he will declare to you the things that are to come. . . . He will take what is mine and declare it to you" (John 16:13–15). Our knowledge of Christ is not based on any human capacity; it is a miraculous gift of the Holy Spirit. Yet it is through the witness of scripture that the Spirit leads us in every new age.

3

The Final Form of Scripture

Our theological affirmation of canon also involves confessing the author-ity of the final form of the biblical witness. In a sense, this confession is in full continuity with the historic mainstream of Christian tradition. The church has everywhere and always regarded the Christian scriptures as shaped by the synagogue and the early church to be the authoritative witness to God's eternal will. Almost by reflex, the church's exegesis of scripture has operated within the limits established by the canonical shape of scripture, even though it was not always a conscious decision. That reflex accounts for the clear family resemblance that runs through the history of exegesis, despite considerable variety. Yet in another sense, our contemporary affirmation of the authority of the final form of the biblical witness is a new moment of Christian confession, and full credit goes to Brevard Childs for his brilliant insight into canon. According to Childs, canon is not simply a list of books sanctioned for use by the church; much more is involved. Canon describes a process in which the biblical books were shaped—often by unnamed editors in the com-munity—for the purpose of serving as the instrument by which every new generation of God's people might be confronted by the living claim of God. Or better, canon is the result of that process of active shaping of scripture for the purpose of rendering it theologically useful for the role it plays. The process itself was not canonized; adherence to canon therefore does not mean continuing that process by our own creative reshaping of the text. On the contrary, the process came to an end, and the canon of sacred scripture was born, as confessed by the early church; from that time forth there is an absolute distinction between scripture and ongoing interpretation.

The theological clues for seeking out the divine will are built into the very theological shaping of scripture, in a variety of different ways. Christian theology is committed to canon; it is committed to hearing the biblical word in the theological context of the canonical shape it received from the synagogue and the early church. Their shaping of the text was a construal of faith, through direct encounter with the activity of God. The activity of God has not in any way whatsoever come to an end. God continues to manifest himself; God continues to act with stunning surprise and overwhelming glory; God continues to encounter the church, bringing life and light to all who believe and obey; God continues to make known his marvelous and indeed utterly strange will. Divine self-revelation is not limited to the biblical past but continues fully in the present. Nevertheless, for us today God makes himself known solely through the instrument of scripture as it is shaped for that purpose. Our confession of faith is to accept the final form of scripture as our authority, to affirm our unyielding allegiance to the subject matter of which it speaks, and to turn again and again to the canonical text for illumination and discovery.

It is also essential to observe that the final form of scripture is not identical to the latest stage in its redactional history. Dogmatic theology affirms the use of historical critical tools in biblical scholarship. The broad legacy of the religious right is to reject those tools as such, or at least to mold them toward a preestablished conservative position, which is a form of historical obscurantism far removed from biblical faith. On the other hand, dogmatics joins biblical theology in its criticism of the theological misuse made of historical criticism on the religious left. The final form of the text is not the same as the end product of its oral history, tradition history, literary history, and redactional history. Though knowledge of these trajectories may very well add needed precision to the study of the final form, the authority of scripture lies in the shaped text, not in the shaping process. The final form of the text reverberates with a theological dynamic that is not the same as the added layers behind it, including the final layer; and appeal to scripture always and only means appeal to the final form, not to the historical layering. To be sure, concern with the final form is not a chronological concern, as if only one moment in the life of the text were exegetically relevant. Canon honors and accepts the lengthy history of oral and written transmission that produced our Bible. Rather, the final form is a *theological* concern; at all stages of its growth, canon is concerned with the role of scripture as a witness to the living God who evoked it.

Moreover, dogmatic theology joins biblical theology in rejecting any form of ostensive reference in the interpretation of scripture. Such interpretation is common to both the religious left and the religious right, though the final results are different. Ostensive reference means any approach to scripture in which the text is used as a source to reconstruct critically a reality known fully only from a standpoint outside the witness of the text. Such an approach invariably abandons the confessing faith of the church: on the left in order to critique the gospel, on the right in order to offer rational support for the gospel. But either way, ostensive reference is a misuse and mishearing of the canonical witness of scripture. The inherent theological dynamic of the text is ignored in favor of a rational-experiential foundation, which is then used to separate the text from the genuine subject matter of which it speaks. Against such a view, the church confesses that the final form of the text alone contains the authentic avenue to the true subject matter of the Bible and equally rejects both liberal and conservative forms of ostensive reading.

I think it is worth pointing out here the clear advance that Childs's work on scripture represents in relation to Karl Barth. There is a clear family resemblance between Barth and Childs. Indeed, it is not too strong to suggest that Childs's biblical reflection is virtually unthinkable without Barth. Nevertheless, it is not the case that Childs simply provides a supporting structure of biblical study for Barthian theology. There is a positive theological advance that must be carefully noted. Despite Barth's undeniable genius in interpretation of scripture, and despite Barth's lasting contribution to the future of church theology, the fact remains that Barth never fully solved the problem of scriptural interpretation in theology. The limits of Barth's work can be seen almost immediately in his description of the exegetical process, which moves in the threefold form of a historical phase, reflective phase, and final phase of appropriation.[1] It is in the movement from the first to the second that the trouble occurs. For Barth, there is a giant gap, a virtual leap, from a historical reading on general hermeneutical grounds to a moment of theological reflection. The problem that thus arose among those who followed in Barth's steps was theological validation: how does one measure the validity of theological reflection on the basis of scripture when the gap is so wide that no real connection is visible? Barth never solved this problem. Childs has shown that scripture itself anticipates the problem and provides its own solution. The final form of scripture provides the theological framework for ongoing theological reflection. The Old and New Testaments, though certainly embedded in the history of Israel and the early church, were rendered and shaped as a

1. *CD*, 1/2, 722–40.

vehicle for ongoing theological reflection in the community of faith that treasures them. There is a link—missing in Barth, even though present in scripture—between analysis of the text of scripture and theological reflection on its content. That link is the theological shape of the text, which guides the reader toward its genuine appropriation in every new age of the church's future. The theological framework of the text does not in the least predetermine what will be found; there is and always will be a need for the utmost use of creative imagination in the search for God's living will in scripture. The theological shape of the biblical witness serves rather as a faithful and reliable guide to mark the path of movement from the witness of the text to the subject matter of which it speaks. Dogmatic theology henceforth must confess and adhere absolutely to the guidance it receives from the final form of the text, for without such adherence there is no true hearing of the divine word.

Several theological insights follow from observing the authority of the final form of scripture. First, we continue the historic affirmation of the perspicuity of scripture. The divine Word in sacred scripture is ultimately clear. That is not to say that it is obvious; on the contrary, the church has always recognized that the gift of clarity in scripture calls forth strenuous and joyful labor in the church. John of Damascus speaks for countless generations of Christians in his appealing description of the attention required: "Let us not knock carelessly, but rather zealously and constantly. . . . For thus it will be opened to us. . . . Let us draw of the fountain of the garden perennial and purest waters springing into life eternal."[2] If the clarity of scripture is a gracious gift of the Spirit, it is also a requirement for eager and serious response. Nevertheless, the clarity of scripture means the universal availability of the biblical word of hope and promise. True insight will be given to whoever asks; whoever seeks will find; to whoever knocks it will be opened (Matt. 7:7). However necessary the theological training of the academy for the good of the church, no professor of biblical studies or theology ever adds to the inherent clarity of the divine Word, which is openly manifest for all with ears to hear (Matt. 13:9).

The issue of the clarity of scripture as canon has of course received sharp criticism among biblical scholars. One of the charges commonly leveled against Childs from the religious left, especially by James Barr, is the charge of "theological fundamentalism."[3] It is Barr's oft-repeated contention that even to speak of a confessional reading of scripture is by definition to fall into the trap of fundamentalism. How does the criticism of Childs by Barr sound when considered outside the field of biblical

2. John of Damascus, 89.
3. Barr, 437.

studies, in the complementary yet different field of dogmatic theology? One can only be disappointed to observe the lack of serious and informed engagement by Barr with the history of Christian tradition. His criticism of Childs is made without any reference to, or apparent account taken of, the long history of Christian engagement with the Bible. In Childs's work on biblical theology, the classical approaches of Irenaeus, Origen, Augustine, Thomas Aquinas, Martin Luther, and John Calvin are described in detail, including contemporary research on these figures.[4] Indeed, Childs is well known for his exhaustive understanding of the history of exegesis, including the dogmatic tradition. By sharp contrast, Barr's recent work on biblical theology starts with Ludwig Koehler and ends with Walter Brueggemann! From Barr's narrow historical vantage point, the connection between Childs and the long legacy of Christian wrestling with scripture is scarcely visible. Barr is apparently unaware that the theological features he objects to so strenuously in Childs are shared not by modern fundamentalists, who likewise reject the canonical approach, but by the historic mainstream of the Christian church. One can only ask of Barr: did "real" biblical theology begin only in the twentieth century? Are all prior figures to be dismissed out of hand as "fundamentalists" for reading the Bible theologically, including the church fathers, the scholastics, and the Reformers? Surely the myopic limitation and arrogance of such a view are self-evident.

The confession of canon recognizes that there are clear theological lines drawn within scripture itself beyond which the gospel is distorted and twisted. The creeds and confessions of the church trace the contours and boundaries of those lines. Childs's work shows that the church's hearing is in fact an echo of the theological shape of the biblical testimony. It is to the tracing of these lines that Barr, and indeed the religious left generally, objects in the presentation of Childs. For Barr, the very notion of a boundary line of theological truth is anathema. Of course, the error of fundamentalism is to draw lines where none are found in scripture. Puritanical legalism is always to be guarded against. But the surest defense against fundamentalism is not to deny the theological reading of scripture, as Barr contends. Quite the contrary, the surest defense against all forms of fundamentalism is precisely the theological interpretation of scripture based on canon. It is one thing to object that lines have been drawn in the wrong place; that is the basis for the church's absolute no to fundamentalism. It is quite another to deny that scripture should be read theologically. The marvel of it all is that Barr is apparently unaware how truly idiosyncratic and reactionary his criticism

4. *BTONT,* 1/3.

of Childs sounds when heard against the backdrop of the church's long engagement with the Bible.

Here Luther's debate with Erasmus in *The Bondage of the Will* is illuminating. Luther argued, against Erasmus, for the inherent clarity of scripture. Scripture needs no teaching office or magisterium to ground or explain its clarity; on the contrary, scripture is its own interpreter (*sacra scriptura sui ipsius interpres*). To deny, as Erasmus does, that scripture has a clear subject matter is in fact to ignore the clear affirmation of faith: "For what still sublimer thing can remain hidden in the Scriptures, now that the seals have been broken, the stone rolled away from the sepulcher, and the supreme mystery brought to light, namely, that Christ the Son of God has been made man, that God is three and one, that Christ suffered for us and is to reign eternally? . . . Take Christ out of the Scriptures, and what will you find left in them?"[5] Thus for Luther, the issue of scripture's inherent clarity is ultimately christological. Scripture is clear when read in the light of its substance, which is the risen Christ. Bernhard Lohse summarizes Luther's viewpoint: "Scripture interpretation that does not produce such theological interpretation in the real sense fails its task, though it may yield considerable information in detail."[6] For Luther, the inherent clarity (*claritas externa*) of scripture is not obvious; rather, it requires the inner working of the Holy Spirit (*claritas interna*) in order to be recognized and affirmed: "If you speak of the internal clarity, no man perceives one iota of what is in the Scriptures unless he has the Spirit of God. . . . If, on the other hand, you speak of the external clarity, nothing at all is left obscure or ambiguous, but everything there is in the Scriptures has been brought out by the Word into the most definite light, and published to all the world."[7]

Luther and Childs are in complete agreement—despite the different times and the different tools used—that scripture bears witness to Jesus Christ and that the light Christ sheds on the true meaning of scripture is plain to see. Its clarity is not recognized by autonomous human reason and experience; it is recognized only by faith, which is a gift of the Spirit. Barr repeatedly attacks Childs in rather vehement terms for importing into scripture his own views, a charge of course which both Rome and Erasmus leveled at Luther. Barr, like Erasmus, would prefer humble reticence: "As for involvement in what are commonly called 'the burning issues of the day,' biblical studies are of course a factor in the mind of religious communities. But the Bible does not, in most cases, give in itself a decision on such matters."[8] Barr, like Erasmus, would keep

5. *LW,* 31:25–26.
6. Lohse, *Martin Luther's Theology,* 195.
7. *LW,* 33:28.
8. Barr, 607.

silent when scripture speaks clearly. Nevertheless, denial of the theological clarity of scripture is indeed a direct contradiction of faith in the exalted Christ, in whose light truth comes to all the earth.

Where does the denial of the clarity of scripture come from? According to the book of Isaiah, the failure to understand the scriptures is itself a form of supreme divine judgment upon God's people: "For the LORD has poured out upon you a spirit of deep sleep; he has closed your eyes, you prophets, and covered your heads, you seers. The vision of all this has become for you like the words of a sealed document. If it is given to those who can read, with the command, 'Read this,' they say, 'We cannot, for it is sealed.' And if it is given to those who cannot read, saying, 'Read this,' they say, 'We cannot read'" (Isa. 29:10–12). God hardens the hearts of his people, so that they cannot even read the very scriptures in which his truth is revealed. Of course this judgment comes in the form of a terrifying paradox; but it is the same paradox that canon itself recognizes and confesses. The true substance of scripture is clear, but it is not obvious; it is fully clear for those who have eyes to see and ears to hear. "For to those who have, more will be given, and they will have an abundance; but from those who have nothing, even what they have will be taken away" (Matt. 13:12).

Second, on the basis of the final form of scripture we likewise continue the historic church's affirmation of the scope of scripture, which is the one goal of the biblical witness. In the end, sacred scripture is about one and only one thing, and that is Jesus Christ, the Lord of all creation and Redeemer of all humanity. Here again, we join our voice with the chorus of the ecumenical church. The Barmen Declaration begins with the resounding declaration "Jesus Christ, as he is attested for us in Holy Scripture, is the one Word of God which we have to hear and which we have to trust and obey in life and in death."[9] As is well known, these words of confession were not idle speculation but came at a time when the confessing church stood against Hitler at the cost of life itself. Or again, from the *Catechism of the Catholic Church* comes a similar declaration: "Different as the books which comprise it may be, Scripture is a unity by reason of the unity of God's plan, of which Christ Jesus is the center and heart, open since his Passover."[10] Or again, Cyril of Alexandria speaks of the "mind of the Scriptures."[11] The modern ecumenical church is in full agreement that scripture points ultimately to one scope, which is Christ the risen and exalted Lord. Nor is the christological scope of the biblical message an exclusively modern insight, for indeed it is the

9. Thesis 1, in Leith, 520.
10. *Cat*, 32.
11. Cyril, 69.

ultimate message of the universal church of all ages, grounded in the
basic confession of canon. Hugh of St. Victor makes the essential point
crystal clear: "All Sacred Scripture is but one book, and that one book
is Christ, because all divine Scripture speaks of Christ, and all divine
Scripture is fulfilled in Christ."[12]

The scope of scripture is not a christological proposition but Christ
the risen Lord himself, the true subject matter of all scripture: "Then
beginning with Moses and all the prophets, he interpreted to them the
things about himself in all the scriptures" (Luke 24:27). The religious right
looks in vain when it searches the scriptures for support for principles
of moral value; the religious left likewise looks in vain when it searches
the scriptures for examples of liberation from the oppressive structures
of human hierarchy. The confessing church points to the beacon of light
that draws the reader from the complexity of the text to the ultimate
simplicity of its content: "Again Jesus spoke to them, saying, 'I am the
light of the world. Whoever follows me will never walk in darkness but
will have the light of life'" (John 8:12). Now, the scope of the text does not
cancel out the rich variety of the scriptural witness. It is not as though
the simplicity of the text comes only after scripture has been filtered
through a systematic arrangement of propositions. The scope of scripture
is not an intrasystematic principle; here we must part company with the
notion of "fundamental articles" in scholastic Protestantism in both its
later Lutheran and Reformed manifestations.[13] Rather, the entire witness of scripture in all its variety points beyond itself to a divine reality
whose ultimate simplicity is the invitation of faith itself: "Come to me,
all you that are weary and are carrying heavy burdens, and I will give
you rest. Take my yoke upon you, and learn from me. . . . For my yoke is
easy, and my burden is light" (Matt. 11:28–30). The variety of scripture
is to be carefully preserved not despite the simplicity but precisely for
the sake of it.

Third, the final form of the text brings with it confession of the dialectical relation of Old and New Testaments. There is one Christian scripture, but it retains the form of two distinct Testaments, Old and New.
Theological reflection on their interrelation has accompanied dogmatic
theology since the very beginning. The early church simply assumed that
the Old Testament bears witness to Christ. It did not need to be Christian-
ized in order to make its witness, for the Old Testament itself is Christian proclamation. In other words, the effort was to assert the absolute
integrity of the Old Testament in its own inherent theological validity,
together with the unbreakable unity of Old and New through the one

12. Cited in *Cat*, 37.
13. See Heppe, chapter 3, and Schmid, chapter 5.

subject matter of Jesus Christ. The entire promise of the Old Testament is perfectly fulfilled in the New. The great threat to the church's teaching came from two sources. The first was Marcion, who rejected the Old Testament in its entirety as inferior to the Christian message. Even the New Testament was severely truncated in order to mesh with Marcion's conception of the truth. The other threat came from certain forms of Gnosticism which, though they did not reject the Old Testament entirely, cast aside several parts and insisted on spiritualizing the rest. Behind this Gnostic move was their conviction of an unknown supreme being beyond the Demiurge who fashioned the present material universe.

In response to this threat, catholic theologians affirmed and defended the unitary substance of the two Testaments of scripture, despite the discontinuity of form. At stake was the unity of God, the unity of redemption and creation, the identity of Christ, the theological validity of the law, and the definition of human life. Irenaeus and Origen led the way in the orthodox defense of the twofold canon against heresy. According to Irenaeus, "The whole range of the doctrine of the apostles proclaimed one and the same God, who removed Abraham, who made to him the promise of inheritance. . . . Both the Mosaic law and the grace of the new covenant . . . were bestowed by one and the same God for the benefit of the human race."[14] Marcion splits the person of God into one who loves and one who judges, and "on both sides, he puts an end to deity. For he that is the judicial one, if he be not good, is not God, because he from whom goodness is absent is no God at all; and again, he who is good, if he has no judicial power, suffers the same [loss] as the former, by being deprived of the character of deity."[15] Marcion's rejection of the Old Testament automatically obscures the identity of God. Clearly the unity of the Testaments goes beyond a mere literary question and strikes at the heart of Christian faith itself.

Origen likewise insists on the unity of the Testaments, though in different concepts from those of Irenaeus. For Origen, all theology is based on the words of Christ. However, "by the words of Christ we do not mean those only which He spake when he became man . . . for before that time, Christ . . . was in Moses and the prophets."[16] All biblical writers were filled with the Spirit of Christ, and therefore all together speak of the one Lord. For Origen, it is necessary to be led from both Testaments to the risen Lord whose words they constitute. The understanding of the unity of the Testaments in the early church was encapsulated in the classic formulation of Augustine: "In the Old Testament there is a

14. Irenaeus, 434.
15. Ibid., 459.
16. Origen, 239.

veiling of the New, and in the New Testament there is a revealing of the Old."[17] In summary: "The church read the Old Testament in the light of its fulfillment in Jesus Christ, even as it also understood Jesus Christ from the point of view of the Old Testament."[18]

A full survey of the relation of Old and New Testaments in the Christian tradition goes beyond the scope of the present volume. However, it is helpful to reflect briefly upon another pivotal moment: the rediscovery of the Old Testament in the theological development of the young Luther (for what follows, see the still remarkable study by James Samuel Preus, *From Shadow to Promise*). Despite the best intentions of the church during the medieval period, and despite several noble efforts to overturn the prevailing trend, it seems clear that the medieval church lost the full theological vision of the early church in reading the Testaments dialectically. The dialectic was replaced by a unilinear interpretation moving forward from the Old Testament into the New. The result was that the Old Testament was thought to simply provide "shadow images," in the fine formulation of Preus, of New Testament realities. The hermeneutical weight fell entirely upon the New Testament, while the Old was limited to providing useful examples corroborating New Testament teaching. An essential part of the development of the Reformation—indeed Preus makes a careful case for the theological recovery of the legitimacy of the Old Testament as the decisive turn in the young Reformer's thinking—was Luther's struggle and eventual success at hearing the Old Testament itself, with its own theological integrity. No longer is the Old Testament for Luther a shadow image of the reality of the New. Now, the Old Testament is a full promise of the New, and more important the same promise that even now the Christian grasps in faith. In other words, there is a direct existential bearing of the Old Testament on the Christian life today. Thus, it is not so much that Luther's new understanding of faith brought with it a changed conception of the importance of the Old Testament for Christian existence; rather, Luther's fresh hearing of the witness of the Old Testament brought with it a new understanding of faith in the word of promise. In the words of Preus, "For Luther, the faith of the Old Testament people has—quite unexpectedly—ceased to be carnal, just a *figura*. It has become a model for Christian faith!"[19] The lesson here is not a cavalier dismissal of all medieval exegesis. The lesson rather is that serious theological reflection on the Bible—such as dogmatics must certainly entail—has always involved a fresh encounter with the

17. Augustine, *The Catechising of the Uninstructed*, 287.
18. Lohse, *Short History*, 25.
19. Preus, 199.

Old Testament witness in its own theological integrity as a direct claim upon Christian faith and life.

Both the religious left and the religious right have strayed from the church's confession of the dialectical relation of Old and New Testaments. On the left, the error is clearly seen already in a figure like Schleiermacher. Because of his philosophical definition of the nature of human piety and his anthrolopological charting of comparative religion, Schleiermacher concludes that Christianity has only a "historical connexion" with Judaism, which he defines as the "Mosaic institutions."[20] Even here it is important not to be too exclusive, according to Schleiermacher, for heathen elements also made their contribution to Christian development. He states: "The truth . . . is that the relations of Christianity to Judaism and Heathenism are the same."[21] In other words, Christian faith based on the New Testament has only the relation of having been influenced in its historical development by the Old Testament; there is no direct bearing of the Old Testament upon questions of faith and life in the Christian community of faith. Schleiermacher's conception has direct implications for the Christian reading of the Old Testament, as he makes very clear: "Hence the rule may be set up that almost everything else in the Old Testament is, for our Christian usage, but the husk or wrapping of its prophecy, and that whatever is most definitely Jewish has least value."[22] All of this leads to the astonishing summary declaration of Schleiermacher on the issue of the twofold Christian Bible: "Hence the Old Testament appears simply a superfluous authority for Dogmatics."[23]

I do not think it is too severe at all to suggest that this is more than a simple error of judgment. Despite the failure of good intentions in the medieval period noted above, even the worst neglect of the Old Testament in the darkest periods of biblical study never led to anything remotely like such a declaration. Not since Marcion has such a direct elimination of the Old Testament as authority for the church been sponsored on supposedly Christian theological grounds. Schleiermacher's attempt to remove the Old Testament as a direct authority for the Christian church carries him, and liberalism after him, outside the circle of Christian confession. Moreover, the modern formulation "the Hebrew Bible" is simply a further development along the same theological trajectory. It is one thing to defend the theological legitimacy of the Old Testament witness in its inherent integrity as authority for the church. That is not only important but vital for Christian mission and proclamation. It is quite

20. Schleiermacher, 60.
21. Ibid., 60–61.
22. Ibid., 62.
23. Ibid., 115.

another to sever the Old Testament from its christological substance. From its beginning, everywhere and always, the church has confessed that the one, selfsame, ontologically identical subject matter of both Testaments of scripture is Jesus Christ himself. The gospel itself is at stake in avoiding the error of the religious left. The risen Lord appears to the disciples with the amazing declaration "These are my words that I spoke to you while I was still with you—that everything written about me in the law of Moses, the prophets, and the psalms must be fulfilled" (Luke 24:44). Insofar as it is incapable of making good on this invitation to search the Old Testament as a direct authority for the Christian community, liberalism is preaching another gospel (Gal. 1:6–9).

The failure of the religious right to grasp the church's dialectical understanding of the relationship between the two Testaments is nowhere more evident than in the widespread and popular movement of "dispensationalism." Made vastly popular by the Scofield Reference Bible and taught in such institutions as Dallas Theological Seminary, dispensationalism divides the Bible into a series of several epochs or "dispensations." Each of the biblical ages is constituted by a different moment of the divine government of the world, a different responsibility laid upon human beings, and a special divine revelation characterizing that age.[24] While the basis of faith remains the same throughout the Bible, the content of faith changes from one epoch to the other.[25] The final epoch, known as the kingdom of God, was offered by Jesus; but it was refused and therefore was postponed until the end of time.[26] One byproduct of this schematization is that the Sermon on the Mount, which falls under the "Kingdom of God" dispensation, while relevant to contemporary times, has its real application only in the final age, which is yet to come. It does not apply today directly, but only indirectly at best.[27]

Ryrie does his best to defend dispensationalism against the charge of heresy; he clearly has the best of intentions to honor the authority of both Testaments of scripture. Nevertheless, there can be no doubt that dispensationalism falls well outside the circle of orthodox Christian confession concerning the authority of scripture. What is particularly troublesome is Ryrie's strange argument that the opposing view—he calls it "covenant theology"—was unknown to the early church and the medieval church and never even mentioned by the Reformers.[28]

The theological affirmation of canon brings with it a rejection of dispensationalism. First, the church's confession that both Testaments

24. Ryrie, 36–37.
25. Ibid., 123–24.
26. Ibid., 165.
27. Ibid., 105–9.
28. Ibid., 179.

of scripture bear witness to the selfsame subject matter is not a special "covenant theology," as Ryrie contends; it is the basic confession of the church of all times and places, founded on scripture itself. Christ the risen Lord "opened their minds to understand the scriptures" (Luke 24:45); scripture is nowhere divided into a series of discrete epochs and periods in terms of the substance of faith, for the one content of true faith for all humanity of all times and places is Jesus Christ himself, whose authority over all reality is the true substance of both Testaments. Denial of the one scope of scripture is a direct assault on the gospel itself, for "Jesus Christ is the same yesterday and today and forever" (Heb. 13:8).

Second, it is a sheer error of historical theology to suggest that confession of the unitary substance of the Bible is a modern reaction to dispensationalism and is absent from classical theology. Indeed, there is no more crucial affirmation of dogmatics from the moment of its birth to the present day than the position denied by dispensationalism: that Jesus Christ is the one subject matter of both Testaments of scripture. Calvin spells this out in illuminating detail in the *Institutes* (2.10), in a section that begins with the resounding statement "Now we can clearly see from what has already been said that all men adopted by God into the company of his people since the beginning of the world were covenanted to him by the same law and by the bond of the same doctrine as obtains among us."[29] There are of course for Calvin crucial elements of difference between the two Testaments, but these differences are in terms of mode of administration, not content: "The covenant made with all the patriarchs is so much like ours in substance and reality that the two are actually one and the same."[30] Nor is Calvin expressing here a theological principle limited to Reformed theology; modern Roman Catholicism stresses the exact same point: "The unity of the two Testaments proceeds from the unity of God's plan and his Revelation."[31] It is important for dogmatic theology based on canon to make room for the true theological range of voices in the church; nevertheless, dispensationalism sets itself far apart from that legitimate range when it shatters the unitary substance of the Bible.

Third, the faith itself is seriously denied by the unscriptural fiction of a "postponed kingdom." Christ the risen Lord directly tells his disciples: "All authority in heaven and on earth has been given to me" (Matt. 28:18). The absolute rule of Jesus Christ over all reality is present, direct, and pervasive, and extends throughout the entire universe. "The kingdom of God is among you" (Luke 17:21)—for Christ himself is the true mystery

29. Calvin, 1.428.
30. Ibid., 1.429.
31. *Cat*, 38.

of the kingdom of God. The Sermon on the Mount is the call to discipleship in the present for all who follow him; it is in no sense whatsoever
reserved for a future age, nor has it ever been read that way by any major
theologian in the mainstream of Christian tradition. There is no true
Christianity except where the teaching of the Sermon on the Mount is
not only accepted but put into practice: "Not everyone who says to me,
'Lord, Lord,' will enter the kingdom of heaven, but only the one who
does the will of my Father in heaven" (Matt. 7:21).

And finally, dispensationalism errs in suggesting that God has two
separate purposes for the world, one for Jews and the other for Christians. According to L. S. Chafer, one of the primary architects of dispensationalism, God's purpose is twofold: "The dispensationalist believes that
throughout the ages God is pursuing two distinct purposes: one related
to the earth with earthly people and earthly objectives involved which is
Judaism; while the other is related to heaven with heavenly people and
heavenly objectives involved, which is Christianity."[32] There can be no
more serious threat to the gospel, which without ambiguity declares one
divine redemptive purpose for both synagogue and church, and indeed
for the whole creation: "For I am not ashamed of the gospel; it is the
power of God for salvation to everyone who has faith, to the Jew first
and also to the Greek" (Rom. 1:16). The apostle Paul affirms an absolute
and unbreakable ontological bond between Israel and the church: "They
are Israelites, and to them belong the adoption, the glory, the covenants,
the giving of the law, the worship, and the promises; to them belong the
patriarchs, and from them, according to the flesh, comes the Messiah,
who is over all, God blessed forever. Amen" (Rom. 9:4–5). The ontological bond between Israel and the church is severed by dispensationalism,
and the gospel itself is lost in the process.

It is worth observing that the failure to grasp the genuine dialectic of
Old and New Testaments by the religious left and the religious right in
fact shares an underlying error. Both are built on biblicism, which limits
theological attention to the verbal sense and fails to move from the witness of the text to the subject matter to which it refers. The church has
always been able to wrestle with the continuity and discontinuity of the
two Testaments because it has reflected upon the substance of which they
testify. The biblicism of modern liberalism and evangelicalism cannot
engage in such reflection, because neither penetrates to the reality to
which the biblical witness points. Yet it is precisely the role of the Spirit
to lead the reader from the text to the reality: "When the Spirit of truth
comes, he will guide you into all the truth" (John 16:13).

32. Quoted in Ryrie, 45.

We today certainly share the same theological dialectic of Old and New Testament as the early church, as encapsulated in the Augustinian dictum: The New Testament is concealed in the Old; the Old Testament is revealed in the New. This is not a peripheral issue for dogmatics but indeed is at the heart of church confession. Both Testaments of scripture bear witness to Jesus Christ, each in their different ways. Moreover, we also share Luther's insistence that the Old Testament be heard on its own terms, which was also stressed and developed further by Calvin. The temptation posed by medieval allegory was to render the independent witness of the Old Testament to Christ null and void and thus to lose the rich variety of biblical witness according to both its challenge and its promise. Indeed, with the development of modern study of scripture, we can now approach the text of the Old Testament even more closely than the Reformers did and should strive to expand and deepen the church's hearing of the Old Testament on its own terms as a direct address to the contemporary community of faith. Such a commitment is no longer a "Protestant" issue but is clearly shared by the wider Christian community. The *Catechism of the Catholic Church* stresses, for example, precisely this point: "Christians venerate the Old Testament as true Word of God. The Church has always vigorously opposed the idea of rejecting the Old Testament under the pretext that the New has rendered it void (Marcionism)."[33] It is also essential to recognize that dogmatic reflection on the canon of scripture in its final form is not identical to New Testament theological reflection on the Old Testament. Only a narrow biblicism would misconstrue the issue in that manner. While we approach the Old Testament from the standpoint of the gospel, we also return to the Old Testament witness in its own integrity in order to understand the same gospel more fully. Clearly a dialectical grasp of the relationship between the Testaments involves complex theological movement in two different directions simultaneously, a movement that cannot be reduced to a single interpretive formula or technique, even that of promise and fulfillment. The gospel is inconceivable without the Old Testament, yet the event of Jesus Christ is radically new and is itself the only true access to the meaning of the Old Testament. We in the church today are invited to discern anew in both Testaments the presence of the exalted Lord and his ever fresh claim upon human life. "Therefore every scribe who has been trained for the kingdom of heaven is like the master of a household who brings out of his treasure what is new and what is old" (Matt. 13:52).

33. *Cat*, 35.

Part II ❉

The New
World of God

4

Faith Seeking Understanding

In the fall of 1916, the young Swiss pastor Karl Barth delivered an address in the church at Lentwil, whose title, loosely translated into English, was "The Strange New World within the Bible."[1] Looking back, it is now clear that this address represents a revolutionary break with modern theology, as practiced on both the theological left and the theological right. In this profound address Barth began a search, beyond human piety and morality, for the truth of God spoken in scripture. Barth opened a new and powerful understanding of scripture that completely reoriented the task of interpretation. As he expressed it in his stunning formulation: "It is not the right human thoughts about God which form the content of the Bible, but the right divine thoughts about men. The Bible tells us not how we should talk about God but what he says to us."[2] It was a search that would eventually lead him to the writing of the *Church Dogmatics* and would include his radical denial of all natural theology. Barth's theological work represents the application of the Reformation insight into justification by faith to the realm of theological knowledge. There is no going back behind Barth, yet there is much left to be done.

In the latter half of the twentieth century, a book appeared bearing the title *Biblical Theology in Crisis*, by Brevard Childs. Certainly in continuity with Barth, and yet with a very different voice shaped by concerns in the

1. Barth, "Strange New World," 28–50.
2. Ibid., 43.

field of biblical studies, Childs likewise broke entirely fresh ground with an astonishingly new vision of scripture, leading finally to his epoch-making treatise *Biblical Theology of the Old and New Testaments*. Childs successfully demonstrates that the only way forward for the church is through a fresh vision of scripture. Childs's work in biblical theology must now be met by renewed effort of dogmatic reflection on scripture. Dogmatic theology must now make good on the vision of scripture it has learned from biblical theology. That vision of scripture must retain its critical edge as well. It is not possible for the church to return to a style of theology prior to Barth's revolutionary insight, nor prior to Childs's fresh vision of the issue of canon.

The basic approach to theology that underlay both the work of Barth and the work of Childs, and that constitutes the fundamental direction of dogmatic theology, is faith seeking understanding. Faith seeking understanding is not a single method of theology but in fact allows for variety and flexibility in theological method. Faith seeking understanding is a critical theological stance that locates theology in the confessing church of Jesus Christ. To adopt the approach of faith seeking understanding means to approach questions of theology from a certain vantage point; it also means the decision to reject an alien vantage point, that of natural theology. Natural theology is the attempt to locate the critical standpoint of theology outside the church, or at best to coordinate the confessing faith of the gospel with such a standpoint. While there is a great deal of latitude in the vision of faith seeking understanding, there is also crystal clarity about the choice concerning natural theology. Faith seeking understanding means a direct, absolute denial of all natural theology. There are times when the affirmation of the gospel requires a corresponding denial of its opposite; natural theology constitutes such an either/or decision for the life of the contemporary church. Indeed, the confessing church has already spoken on this issue by its radical denial of natural theology in the Barmen Declaration: "We reject the false doctrine, as though the Church could and would have to acknowledge as a source of its proclamation, apart from and besides this one Word of God, still other events and powers, figures and truths, as God's revelation."[3] The task of the church today is not to turn back the clock behind the Barmen Confession but rather to explore further the profound theological issues that are at stake.

Canon is more than a list of sacred books, though it certainly circumscribes the textual basis for all Christian proclamation and theology. Canon is the theological context in which dogmatic theology is carried out. The orientation of dogmatics to the reality of canon brings with it

3. *Conf*, 257.

a particular approach in theology, which is faith seeking understanding. By "approach" I do not mean technique or a schematic set of principles. I mean rather the comprehensive orientation of dogmatic theology as a whole. Dogmatic theology is an activity of the Christian church, based on faith. The confession of canon is not grounded on some higher philosophical or theological principle; canon is not locked into a broader theological system. Rather, the confession of canon is the entry point for all dogmatic work, for it describes the location in which the treasure of truth can be sought and found. Dogmatic theology begins by accepting and affirming canon as the proper location of divine truth. In doing so, dogmatic theology simply shares the one faith of the universal church, grounded in the supreme authority of Jesus Christ, the one Head of the church. To practice the approach of faith seeking understanding means therefore to begin dogmatic theology with a willing acceptance of canon. There is no other way. It is not as though the theological approach came first and then the reality of canon. It is not as though the confession of canon were one option among others for the method of faith seeking understanding. On the contrary, the approach is implied in the affirmation of canon, as canon necessarily brings with it a new approach. Here we must not only wholeheartedly accept the reorientation of theology provided by Barth; we must also stress the absolute ontological claim of canon as described by Childs. There is no other basis for true dogmatic theology in the present, nor is there any other valid link in the present to the grand heritage of dogmatic theology in the universal Christian church of the past. The confession of canon is normative for the Christian church, as its primary confessions make clear. To begin dogmatic theology with faith in Jesus Christ is to begin with canon; to begin with canon is to begin with faith in Jesus Christ. To confess Christ is to confess canon, and to confess canon rightly is to confess Christ. To borrow the phrase of Neil B. MacDonald, canon constitutes the *conceptual foundation* for all valid Christian theology.[4]

Faith seeking understanding also means hearing the living Word of God in the present. Scripture is not a dead letter; scripture is the instrument by which Jesus Christ the risen Lord encounters each new generation of the church for the sake of the world. Through the gracious gift of the Spirit's guidance, scripture serves every new age as a living witness to God's active will for human life. While there is only one gospel for the whole of humanity of all times and places, that one gospel is sounded forth in a new way for every new generation of the church. Every new generation of the church strives with all its might to be faithful to Christ in mission to the world. If it is to serve its proper purpose, dogmatic

4. MacDonald, 115.

theology must join in that challenging yet enlivening effort. It must give aid in the church toward that effort. Faith seeking understanding is therefore a commitment to the task of hearing the Word of God spoken afresh to the contemporary world. It does not mean simply accumulating the wisdom of the past, though it certainly cannot be undertaken without guidance from the past. Indeed, it cannot be done at all without that guidance. Nevertheless, unless dogmatic theology seeks to hear the living voice of the Lord of the church and the world anew, it is not faith seeking understanding. Dogmatic theology therefore affirms the unbreakable connection between Word and Spirit, a connection that can never be collapsed into one. The creative interplay of the two is the mysterious movement in which dogmatic theology is drawn toward a fuller understanding of the true reality of God.

Faith seeking understanding means a movement of understanding in which there is an inversion of truth between knower and known. The human person can and must seek after God by faith, and yet in the mystery of the search it becomes clear that the divine Person is in search of humanity. The human search itself is but a living response to a divine search for humanity that precedes it, accompanies it, and draws it forward. By faith we ask for the gift of greater understanding of the full majesty of God's being and will for the world; and yet in the mystery of divine presence it becomes clear that God himself puts human life into question through the gift and demand of his gracious rule, and himself provides the answer to the question he poses. By faith we knock at the door of divine truth; yet in the mystery of God it is Christ himself who knocks at the door of human hearing: "Listen! I am standing at the door, knocking; if you hear my voice and open the door, I will come in to you and eat with you, and you with me" (Rev. 3:20). The inversion of truth in no way denies the need for supreme human effort in the quest for understanding; faith is not idle or distracted but does indeed seek understanding through concentrated activity. Yet the process is turned on its head by the living Lord, who never follows but only leads: "Not that I have already obtained this or have already reached the goal; but I press on to make it my own, because Christ Jesus has made me his own" (Phil. 3:12). Above all, the inversion of truth means that the very quest by which faith seeks understanding is itself part of the wondrous gift of the knowledge of God. In the language of hymnody, "'Twas grace that taught my heart to fear, and grace my fears relieved" ("Amazing Grace").

Faith seeking understanding means letting God be God; letting God define for us the true nature of his own reality. Dogmatic theology categorically rejects any attempt to define the concept of God on the basis of any prior ontological or philosophical foundation and then to use such a concept in theological reflection. God alone defines himself; God alone gives true knowledge of himself. As John Calvin aptly stated, "God alone is a fit witness of himself in his Word."[5] Or, in the similar phrase of Thomas Aquinas, "God is not in a genus" (*Deus non est in aliquo genere*).[6] God can be known only in reference to his own perfection. What that means in practice for contemporary dogmatics is a close relationship to the field of biblical theology. Biblical theology, which uses the exact same approach of faith seeking understanding, trains the church to move from the manifold witness of scripture to the one reality of which it speaks. Here is the crucial check in dogmatics against any form of nontheological foundationalism, for dogmatic reflection does not start with its own resources but with the findings of biblical theology. And yet it does not simply repeat biblical theology; rather, beginning with the understanding of God on the basis of scripture that it has learned from its conversation partner in theological labor, it returns to the same scripture in the light of the divine reality. It seeks to give greater depth, precision, and clarity to the church's understanding of the living reality of God by interpreting scripture in the light of the reality of which it speaks. There is thus an economical division of labor in which the new world of God is explored jointly for the sake of praise to God in witness to the world. The hermeneutical circle of faith seeking understanding in its proper sense is thus the economy of shared effort between biblical theology and dogmatic theology.

If it does not so much focus on moving from witness to subject matter, which is the primary concern of biblical theology, what then is the aim of dogmatic reflection on Holy Scripture? Granted that we return to the witness of the text in light of the reality of which it speaks; what is the goal of understanding in our return to the text? The special aim of dogmatics is reflection upon the inner logic of the subject matter of scripture. God is a communion of love in the eternal reality of his inner being. God seeks to establish a relationship of love with the reality of creation that came from his creative power. On the one hand, the entirety of scripture speaks with one voice of the living God, for all scripture is inspired by the same Spirit. On the other hand, there is a profound and manifold variety in scripture that cannot and must not be lost without grave peril to the truth of faith. Dogmatic theology assumes the unity of the biblical witness, for there is one risen Lord Jesus Christ of whom both Testaments bear witness. It also seeks to preserve the variety, for the manifold truth of scripture undercuts every human rationalistic scheme for reducing the divine claim to simplistic formulas and slogans.

5. Calvin, 1.79.
6. *ST*, 1.17–18.

We must think dialectically, not organically. On the one hand, dogmatics is not moved by imperialistic claims to truth on the part of ancient or modern canons of logic. They have no authority whatsoever in Christian theology. The effort of dogmatics is not toward rationally improving the findings of biblical theology by turning them into a propositional system. On the other hand, the tools of critical rationality are employed in the service of the gospel, toward discerning the coherent shape of biblical truth. The effort of dogmatics is to retrain human thinking and acting to fit the inner logic of the new world of God. The time-honored method for dogmatic reflection is thus the loci method, in which the inner logic of divine truth governs and guides human thinking to new discovery of the living divine will. In dogmatic theology, we are eager to allow the inner logic of the subject matter of scripture to declare itself in the grandeur of its own beauty and truth and never to diminish that grandeur through human ideology. Knowledge of God is a gracious gift of the Holy Spirit; that same Spirit works to undermine every human attempt to capture the truth of God for an unworthy purpose. The ultimate test is whether the unfolding of divine truth in dogmatic reflection provides genuine illumination of scripture and a further invitation to return to scripture for a fresh hearing of the word of Christ spoken in the contemporary world.

As we seek to discover and chart the inner logic of divine truth, the movement is always from the reality of that truth to the unfolding of its genuine content. Dogmatic theology never seeks to establish prior conditions for the possibility of understanding God. There are no such conditions, for the knowledge of God's will is a gracious divine miracle grounded only in the electing love of God. Thus, faith seeking understanding does not start with what is unknown and proceed to what is known, nor does it move from what is humanly possible to what is divinely revealed. Rather, it begins always with what is known through Word and Spirit and seeks greater understanding through a process of rational inquiry, imaginative investigation, eager searching. It begins with what is divinely possible even though humanly impossible and then seeks to understand in a new way the gift of divine presence in human life. Faith seeking understanding insists upon hearing the Word of God address the contemporary world, but it rests upon the marvelous and unheard truth that God himself on his own initiative wills to communicate his purpose in a fresh way to the world of today. Contemporaneity with the living Christ is not grounded in a preestablished understanding of human life in the present; rather, it is only the living Christ himself who shows his disciples the fresh call of discipleship for a new humanity in the world today. There is a search, and it requires every last ounce of effort, the deployment of every conceivable resource, the expenditure of one's whole existence, including rigorous rationality and fresh imagination. But the search takes place not on the basis of a human capacity but on the basis of a freely given divine promise. In the end, faith seeking understanding is a theology grounded solely in the promise of Christ: "When the Advocate comes, whom I will send to you from the Father, the Spirit of truth who comes from the Father, he will testify on my behalf" (John 15:26). Faith seeking understanding is not a conversation about God, as if God were an idea or a theological principle; it is ultimately a fresh encounter with the living Lord of all reality.

The great enemy of faith seeking understanding, and therefore of the confessing church of Jesus Christ, is natural theology, which is practiced alike on both the religious left and the religious right. Natural theology is the attempt to correlate the message of scripture with self-affirming human experience. Some feature of human reason and experience is isolated and analyzed in order to provide the link between human capacity and divine truth. A method or principle is then used to "reinterpret" Christian truth for the modern world. Natural theology can take the more aggressive form of "proofs" for the gospel; it more often takes the milder form of establishing the "meaning" of faith. Either way, it is to be condemned on the grounds of dogmatic theology. It is worth noticing that the motive behind natural theology is most often well intentioned. There is the well-meaning desire on the part of those who practice it to make the gospel relevant to the modern person and to do whatever can be done to remove the stumbling block of doubt. And precisely here is the grave error, for the gospel is a stumbling block to unbelief (1 Cor. 1:23). To be received, the gospel requires the response of faith. Natural theology takes doubt far too seriously; it puts the gospel on the defensive and without realizing its error subtly but drastically changes the radically new message of scripture into something very different. Yet the gospel is never on the defensive; it always moves forward on the offensive: "Indeed, we live as human beings, but we do not wage war according to human standards; for the weapons of our warfare are not merely human, but they have divine power to destroy strongholds. . . . We take every thought captive to obey Christ" (cf. 2 Cor. 10:3–5). Natural theology is a direct violation of Christ's proscription in the Sermon on the Mount: "Do not give what is holy to dogs; and do not throw your pearls before swine, or they will trample them under foot and turn and maul you" (Matt. 7:6).

How extensive is natural theology in modern religious thought? It is in fact endemic to the entire period from the post-Reformation period of scholastic orthodoxy to the present. It has its origins in the Protestant scholastic response to Cartesianism, which without realizing it abandoned the position of the Reformation while trying to preserve and defend it. Natural theology is the guiding endeavor of the famous works of modern religious discourse: John Locke's *The Reasonableness of Christianity*, David Hume's *Dialogues Concerning Natural Religion*, Gotthold Ephraim Lessing's *The Education of the Human Race*, Immanuel Kant's *Religion Within the Bounds of Reason Alone*, Friedrich Schleiermacher's *Speeches on Religion*, G. W. F. Hegel's *Lectures on the Philosophy of Religion*, Charles Hodge's *Systematic Theology*, Albrecht Ritschl's *The Christian Doctrine of Justification and Reconciliation*, Adolf von Harnack's *What Is Christianity?* Paul Tillich's *Systematic Theology*, Rudolf Bultmann's *Jesus Christ and Mythology*, Jürgen Moltmann's *The Theology of Hope*, Wolfhart Pannenberg's *Revelation as History*, and so forth. Works such as these have the appearance of great variety, and even clear conflict, in theological content. Nevertheless, appearances deceive, for underlying them all is the same method of correlation that always shows itself wherever natural theology has intruded into dogmatics. All are essentially apologetic works, not genuine dogmatic theology, the only difference being the variation in philosophical resources that are used from one figure and movement to the other.

Furthermore, the exact same logic appears in the various works of liberation theology, whose quarrel with "modern" theology is most certainly not a quarrel with natural theology, but simply an extension of modern natural theology into the counter-cultural movements of the late twentieth century. One finds the identical correlation of self-affirming human experience and the Christian message, which characterizes the modern works mentioned above, in such "postmodern" theologies as Rosemary Radford Ruether's *Sexism and God-Talk*, Gustavo Gutiérrez's *A Theology of Liberation*, James Cone's *God of the Oppressed*, and Cornel West's *Prophesy Deliverance*. The difference is only in the way human experience is defined, for now various forms of Marxism, feminism, and racial ideology provide the starting point for theological reflection. The quarrel of high cultural and countercultural theology is a quarrel within natural theology.

Several points are to be emphasized in coming to grips with the natural theology of the modern period. First of all, the same efforts characterized both conservative and liberal tendencies in theology. Conservatives and liberals alike fell into the same trap. Thus, while the surface shows a longstanding conflict between "traditionalists" and "progressives" in modern theology, the reality is very different. Both conservatives and liberals are quintessentially modern; both represent a radical break from the theology of the reformers and the historic tradition of the church that lay behind it.

Second of all, there were protests against natural theology all along: one thinks of Blaise Pascal's *Pensées*, Søren Kierkegaard's *Philosophical*

Fragments, or Martin Kaehler's *The So-Called Historical Jesus and the Historic Biblical Christ*. Despite the clear dominance of natural theology in the modern period, the church was never left without a witness to the truth of the gospel. These protests finally culminated in the explosive breakthrough of Karl Barth, who opened a new era for church theology, though obviously the old dies hard.

Third, the contrast between the dogmatic theology of the church and natural theology has nothing to do with the issue of contemporaneity. Dogmatic theology insists upon the contemporary address of the church and world by the living voice of the gospel. Indeed, among the various fields of church theology, dogmatic theology is one of the most concerned with contemporaneity. However, it does not address that concern on the basis of a systematic hermeneutical principle of correlation or any other such principle. Contemporaneity is a gift of the Holy Spirit, who "tears down the walls" separating the biblical world from our world through the miracle of his presence. Through the guidance of the Spirit, Jesus Christ makes a direct, immediate, and absolute claim upon the whole life of the church in the contemporary world through the witness of scripture. There is no "correlation"; there is only radical obedience.

> To another he said, "Follow me." But he said, "Lord, first let me go and bury my father." But Jesus said to him, "Let the dead bury their own dead; but as for you, go and proclaim the kingdom of God." (Luke 9:59–60)

And finally, the church's rejection of natural theology must include a rigorously dialectical understanding of the use of philosophical and cultural tools. As a nontheological foundational epistemological basis for dogmatics, any form of human philosophy, from Aristotle to Wittgenstein, is absolutely to be rejected. To any that would set the agenda or determine the parameters of Christian truth, our answer is simply *no*! However, as a set of tools that may bring some clarity in the process of faith seeking understanding, any form of human philosophy and culture may be legitimately brought to bear upon the questions at hand, provided the usage is in accordance with the inner logic of the subject matter as learned from the scriptures. The church theologian should be fully educated in the history of human culture and fully conversant with issues of the day, but the theologian is absolutely free from the imperialistic claim of any human system.

Four brief examples will illustrate the church's necessary condemnation of natural theology. Through philosophical and sociological analysis, Schleiermacher is led to conclude that piety is a form of "immediate self-consciousness."[7] In particular, piety is a form neither of knowledge nor of moral activity, but a modification of human feeling. Dogmatics is thus the systematic correlation of the content of human feeling, or self-consciousness, with the consciousness of God present to that realm of feeling. What kind of feeling? At times we feel partially dependent on another; at times we feel partially active in relation to the other. But through self-analysis we also recognize a feeling of absolute dependence, which is in fact the nature of true piety. Indeed, the religious feeling of being absolutely dependent is the "co-existence of God in the self-consciousness."[8] Christian theology assumes a necessary correlation of self-consciousness and God-consciousness as the basis for its approach to all aspects of Christian belief and life. From this perspective, Schleiermacher then seeks to relate all aspects of Christian doctrine to the philosophically defined reality of human piety.

No doubt Schleiermacher thought he was acting in the interests of Christianity by composing his formulation of the matter. However, his fundamental orientation cannot be sustained in the light of scripture. The true God of Christian faith is in no way whatsoever "co-existent" in the self-consciousness. The true God of Christian faith brings the radically new world beyond all possible human self-consciousness: "So if anyone is in Christ, there is a new creation: everything old has passed away; see, everything has become new!" (2 Cor. 5:17). At issue here is the holiness of God, which is not primarily a moral characteristic of God but rather the sheer self-separating majesty of God in his own self-defined splendor. God's holiness is his transcendent otherness, neither given to nor presupposed by the world or human self-consciousness but reigning supreme over all reality: "Holy, holy, holy is the LORD of hosts; the whole earth is full of his glory" (Isa. 6:3). Furthermore, feeling is not a self-grounded human prerogative into which God himself must fit. The radical call of discipleship transforms human emotion as well. As the Psalms fully illustrate, the entire range of human emotion is taken up into the love and praise of God in every dimension of life. Moreover, while the true God certainly lays claim to human emotion, he also lays claim to human intellect, human decision, even the human body: "You shall love the LORD your God with all your heart, and with all your soul, and with all your might" (Deut. 6:5). The call of Christ claims the whole person. Schleiermacher's natural theology, far from being a limited entry point to a true understanding of faith in the modern world, in fact seriously misunderstands the radical claim of the gospel upon human life in the present. In seeking to make the Christian faith palatable to the

7. Schleiermacher, 5.
8. Ibid., 126.

"cultured among its despisers," Schleiermacher unknowingly distorts the very truth he sincerely means to confess.

Second, according to Hodge nothing contrary to human reason or human moral nature can be true. The theologian therefore is required to assume the validity of all laws that God has impressed upon human nature. No objective revelation can possibly contradict these laws of human nature. Included in these laws are those beliefs that are self-evident, as well as all truths that stand the test of universality and necessity, as well as the absolute requirement for consistency. God himself must obey the law of human nature. On this basis, natural theology must be absolutely affirmed. Hodge concludes: "It cannot, therefore, be reasonably doubted that not only the being of God, but also his eternal power and Godhead, are so revealed in his works, as to lay a stable foundation for natural theology."[9]

Of course Hodge considers himself to be following the biblical mandate and is completely unaware of the astonishing rationalism that his position represents. He is seeking to introduce a measure of objectivity into theology over against the perceived subjectivism of liberalism; he never realizes that he has purchased a false objectivity at the price of losing entirely the true object of the Bible, the living God, who approaches humanity only as a self-grounded, self-giving, self-moving Subject.

Against Hodge it must be stated that a natural theology based on the self-grounded claim of human nature in relation to the divine can not only be doubted, it can and must be radically denied, and is so by scripture itself. Paul forthrightly declares: "For the message about the cross is foolishness to those who are perishing, but to us who are being saved it is the power of God. For it is written, 'I will destroy the wisdom of the wise, and the discernment of the discerning I will thwart.' . . . For God's foolishness is wiser than human wisdom, and God's weakness is stronger than human strength" (1 Cor. 1:18–19, 25). In setting rational and moral conditions for the self-revelation of God—Hodge's very modern version of correlation, despite his conservative ideology—Hodge has at best domesticated the gospel beyond all recognition and at worst has fallen into the trap of self-idolatrous human arrogance. Hodge is certainly right that God is revealed in nature; he wrongly concludes from this, however, that God is known from nature. That is, given the ontic reality of revelation in nature, he proceeds to the noetic method of natural theology. What he fails to reckon with is the fact of sin; the fall makes an absolute break between the ontic and the noetic, for human reason and moral experience are now the captive of human corruption. All that the "the laws of human nature" are now able to produce is nothing but

9. Hodge, 1:25.

the darkness of human wickedness: "They have all gone astray, they are all alike perverse; there is no one who does good, no not one" (Ps. 14:3). To insist that God meet the laws of human nature is in fact a terrifying denial of God's holiness, a sheer affront to the divine majesty. God is revealed in nature, but he is not known from nature, because the human knower is captive to sin. Indeed, the pitiful figure of Hodge's theologian insisting that God himself be conformed to the requirements of human nature would be laughable, if it were not so tragically in error.

What is particularly disturbing about Hodge's shocking theological hubris is that it comes purportedly from the soil of John Calvin, who more than any other theologian in the classical period saw the dangers of natural theology. Because of the universality of sin, according to Calvin, human piety is in no way a reliable guide to the true reality of God. On the contrary, human experience as a whole is nothing but a factory of idols: "No mortal ever contrived anything that did not basely corrupt religion."[10] The only role of God's revelation in nature is to render us without excuse; in no way does it serve as the basis for a theology of correlation: "But although we lack the natural ability to mount up unto the pure and clear knowledge of God, all excuse is cut off because the fault of dullness is within us."[11] Hodge's foray into natural theology is not only a corruption of scripture; it is in fact a catastrophic denial of the Reformed faith he endeavored to espouse.

Third, it is likewise essential to register a forthright protest against the natural theology of Roman Catholicism. As taught in the system of Thomas Aquinas (*Summa Theologiae* 1.2), affirmed at Vatican I (C.2), and reaffirmed in a more recent comprehensive summary of Roman Catholic thought, the "desire for God is written on the human heart."[12] Because of the human capacity to know God, the existence of God can be proved, both by the realities of the surrounding creation and by the structure of the human self. The human person, through self-knowledge, is led to the contemplation of divine being: "With his openness to truth and beauty, his sense of moral goodness, his freedom and the voice of his conscience, with his longing for the infinite and for happiness, man questions himself about God's existence. In all this he discerns signs of his spiritual soul. The soul . . . can have its origin only in God."[13]

Roman Catholic theology clearly affirms natural theology, but does it accurately record the position of Thomas Aquinas? Is the natural theology of Thomas foundationalist? Is it true natural theology? It is of course possible to read him differently, as more of a biblical theologian based

10. Calvin, 1.65.
11. Ibid., 1.68.
12. *Cat*, 13.
13. Ibid., 15.

in the community of faith. On that reading, his famous proofs for the existence of God are not so much proofs in the rationalistic sense as they are fundamental definitions of God's reality, derived from scripture. However, against such a reading it must be clearly recognized that Thomas is openly read as a natural theologian in the Roman Catholic tradition, which makes the affirmation of natural theology a fundamental article of faith. One must surely ask: Is Thomas simply misunderstood by his own disciples? Moreover, does not Thomas clearly enunciate the basic principle that all natural theology follows, that God is known from his effects, of which he is the cause: "Hence the existence of God, in so far as it is not self-evident to us, can be demonstrated from those of His effects which are known to us"?[14] In my opinion, it is impossible to deny that Thomas employs a natural theology, which in the end leads to the unfortunate affirmation of Vatican I: "If any one shall say that the one true God, our Creator and Lord, can not be certainly known by the natural light of human reason through created things: let him be anathema."[15] In fact, God cannot be known by the natural light of human reason; he is known only from his Word heard in faith: "For I am not ashamed of the gospel; it is the power of God for salvation to everyone who has faith. . . . For in it the righteousness of God is revealed through faith for faith" (Rom. 1:16–17).

Nicholas Wolterstorff presents an alternative reading of Thomas that seeks to cast him in a more positive light. In his essay "The Migration of the Theistic Arguments: From Natural Theology to Evidentialist Apologetics," Wolterstorff describes what he considers two very different projects for natural theology in Thomas Aquinas and John Locke. Between the time of Thomas and the time of Locke, the social horizons have shifted; the philosophical resources have vastly altered; the overall place of theology in the cultural landscape has dramatically changed. Consequently, Locke is using natural theology as evidence to meet the challenge of modern skepticism. Locke is a foundationalist, for whom belief is permitted only on the basis of good reasons. Wolterstorff is critical of foundationalism and hence rejects the evidentialist approach: "Significant alterations in our social or intellectual situation will make evidentialism seem irrelevant or implausible or unimportant."[16] By contrast, according to Wolterstorff, Thomas works with a variety of projects in his natural theology, which need to be properly discerned and evaluated. First of all is the task of clarifying the nature of *scientia*, a task that the believer shares with the unbeliever. Second is the task of

14. *ST*, 1.12.
15. Schaff, 2:252.
16. Wolterstorff, 55.

moving the believer to accept the content of revelation even when the authority of revelation is denied. Third is the task of transmuting the faith of the believer into sight. The third project is the key; for according to Wolterstorff, this use of natural theology within the structure of theology for the believer puts Thomas directly in the camp of Augustine and Anselm, embracing the method of *fides quaerens intellectum*. Wolterstorff presents the best possible case for this reading of Thomas and carefully lays out the textual evidence.

Despite the attractive qualities of his argument, there are two objections that make it impossible to sustain. The first objection, and less important, is the continuing controversy over historical interpretation. Even in the more limited sense of the medieval period, does not Thomas clearly assume a proof for the existence of God based on reason alone? Despite the clear and vast philosophical differences from Locke, from the point of view of theological function, where does the *theological* difference truly lie? Wolterstorff twice critiques Barth for failing to recognize the differences between classical and modern natural theology; but Barth was clearly measuring Thomas by a very different standard from Wolterstorff's, a standard in which the rigorous method of faith seeking understanding is seen in a medieval figure like Anselm but not in Thomas. I am not convinced by Wolterstorff's easy dismissal of Barth's weighty concerns. Furthermore, while Wolterstorff seems to appeal approvingly to the great medievalist Étienne Gilson, Gilson himself read Thomas very differently. In his classic summary *Reason and Revelation in the Middle Ages*, Gilson divides the medieval period into three camps. The first camp, arguing for the primacy of faith, includes figures such as Augustine and Anselm. The second camp—nowhere mentioned in Wolterstorff's own survey—is philosophical rationalism based on the primacy of reason, including the Spaniard Averroës and his many Latin followers such as Siger of Brabant and Boethius of Dacia. The third camp, of course, argues for the harmony of reason and revelation, of which Thomas is the shining light. The point is this: in Gilson's analysis Thomas Aquinas is notably *absent* from the group embracing faith seeking understanding, based on the Augustinian motto *credo ut intellegam*, I believe in order to understand. By sharp contrast, Wolterstorff puts Thomas squarely in the Augustinian-Anselmic line: "Aquinas stands in the great Augustinian/Anselmic tradition of *fides quaerens intellectum*."[17] I agree that certain fine texts in Thomas seem to point that direction; I wonder, however, whether Wolterstorff's desire to put him there has blinded him to other texts in Thomas that point in a very different direction.

17. Ibid., 72.

But far more important than the historical argument is the theological one. Wolterstorff isolates and affirms in Thomas a role for natural theology in the church. Wolterstorff seems willing to criticize natural theology on the boundary between belief and unbelief but tries to rescue natural theology as a churchly enterprise. Thomas uses natural theology for the "transmutation" of faith into vision. Here I can respond only with a vigorous denial. To speak of using natural theology in the church is not to improve its standing and validity. On the contrary, it is even to make the egregious error of natural theology all the worse by covering it over with layers of spirituality and piety. Natural theology is far more dangerous in ecclesiastical form than it is in the relatively harmless chatter of skepticism. The golden calf was not constructed by the impious but by the supremely pious! It is *precisely* in its churchly form that we must reject natural theology, for the sake of the church. The fundamental issue is the cross of Jesus Christ, which radically cancels out any approach to God apart from faith in the gospel, even a supposedly Christian one. In the light of the cross we dare not hide but confidently proclaim the utter foolishness of the gospel, which cannot be removed without removing the stumbling block of faith: "For the message about the cross is foolishness to those who are perishing, but to us who are being saved it is the power of God. . . . For I decided to know nothing among you except Jesus Christ, and him crucified" (1 Cor. 1:18; 2:2). In dogmatic theology we use the resources of human reason and imagination, but we use them to move from faith to faith; we do not in the least use them to transmute faith into sight, for to do so is the height of folly: "Where is the one who is wise? Where is the scribe? Where is the debater of this age? Has not God made foolish the wisdom of the world? For since, in the wisdom of God, the world did not know God through wisdom, God decided, through the foolishness of our proclamation, to save those who believe . . . for God's foolishness is wiser than human wisdom" (1 Cor. 1:20–21, 25). Natural theology is most dangerous in its ecclesiastical form and must above all else be combated in the church for the church. "For we walk by faith, not by sight" (2 Cor. 5:7).

Roman Catholicism makes the same error of modern neo-Protestantism in assuming a correlation of God-consciousness and human self-consciousness. It makes the same mistake of modern Protestant evangelicalism in ignoring the sharp break of the ontic and noetic introduced by the fact of human perversity after the fall. Why do I not therefore condemn Roman Catholicism as heretical for its natural theology, as I certainly do liberalism and evangelicalism? The Roman Catholic Church employs natural theology as an unfortunate tactic despite its clear-headedness on other issues. Roman Catholic doctrine would never compromise the

doctrine of the Trinity, as Schleiermacher was surely led to do because
of his natural theology; nor would it lapse into an open Pelagianism, as
modern evangelicalism has done as a result of its natural theology. The
reason is the creedal heritage of Rome, which prevents it from errors
that its own natural theology inadvertently introduces. Thomas Aquinas
was certainly doing natural theology; however, just as clearly the primary
center of gravity in his system is located not in natural theology but in
the divine self-knowledge that is graciously communicated to humankind
in the articles of faith. Indeed, Thomas elsewhere delivers a brilliant and
convincing statement of the necessary logic of faith seeking understanding: "Hence Sacred Scripture, since it has no science above itself, can
dispute with one who denies its principles only if the opponent admits
some at least of the truths obtained through divine revelation; thus we
can argue with heretics from texts in Holy Writ, and against those who
deny one article of faith we can argue from another. If our opponent
believes nothing of divine revelation, there is no longer any means of
proving the articles of faith by reasoning, but only of answering his objections—if he has any—against faith."[18] Thomas sees very clearly that the
basic principles of theology are taken from scripture alone, and he is thus
a canonical theologian in every sense: "As other sciences do not argue in
proof of their principles, but argue from their principles to demonstrate
other truths in these sciences: so this doctrine does not argue in proof of
its principles, which are the articles of faith, but from them it goes on to
prove something else."[19] Thomas Aquinas is a confessing theologian of the
church with a basic dogmatic stance oriented toward scripture as canon,
who despite his own best insights wrongly deployed the tactic of a natural
theology. For him, and for Roman Catholicism after him, natural theology
is a tactic, not a grand strategy; it is not epistemologically foundational,
even though it contradicts the true foundation of faith; it is an error, not
a heresy. Nevertheless, it is an error that must be removed for the sake
of the ecumenical consensus of the universal church. We therefore can
but appeal to the Roman Catholic communion to be corrected by its own
creedal affirmation, which all Christians alike share, and forsake the error
of natural theology, even in its attenuated Thomistic form.

Fourth, I think it is worth pointing out that at least one prominent
evangelical theologian rejected natural theology entirely, and that is Carl
F. H. Henry. In his comprehensive systematic theology, Henry devotes a
full chapter to "the rejection of natural theology."[20] His final conclusion
makes clear the theological basis for his rejection: "We reject natural

18. *ST*, 1.5.
19. Ibid.
20. Henry, 104–23.

theology because of the express nature of supernatural revelation, because of man's epistemic nature and because of the invalidity of empirically based arguments for theism."[21] I can only wholeheartedly agree
with Henry's rejection of natural theology, a courageous stand that runs
counter to the trend of the theological tradition he represents. However,
I am convinced that the primary problems of natural theology unfortunately resurface in his work, indeed in the very next chapter, "The
Image of God in Man."[22] Henry defines the divine image in humanity
as a rational and moral capacity for relationship to God: "The divine
image, a cohesive unity of interrelated components that interact with
and condition each other, includes rational, moral and spiritual aspects
of both a formal and material nature."[23] The laws of logic are part of the
divine image: "If man made any sense of his own experience, the laws
of logic must intrinsically have qualified the *imago Dei*."[24] Consequently,
reason has a foundational role to play in all theology: "Reason illumi-
nates divine revelation by furnishing the concepts for truth not only
about man and nature but also about God."[25] Finally, the divine image
includes the moral nature of humankind: "Man's very self-constitution
is stamped with the conviction that the distinction between good and
evil is not merely an arbitrary and optional contrast but is genuine and
objective."[26] How are we to respond?

Despite my desire to agree with Henry as an ally against natural
theology, his position shows unfortunately the same strains of serious
weakness as the older evangelical approach of Hodge. At its most basic
level, the profound problem with Henry's position is that it is thoroughly
unbiblical, despite his affirmations of the role of scripture in church and
theology. First, there is not the slightest evidence in scripture that the
divine image is to be equated with the rational and moral constitution of
humanity—not a single verse. The system of "revelational theism" may
require the equation in order to be logically neat and tidy, but here the
"system" must yield to the binding authority of scripture as norm of faith.
In the Bible, the divine image is a mystery that points to relationship
with God as constitutive of humanity, yet it leaves the exact determination of that relationship an abiding mystery. There is a tension in human
existence that is unnamed and unnamable; humanity has its origin from
the earth yet is made like unto God: "Moreover, he has put a sense of past
and future into their minds, yet they cannot find out what God has done

21. Ibid., 123.
22. Ibid., 124–42.
23. Ibid., 125.
24. Ibid., 126.
25. Ibid.
26. Ibid.

from the beginning to the end" (Eccles. 3:11). Henry's position dissolves the tension and therefore loses the biblical mystery. Second, Henry fails to reckon with the inherent ambiguity of human rationality, especially in the Old Testament. On the one hand, a figure like Joseph can show gifts of wise ordering by organizing grain relief for the entire nation of Egypt and beyond: "So Pharaoh said to Joseph, "Since God has shown you all this, there is no one so discerning and wise as you"" (Gen. 41:39). On the other hand, when the Assyrian empire arrogantly plans world dominion, Isaiah announces the complete overruling of its plans by the sovereign action of God: "I will break the Assyrian in my land. . . . This is the plan that is planned concerning the whole earth; and this is the hand that is stretched out over all the nations" (Isa. 14:25–26). In the Bible, reason is a strictly neutral capacity that may at times bring good but may just as often lead to moral disaster. Henry shows no awareness of the deep biblical insight into human frailty: "There is a way that seems right to a person, but its end is the way to death" (Prov. 14:12). And third, once again there is no biblical evidence for Henry's equation of human conscience with the moral voice of God in human experience. Conscience, rather, in the apostle Paul is the ability of self-reflection and plays only the role of evaluating moral choices when several legitimate options are available. The content of moral norms comes exclusively from the Word of God, not from conscience. How utterly different is Henry's appeal to the "self-constitution of human nature" from the sterling cry of Luther at the Diet of Worms: "I am bound by the Scriptures I have quoted and my conscience is captive to the Word of God."[27]

27. Lohse, *Martin Luther's Theology*, 200.

5

The Subject Matter of Scripture

Dogmatic theology is a theological discipline of the community of faith. The role of dogmatics in the community of faith is theological reflection on the subject matter of scripture. Its focus is upon discerning and explicating the inner logic of that subject matter, as an aid to faithfulness in the proclamation of the gospel and the service of God in the world. Biblical theology seeks to guide the church to move from the witness of the text to the reality of which it testifies. Dogmatic theology completes the hermeneutical circle of faith seeking understanding by returning to the text of scripture in light of the subject matter. And so we are now in a position to ask: what does it mean to reflect theologically upon the inner logic of the subject matter of scripture?

It is helpful to recognize at the outset that we are not asking a new question. While we must both ask and answer the question anew in our own generation and with the special problems and possibilities of the horizon of our times, it is essential to recognize that every generation of the church has sought to participate in the same labor of dogmatic inquiry. This is not the context for a full treatment of the history of the church's inquiry concerning the subject matter of scripture and the way to unfold it. Instead, I will focus on one remarkable treatment from the period of the early church, as a way of getting some initial bearings.

Augustine's *On Christian Doctrine* is a profound and brilliant encapsulation of the primary effort of dogmatic work in the patristic period. According to Augustine, theology is focused on the interpretation of scripture. Finding the true subject matter of scripture is not chaotic; rather, it is a disciplined inquiry that is governed by a specific set of rules (*praecepta*). The purpose of his treatise is to transcribe and explain those rules to students of scripture, "so that they may profit not only from reading the work of expositors but also in their own explanations of the sacred writings to others."[1] To those who consider such rules unnecessary in light of the charismatic gift of interpretation, Augustine is adamant: "We should beware of most proud and most dangerous temptations of this kind."[2] The bond of charity itself requires that rules of discipline be taught and learned in the community of faith, for these rules bind members together in a common enterprise. Interpretation of scripture requires two comprehensive matters of study and discussion: how to discover the true substance of scripture and how to communicate that substance to others. Augustine begins with the first and orients his presentation around the distinction between sign and thing.

Doctrine involves two levels: signs and the things to which those signs refer. Words are signs, which signify reality: "for no one uses words except for the purpose of signifying something."[3] The triune God is the ultimate reality to which scripture refers, but God is also the way to discover that reality: "Although He is our native country, He made himself also the Way to that country."[4] The test of whether the true reality of scripture has been rightly discerned comes in the form of the twofold command of love: "Whoever, therefore, thinks that he understands the divine Scriptures or any part of them so that it does not build the double love of God and of our neighbor does not understand it at all."[5] The rule of charity is valid even when it transcends the specific intention of the biblical author. False readings of one passage are always to be corrected by a fuller grasp of the range of biblical witness as a whole; it is therefore illegitimate to seize on only one proof-text and build a theology around it to the neglect of the remaining portions of scripture.

Augustine then turns from the treatment of "things" to the treatment of "signs." Above all, treatment of signs (the verbal sense of scripture) should be based on familiarity with scriptural usage and a sense of the whole: "He will be the most expert investigator of the Holy Scriptures who has first read all of them and has some knowledge of them."[6] Even granted the need for expertise and careful attention to the signs, it is crucial to remember that the signs are to be studied for the sake of the

1. Augustine, *On Christian Doctrine*, 3.
2. Ibid., 5.
3. Ibid., 8.
4. Ibid., 13.
5. Ibid., 30.
6. Ibid., 40.

things to which they refer: "And they are weaker in that they wish to seem instructed, not in the knowledge of things, by which we are truly instructed, but in the knowledge of signs, in which it is very difficult not to be proud."[7] Most of the signs in the Bible can be properly explained when one reads the obscure places in the light of what is clearly said in other passages. However, in the case of ambiguous signs, explicit rules are needed. Augustine summarizes the seven rules of Tyconius (a Donatist layman whose book *Liber Regularum*, c. 380, exercised enormous influence on Augustine, and through him the entire medieval period), which are to be applied above all in the context of prayer. Augustine concludes the treatise by reflecting upon the proper manner of teaching to others the reality of scripture which has been discovered (book 4). Here too the emphasis throughout is on the ultimate claim of the subject matter: "For it is a mark of good and distinguished minds to love the truth within words and not the words. Of what use is a gold key if it will not open what we wish?"[8]

Several aspects of Augustine's brilliant treatment of theological interpretation are to be noted. First, there is the profoundly sophisticated grasp of the basic problem of dogmatic theology: how to read scripture in the light of the subject matter. One is astonished at the consummate skill with which Augustine, and the Eastern and Western fathers, searched the scriptures for the theological truth that they yield.

Second, there is the dialectical relation of the biblical witness (sign) and the reality of which it speaks (thing). Augustine would never allow the two to be separated, but nor would he ever allow the two simply to be collapsed. Theology and proclamation are defined precisely by the extraordinary joy of labor in relating the one to the other in the unity of their tension through the guidance of the Spirit.

Third, one can only admire the richly holistic manner in which Augustine read the Bible, in a way that clearly yielded a fresh presentation of Christian truth that speaks with as much power and force today as it did then. The paradox is truly astonishing: Augustine wrote as a North African bishop to the problems of late antiquity, and yet his ability to penetrate to the subject matter and relate that subject matter to the listening world is enduring.

Fourth, though it is clear that Augustine insisted upon the absolute integrity of a ruled interpretation of scripture, a disciplined reading broken only by heretics, his understanding of the function of those rules is anything but narrow and restrictive. These rules guard against error and focus the interpretation of scripture where it will be fruitful. But they do

7. Ibid., 47.
8. Ibid., 136.

not in any way inhibit creative and enriching exposition in a variety of directions. Indeed, according to Augustine they make such exposition possible. (Later, Thomas Aquinas, in *Summa Theolgiae* 1.1.10, adds to the theological suppleness of Augustine's approach by observing that not only can a sign signify a thing, so also can one thing signify another thing, thus increasing the range of flexibility for dogmatic reflection.)

Fifth, one is deeply impressed by the absence of biblicism in Augustine. The aim of biblical study is nothing less than to move from the text to the living reality of God himself. Theological interpretation of the subject matter of scripture is both a divine gift of grace and at the same time an imperious and demanding exercise of human endeavor.

And finally, Augustine leaves no doubt that a genuine interpretation of scripture is not a mere academic exercise, leaving the life of the reader untouched. On the contrary, through encountering the true subject matter of scripture the reader is radically transformed by love of God and neighbor.

A similar brilliance and theological sophistication is attached to the Eastern patristic equivalent of *On Christian Doctrine*, the fourth book of Origen's *On First Principles*. Moreover, these two treatises of Augustine and Origen are only a sample of the wider effort of the early church, not to speak of the theological renaissance of Anselm and the succeeding medieval scholastic period or the biblical exegesis and theological reflection of Luther and Calvin and the other Protestant Reformers. What held this entire period together, despite the many tensions in the various theological traditions, was the overwhelming conviction that in the proper interpretation of scripture the reader is being led from the pages of the text to the Creator and Redeemer of life. There are profound arguments back and forth concerning the proper elucidation and application of the truth one finds, but the search for truth is shared by all. Dogmatic theology is in every sense of the word a living prayer to the Lord of all things. The basic point can be summarized by a saying of Luther at the end of the classical period: "God and the Scripture of God are two things, no less than the Creator and the creature are two things" (*Duae res sunt Deus et Scriptura Dei, non minus quam duae res sunt, Creator et creatura Dei*).[9] Of course no one had a higher view of scripture than Luther, for whom it is the all-transforming Word of God. Indeed, the entire period shared the same high view of scripture. In distinguishing between sign and thing, it is crucial to remember that a sign is not a mere symbol of something totally different; a genuine sign always participates in the reality that it signifies. Nevertheless, the role

9. *LW*, 33:25.

of scripture is not to create and redeem; rather, the role of scripture is to lead humankind to the one Creator and Redeemer of the cosmos.

A dramatic hermeneutical shift occurred with the advent of the modern Enlightenment. It was that shift that in the end produced two separate wings of characteristically modern theology: a conservative wing and a liberal wing. The broad consensus about the work of theology that governed the classical approach was jettisoned. The shift allowed the introduction of a newly vigorous natural theology and the eventual separation of dogmatic theology from its historic orientation toward the authority of scripture. Despite the line of protest voices, the shift dominated the modern scene until Karl Barth redefined the strange new world of the Bible.

Augustine and the classical tradition saw church theology unfolding in the creative tension between sign (biblical text) and reality (the living God) and understood theology as an activity of the community of faith for the sake of proclamation of the gospel to the world. Theology is faith seeking understanding because it accepts the authority of scripture and seeks to move from the pages of the Bible to the reality of which it testifies through critical rational inquiry under the guidance of the Spirit. As Martin Luther saw most clearly, the issue is inherently dialectical: theology denies any role whatsoever for reason and experience as a foundation, for the language of faith is grounded solely in God's self-revelation in Jesus Christ, and yet, reason has a role to play within the church's work of faith seeking understanding and plays that role faithfully when it rightly discerns the inner logic of the true substance of the Bible. After the hermeneutical shift, modern theology becomes, as it were, understanding seeking faith. Reason is defined as a self-validating method of critical assessment, into which the Bible and the biblical God must fit. The authority of scripture is not necessarily denied, but it is affirmed only on the basis of a rational assessment of its "claim" to authority. The locus of validation is thus transferred from scripture to reason. The hermeneutical shift overturned and set aside the economy of theology in its classical sense. After the shift, it is human reason (in the Cartesian form of self-constituting human consciousness) that stands as *judge*, as arbiter of truth, between the sign and its reality. The sign and the signified not only are distinguished but now are separated by an act of rational validation. No longer is scripture the sole access to the reality of which it testifies. Now scripture becomes an illustration of truths to which reason has equal, and eventually better, access.

Details changed, of course, as the progress of Enlightenment and post-Enlightenment culture altered, but the hermeneutical shift held constant through all the changes. Conservatives used the modern hermeneutic in order to defend what they considered traditional biblical teaching.

Liberals, by contrast, used the exact same hermeneutic in order to correct what they considered unfortunate and unnecessary elements of the
same traditional teaching. Of course modern skepticism used the same
approach to attack Christian teaching. But all sides equally removed
theology from its center of gravity in the community of faith, turning
the grand tradition of dogmatics into a form of freelance "apologetics."
Either way, conservative or liberal, the autonomous human person became the measure of divine truth.

The shift can be seen clearly already in John Locke's *The Reasonableness of Christianity*, first published in 1695. According to Locke, the
clashing systems of divinity (he wrote, of course, after the breakup of
Christian unity into its Protestant, Roman Catholic, and Eastern Orthodox forms) are inadequate for approaching scripture. As opposed to the
dogmatic tradition, Locke proposes to undertake an interpretation of
scripture that is "unbiased" and "unprejudiced."[10] Locke will offer to the
reader an exposition of scripture based on "the plain direct meaning of
the words and phrases, such as they may be supposed to have had in the
mouths of the speakers, who used them according to the language of that
time and country wherein they lived; without such learned, artificial, and
forced senses of them, as are sought out, and put upon them, in most of
the systems of divinity, according to the notions that each one has been
bred up in."[11] It is of great interest that Locke begins his "unbiased"
presentation by attacking the traditional Christian doctrine of the fall.
According to Locke, the biblical view is that death and judgment entered
the entire human race at the fall of Adam, but total moral corruption did
not. No human being is captive to sin because of the fall of Adam. The
idea of total depravity, according to Locke, is an addition to scripture
by the "systems of divinity": "To this, they would have it be also a state
of necessary sinning, and provoking God, in every action that men do.
. . . The reason of this strange interpretation we shall perhaps find in
some mistaken places of the New Testament. . . . But, as I remember,
every one's sin is charged upon himself only."[12] Of course, the absence
of the radical nature of the fall leaves human reason able to perform the
role that Locke assigns to it. Reason is able to confirm all the truths of
religion, but not everyone has the time and leisure to pursue the teachings of reason. Faith is therefore introduced as a pedagogical device for
those without the means to pursue reason: "The greatest part cannot
know, and therefore they must believe."[13] Locke offers a full survey of
Christian teaching on faith, law, Jesus, salvation, God, etc., from the

10. Locke, 24.
11. Ibid., 25.
12. Ibid., 26–27.
13. Ibid., 66.

point of view of his new rational reflection on scripture, which replaces the older schemes of ecclesiastical dogma.

Several aspects of Locke's argument are to be critically noted, for it contains *in nuce* the history of modern theology up to and including the latest trends of liberation theology. First of all, according to Locke the philosopher-critic knows better than the confessing church does its own scriptures. For Locke, the confessional heritage of the church is just so much irrational babble. Armed only with his native wit, he can see better than the historic faith of the church what scripture is really about. Needless to say, a direct denial of the biblical picture of the full cosmological effects of the fall is absolutely essential, for reason must be left able to discern the "signified" on its own. The Pauline witness to the complete captivity of the human person under sin (Romans 7) can have no place in modern theology, liberal or conservative: "For we know that the law is spiritual; but I am of the flesh, sold into slavery under sin" (v. 14). Modern theology is inherently Pelagian.

Second, it is useful to note that the real impetus for the hermeneutical shift is not the innate glamour and attractiveness of reason itself. Rather, modern theology begins as an alternative to the church's confessional conflict. The real backdrop to modern theology is the loss of Christian unity at the time of the Reformation, following up on the earlier division between East and West, not the rise of early modern science and philosophy. At the very least this suggests that the only way beyond modern theology is through a renewed endeavor to articulate and nourish the genuine unity of the church. While I share Locke's frustration with the competing "systems of divinity"—who does not yearn for a united Christendom?—it is crucial to remember that the unity of the church is a gracious divine reality, grounded in the unity of Jesus Christ. The true unity of the church has never been, nor can it ever be, lost. The role of dogmatic theology is to share in the labor of making that unity visibly manifest in the contemporary world, according to the rule of truth. That will not happen by papering over the genuine differences between the historic communions; nor will it happen by replacing dogmatic theology with the rationalism of Locke and his many successors. It will happen only as the church, and in the church dogmatic theology, moves forward to a new vision of scripture as canon and to a fresh encounter with the true subject matter of the biblical witness. Concern for truth, not the rationalism of John Locke, is the way forward to a new era of church life and theology.

Third, it is now clearer than it was perhaps to Locke how captive to self-delusion is the human condition. Despite noble intentions, Locke's portrayal of the gospel is a thin version of Enlightenment rationalism and moralism, far removed from the explosive power of biblical faith.

The same can be said for his successors, up to and including liberation theology, all of which necessarily operate with the illusions of self-
affirming autonomy. It is no wonder that theology separated so decisively
from the historic church, as well as from the field of biblical theology,
for only so could the illusion of an "unbiased" reading of scripture be
maintained. Moreover, it is not an adequate answer simply to acknowledge and embrace bias, as is done by so-called postmodernism. That may
solve the problem of illusion in modern theology, but it only makes error
self-conscious error. It does not replace error with truth. Has modern
autonomous humanity succeeded in offering the world an authentic
voice of the gospel? In the seventeenth century such a vision was perhaps
attractive and alluring in its still undeveloped infancy. After the vicious
brutalism of fascism and communism in the twentieth century and the
horrors of terrorism in the twenty-first, it now seems clear that autonomous humanity is no arbiter of truth; it rather is the ultimate illusion.

And finally, theology for Locke is essentially an "objective" exercise, a
free act of disembodied reason. That is to say, it has no living connection
whatsoever to the practicing faith of the Christian community—to its
worship, evangelism, care of the poor, or prayer. Again, the contrast with
the classical period is stark. The scriptures are given as the instrument
by which Christ the risen Lord guides each new generation of the church
to the truth of his living command; yet from Locke forward, modern
theology will have nothing to do with the necessary identification of
the theologian with the church or with the necessary acceptance of the
truth of the gospel that that church proclaims to the world. From the
point of view of the confessing faith, modern theology represents not
the valid criticism of the church from the point of view of the gospel,
as in the Reformation, but a purported criticism of the gospel from the
point of view of human nihilism.

It is no different on the religious right, which represents the other
wing of modern theology. The problem is clearly seen in the *Systematic
Theology* of Charles Hodge and is repeated in countless variations among
evangelicals, fundamentalists, neoevangelicals, conservatives, dispen-
sationalists, and the like. Hodge begins his hermeneutic by separating
scripture from its connection to the living community of faith, including
its confessional heritage. The separation is radical and complete; the
rule of faith encompasses scripture alone and excludes all tradition:
"This excludes all unwritten traditions, not only; but also all decrees of
the visible Church; all resolutions of conventions, or other public bodies, declaring this or that to be right or wrong, true or false."[14] Hodge
furthermore speaks of an innate "right" to read the Bible: "The Bible is

14. Hodge, 1:183.

a plain book. It is intelligible by the people. And they have the right, and are bound to read and interpret it for themselves."[15] Hodge makes clear on what basis this individual "right" is to be exercised: "He [God] has made it obligatory upon every man to search the Scriptures for himself, and determine on his own discretion what they require him to believe and to do."[16] Personal discretion is thus the test of biblical truth. According to Hodge, faith is "personal"; each person must answer for himself, and therefore each must "judge for himself."[17] Above all this means the "right of private judgment" as opposed to the "authority of the parish priest."[18] The reason for his aspersions on the parish minister is spelled out: the preacher of the gospel "is often wicked and still oftener ignorant. This cannot be the foundation of the faith of God's elect."[19] All of this yields three "self-evident" hermeneutical rules, which are not based on human authority: (1) The words of scripture are to be taken in the historical sense, which is the meaning attached to them by the people at the time they were written. (2) Scripture cannot contradict itself, and therefore all seeming contradictions must be logically harmonized. (3) Scripture must be interpreted according to the guidance of the Spirit, which confers a "congeniality of mind" suitable for divine things. These three rules together guarantee what Hodge calls the "divine right of private judgment."[20]

What is crucial to notice at the outset is that Hodge thought he was reproducing a fundamentally Reformation outlook on the Bible, when in fact nothing could be further from the truth. Hodge clearly speaks as a child of the Enlightenment, an obvious theological cousin to the position of John Locke outlined above. Hodge has torn apart the relation of the sign to the signified, the relation of the witness of scripture to the reality of which it speaks. He has substituted for that relation the same self-evident trust in Enlightenment rationality that one finds on the religious left, including the Cartesian ego disengaged from its living relation to the community of faith, the canons of Enlightenment rational logic based on the principle of noncontradiction, and the individual rights of the human mind to determine for itself what is true. No better description could be given of self-affirming human experience than what Hodge himself represents. Luther insisted that where the scriptures contradicted the official teaching of the church, the church is wrong and scripture is right, even if only one individual on earth recognizes

15. Ibid.
16. Ibid., 1:184.
17. Ibid.
18. Ibid., 1:186.
19. Ibid., 1:187.
20. Ibid., 1:187–88.

that to be so. But he argued thus in order to protect and defend the *right of God* over against humanity, not the profoundly modern notion of the right of the individual to define religion for himself or herself. All of the Reformers weighed in mightily against errors that had crept into the official pronouncements of Rome, including the spurious Roman claim of papal infallibility; but the Reformers meant thereby to purify and reform the *confessing church*, not to eliminate the living connection between scripture and church confession altogether. Elimination of church confession was the agenda of the Enlightenment, not the Reformation; Hodge is clearly unaware of his very real connection to the rationalism he otherwise claims to despise.

Furthermore, according to John Calvin we need the "spectacles" of scripture to see the reality of God, precisely because human sin makes reason and experience vulnerable to idolatry; yet Hodge would approach God on the grounds of reason and even insist that the divine speech in scripture fit into the tidy, rational system that Hodge claims to be the only right one. For Calvin, this would surely be to turn the biblical world upside down, with disastrous consequences. For Hodge, the presence of the Spirit is understood anthropologically, as the conferral of "spiritual discernment"[21]; for the Reformers, the Spirit is always understood christologically, as the living presence of Christ sounding forth his Word afresh with overwhelming power to every new generation, bringing sight to the blind. For Hodge, preaching is a form of religious instruction that can have no claim to authority; for the Reformation, the "preaching of the Word of God is the Word of God."[22] As Heinrich Bullinger, author of the *Second Helvetic Confession,* urges, not even an incompetent minister nullifies the inherent validity of God's proclaimed Word: "Wherefore when this Word of God is now preached in the church by preachers lawfully called, we believe that the very Word of God is proclaimed, and received by the faithful; and that neither any other Word of God is to be invented nor is to be expected from heaven: and that now the Word itself which is preached is to be regarded, not the minister that preaches; for even if he be evil and a sinner, nevertheless the Word of God remains still true and good."[23] There is therefore in the Reformation an essential connection between the interpretation of the Bible and the ongoing task of proclamation, just as there is in Augustine; in Hodge, there is none. Hodge entirely neglects the Pauline insistence: "So faith comes from what is heard, and what is heard comes from the word of Christ" (Rom. 10:17). The darkness of the modern period of theology

21. Ibid., 1:99.
22. Second Helvetic Confession C.1, in Leith, 133.
23. Leith, 133.

is just as gloomy on the right as it is on the left. Who cannot hear the voice of Locke's "unbiased" reading of scripture on the basis of private reason, in the almost identical words of Hodge concerning the "right of private judgment"? Does not the biblical God take the "right of private judgment" entirely out of human hands, submitting the entire universe to the far greater right of divine judgment?

> Then Job answered the LORD:
> "I know that you can do all things,
>   and that no purpose of yours can be thwarted.
> 'Who is this that hides counsel
>   without knowledge?'
> Therefore I have uttered what I did not understand,
>   things too wonderful for me, which I did not know.
> 'Hear and I will speak;
>   I will question you, and you declare to me.'
> I had heard of you by the hearing of the ear,
>   but now my eye sees you;
> therefore I despise myself,
>   and repent in dust and ashes." (Job 42:1–6)

If it is true that modern theology has failed, both conservative and liberal, what will come in its place? Two other options were offered to the theological world in the last quarter of the twentieth century and for a time seemed to hold forth promise: the "narrative theology" of Hans Frei and the "cultural-linguistic" approach of George Lindbeck. Indeed, the two are interrelated, as their proponents, both of Yale University, often made clear. Both agreed that modern theology had largely failed; both expressed a certain admiration for the historic tradition of the church; both suggested a strong linkage with Barth. Do narrative theology and cultural-linguistic theology chart a new direction for dogmatic theology?

Frei presented his views in two major works: *The Identity of Jesus Christ*, a reflection on the hermeneutical and exegetical outworking of narrative theology, and *The Eclipse of Biblical Narrative*, a historical analysis of what Frei considered the loss of traditional narrative reading in favor of a modern referential reading. Frei brilliantly identified and critiqued modern referential reading, which is an interpretation of scripture in which critical reason tears apart the meaning and truth of the Bible and intervenes as sole arbiter of genuine understanding. Here reason shares with scripture the role of primary avenue to the substance of the Bible and eventually replaces it. In place of a referential reading, Frei offered the category of "realistic narrative," in which the issue of the biblical reference to a true subject matter is bracketed, if not simply eliminated. The witness of the text and the subject matter of the text are identical; the story of Jesus is about the character in the story, while the character in the story is to be found only in the biblical story and nowhere else. Frei states of the gospel stories: "There is no gap between the representation and what is represented by it."[24] The meaning and truth of the Bible are identical, for the Bible's narrative world is self-contained. According to Frei, it is narrative that ties all of scripture together into a single cumulative story, the unfolding of which is the proper work of theology. Frei's basic approach to narrative theology was reproduced in countless secondary interpretations and gave rise to a vast literature of historical and systematic treatments.

Frei made a crucial and lasting contribution in his critique of the mode of ostensive reference in modern theology. Modernity was wrong to separate sign and reality, witness and subject matter, in order to pursue an alternative mode of access to that subject matter. Modern conservatives and modern liberals made the same mistake, and both are to be roundly condemned, as Frei himself suggests. All apologetics and all natural theology are anathema; every approach to the substance of scripture apart from the witness of scripture is to be denounced. Ostensive reference is a hermeneutical failure, and it is to Frei's enduring credit that he saw through the modern problematic so clearly. When a figure like Carl F. H. Henry continues to defend ostensive reference against a "Barthian" distinction between *Geschichte* and *Historie*,[25] one quickly recognizes the force of Frei's diagnostic analysis of modern theological discourse. Moreover, Frei likewise discerned in a fresh and powerful way the narrative coherence of biblical truth, especially in the classical mode of loci theology. Clearly in some sense classical theology sees the content of scripture as a divine story moving from creation through reconciliation to redemption, as in this brief description from Melanchthon's *Loci Communes*: "Thus the books of the prophets and apostles, arranged as they are, constitute a complete and beautiful story, and a story is a good means of teaching."[26] There is in some sense a sacred story at the heart of Christian confession, and Frei clearly sought to reintroduce that story into the language of theology.

Nevertheless, despite his genuine contribution, I am convinced that Frei's approach fails to lay a solid foundation for the future of dogmatic theology, for several reasons. First, Frei makes a profound confusion that unfortunately pervades all aspects of his historical and systematic treatment. It is one thing to argue against the *separation* of text and reality

24. Frei, *Identity of Jesus Christ*, xiv.
25. Henry, 288.
26. Melanchthon, *On Christian Doctrine*, xlviii.

in the manner of natural theology and apologetics; it is quite another
to suggest that the very *distinction* between the witness of the text and
the reality of which it speaks is theologically illegitimate. Indeed, the
whole of classical theology embraces this distinction and is engaged in
a theological movement from witness to subject matter and back from
the subject matter to the witness. Frei wrongly identified all distinction
between sign and signified with natural theology; he simply failed to
observe that such a distinction is in fact essential to classical theology
as it pursued the method of faith seeking understanding. In fact, the
Christian faith itself is built on precisely this distinction; for we are not
reconciled to God through the verbal witness of the text but through the
act of God in Jesus Christ, of which the text bears joyful witness to the
entire creation. Jesus Christ the risen Lord is the true subject matter to
which the text truthfully refers. Athanasius once objected strenuously in
the battle against heresy: "God cannot save what he does not assume."
The Athanasian principle must be upheld now against narrative theology.
God did not become a text in order to save humankind; God became a
human being of flesh and blood, as told in the story of the Gospels. Let
it be fully affirmed, without any doubt whatsoever: there is no access
to this saving reality apart from the text of scripture. "Sign" and "thing"
can never be separated. But nor can they be simply collapsed without
losing the gospel itself. The distinction between sign and reality is in
fact a distinction of faith seeking understanding, as the whole history of
classical theology shows. The error of modernity was not to introduce
the distinction, as though it had never been there before. That is not the
nature of the "change in interpretation"[27] that Frei correctly sees but
wrongly describes. The error of modernity was to turn the distinction into
a separation based on natural theology, in order to pursue an alternative
rational hermeneutic to that of faith seeking understanding. Modernity is
wrong for making the separation, but Frei is equally wrong for collapsing
the distinction. There must be a *distinctio, sed non separatio*.

Second, Frei's characterization of the classical period, though helpful and discerning, is incomplete. While classical theology articulated
a narrative coherence to biblical truth, "narrative" was not in any way
a privileged genre in classical theology. There are narratives in scripture, so there was clearly reflection upon how to understand them; but
these reflections were not in the slightest way a foundational exercise
for theology, as they are for Frei and as he wrongly suggests they were
before modernity. *Canon*, not the genre of narrative, was always and
everywhere the basis for theology. Classical theology showed an infinitely
richer set of conceptual tools and analytical procedures for expounding

27. Frei, *Eclipse of Biblical Narrative*, 3.

scripture than one would be led to expect by Frei's isolated focus on narrative per se.

Third, in the end is it not clear that "narrative" itself became for Frei and his followers a category of aesthetic natural theology, in which the general hermeneutic of narrativity was imported into theology as a foundational explanatory category? Is this not precisely the error that Frei decried among modern conservatives and liberals? Did not Frei himself, despite his best intentions, speak apologetically to the "cultured among the despisers of religion" on the basis of a shared understanding of narrative? The elimination of reference from theology ties the view of Frei closely with the general drift of postmodern modes of thought; but is postmodernity, by definition, any closer to the gospel than modernity? The strange new world of God in the Bible is neither modern nor postmodern, nor for that matter is it classical; precisely as *God's* new world, it is equally distant from all times and by grace fills time itself: "Jesus Christ is the same yesterday and today and forever" (Heb. 13:8).

Fourth, it is simply historically inaccurate for Frei to appeal to Barth as a forerunner of "narrative theology." Barth made a brilliant distinction between modern history and biblical saga and deployed that distinction in a variety of places in the *Church Dogmatics* (see, for example, his discussion of "Creation, History, and Creation History" in 3/1, pp. 42–94) with supreme skill. It is a theologically necessary distinction, which needs to be maintained and deepened on the basis of faith seeking understanding. But according to Barth it is *not* a distinction between a text that refers and a text that does not refer; it is a distinction between a text whose reference is accessible to universal reason and a text whose reference can be seen only through divine self-revelation with the eyes of faith. Barth states: "Creation comes first in the series of works of the triune God, and is thus the beginning of all the things distinct from God himself. Since it contains in itself the beginning of time, its historical reality eludes all historical observation and account, and can be expressed in the biblical creation narratives only in the form of pure saga."[28] Barth did not attempt to collapse God's work of creation into the story that testifies to it; he attempted rather to show the total difference between the biblical narration of God's creative act and the modern genre of history. Barth's distinction involves a totally different concern from that of Frei and his followers. As Neil MacDonald convincingly shows, for Barth saga is necessary in the Bible for the purpose of bearing truthful witness to an event sui generis, without any analogy whatsoever, and therefore unavailable to "history." Biblical saga makes sui generis historical truth claims, unlike realistic narrative, but the truth claims can

28. *CD*, 3/1, 42.

be received only in faith, unlike critical history.[29] Narrative theology is a vastly different enterprise from the theology of Barth, whose dogmatics is ordered not in accordance with the "narrative universe of the Bible" but in accordance with the loci method of the dogmatic tradition, which allows the richness and variety of biblical form to remain, while yet espousing the one Story of God.

Finally, and perhaps most important of all, in seeking to ground Christian faith in the "story of Jesus" Frei moves in the opposite direction from the kerygma of the early church. For the apostle Paul clearly grounded faith in the risen Christ, not in Jesus of Nazareth: "From now on, therefore, we regard no one from a human point of view; even though we once knew Christ from a human point of view, we know him no longer in that way" (2 Cor. 5:16). Indeed, Jesus Christ the risen Lord is the true subject matter of both Testaments of scripture. When Frei and narrative theologians refuse to speak of a true reality of which the text bears truthful and reliable witness, they are in fact undercutting the Easter faith of the church.

Many of the features of Frei's work are shared by the "cultural-linguistic" approach of George Lindbeck (and vice versa, for in the end each appealed to the other for fundamental theological support). Lindbeck seeks to distinguish between three basic models of doctrine: the classical approach of "propositionalism," the liberal approach of "experiential-expressivism," and the third option, the "cultural-linguistic" approach of postliberalism. Lindbeck makes it fully clear that his "cultural-linguistic" approach is grounded in philosophical and sociological theory, not in dogmatics: "The theory of religion and religious doctrine which [my book] proposes is not specifically ecumenical, nor Christian, nor theological. It rather derives from philosophical and social-scientific approaches."[30] Lindbeck proposes a "rule-theory" of doctrine, the essence of which is that doctrines are not first-order descriptions of reality but second-order grammatical observations of linguistic usage. The Bible must be interpreted intratextually (which is not the same obviously as intertextually); the issue of the true referent according to Lindbeck is simply "irrelevant."[31]

Once again, it is important to recognize the strength of Lindbeck's contribution. At a time when theology was largely oriented toward various philosophical foundations, Lindbeck redirected the attention of theology to the language of faith, as expressed in the creeds and confessions of the church. The confessional heritage of the church is essential to dog-

29. See MacDonald, 106–7n32.
30. Lindbeck, 7.
31. Ibid., 106.

matic theology, and Lindbeck's wide familiarity with church doctrine gives his program a depth largely missing in the various theological approaches of modernity. Moreover, one senses in Lindbeck's work a laudable intention to deepen the ecumenical consensus of the church; and indeed, it is an intention that every genuine dogmatic theologian of the church must share. Lindbeck's approach moves beyond simply rehashing the doctrinal controversies of the past and at least in some sense strives to work toward a measure of consensus, if not full agreement. After Vatican II, a page has clearly been turned in the life of the church; and Lindbeck's proposal rightly caught the spirit of a new day of emerging doctrinal discussion.

Nevertheless, in this case too I remain convinced that Lindbeck fails to offer a fresh start for dogmatics, in light of several serious weaknesses in his approach. First of all, Lindbeck shares with Frei the basic confusion of the issue of reference with the issue of natural theology. As we have seen, natural theology is not an option for the church; any theology based upon it will in fact inevitably distort the gospel of Christ. However, Lindbeck simply assumes that all concern for theological reference necessarily shares a "common framework" with general culture. That assumption is both historically and systematically false. All of the great dogmaticians, from Irenaeus to Barth, who employ the method of faith seeking understanding also speak forcefully about the true reality of which scripture speaks. Barth, for example, whose legacy Lindbeck wrongly claims to share, makes very clear the sheer wonder of faith as it encounters the question of true reference: "He that hath *seen* me hath *seen* the Father." That is it: when we allow ourselves to press on to the highest answer, when we find God in the Bible, when we dare with Paul not to be disobedient to the heavenly vision, then God stands before us as he really is. "Believing, ye *shall* receive! God is *God*."[32] That is not the voice of natural theology; that is the voice of the church's endeavor of faith seeking understanding, raising the rigorous question of true reference to the reality of God on the grounds of the confessing faith of the Christian church. One is stunned to see such massive and prevalent confusion over such a basic issue in a work on Christian doctrine such as Lindbeck's. Concern for the true referent of scripture must in fact be at the heart of faith in any new undertaking in dogmatic theology.

Second, Lindbeck himself, despite his protestations, operates with a clear natural theology. His social-scientific and philosophical assumptions are logically prior to his approach to Christian doctrine and form the basis for his interpretation; his interpretation seeks to correct Christian doctrine on the basis of his methodological approach; and his

32. Barth, 1956, 48.

construction serves as a common basis for discussion on a "religiously neutral" basis. These are the ingredients of quintessentially modern natural theology, whose illusions are now obvious. There is no theologically legitimate act of situating Christian faith foundationally in a broader philosophical scheme, for the gospel is the new world of God; true theological reflection is not based on the standard of a philosophical scheme but solely on the norm of Holy Scripture; and theological speech does not need to be corrected in light of a social-philosophical theory of religious language but in the light of Christ himself, the true content of the gospel.

Third, Lindbeck's approach, by its very nature, eliminates the commission of the risen Christ to his disciples of evangelism. The role of Christians is to help Buddhists become better Buddhists, Marxists become better Marxists, and so on.[33] Evangelism is replaced by interreligious dialogue and cooperation.[34] To be sure, Lindbeck is aware of the confessional affirmation of the *solus Christus* (that salvation is through Christ alone) by all of the historic Christian communions. He endeavors to affirm the *solus Christus* as well as the salvation of nonbelievers by positing a salvific offer of Christ beyond death,[35] but based on what scripture? Such an appeal, however useful to the structure of Lindbeck's system, directly contradicts Christ's parable of the ten maidens, in which the free offer of the divine rule is most certainly not timeless but rather directly impinges upon temporal reality: "Later the other bridesmaids came also, saying, 'Lord, lord, open to us.' But he replied, 'Truly I tell you, I do not know you'" (Matt. 25:11–12). Indeed, Lindbeck (and Frei as well) speaks of the semiotic universe encoded in scripture and of the scriptural world absorbing the universe into itself, whereas the commission of Christ which grounds the Christian church moves in the exact opposite direction, as the church is to carry the gospel outward to the whole of creation: "Go therefore and make disciples of all nations" (Matt. 28:19). I question the ultimate validity of any Christian theology that makes no room for mission.

Fourth, one is dismayed by the lack of historical judgment in Lindbeck's repeated assertions that the ontological Trinity—the eternal reality of the triune God in himself—was and is a moot point for the dogmatic heritage of the church. According to Lindbeck, the doctrine of the Trinity says nothing about who God is in himself; the doctrine of the Trinity is not a first-order description of the reality of God, for all Christian doctrine is intrasystematic, not ontological. Whether or not the Trinity

33. Lindbeck, 54.
34. Ibid., 61.
35. Ibid., 59.

is in reality God is "a narrow issue," one that is "unimportant for theological evaluation."[36] Moreover, according to Lindbeck, this is the view
of the church fathers, including Athanasius, for whom Nicaea was not
about the reality of God but about how Christians should speak about
God. Against Lindbeck's position it must be clearly asserted that *all* of
the Christian creeds of the early church make direct assertions about
the reality of God. The Christian creedal tradition is a matter of life and
death precisely because it is *not* simply a matter of adjusting human
speech patterns according to ruled behavior but because the issue is
right belief about *who God is* and what his will for the world is. The
regula fidei (rule of faith) is also the *regula veritatis* (rule of truth), which
brings to church doctrine a level of seriousness that Lindbeck's account
cannot begin to explain. Athanasius was not merely observing linguistic
convention but was wrestling with the living reality of God for the sake
of the church and the world: "Thus one God is preached in the Church,
'who is over all . . . and through all, and in all'—'over all' as Father, as
beginning, as fountain; 'through all,' through the Word; 'in all,' in the
Holy Spirit. It is a Triad not only in name and form of speech, but in truth
and actuality. . . . Less than these [Persons] the Catholic Church does
not hold, lest she sink to the level . . . of Sabellius."[37] Needless to say,
Athanasius is not pursuing natural theology when he makes this point,
but dogmatic theology based on a rigorous application of faith seeking
understanding. Indeed, must not the question be asked whether Lindbeck, in affirming a kind of agnosticism about the being of God behind
the distinction of the persons, does not himself lapse into an egregious
Sabellianism? Is Lindbeck's position really any different from that of
Schleiermacher, who likewise argued that God has not made himself
known "as He is in and for Himself"?[38] Is Lindbeck's "postliberalism"
really so different from liberalism proper when it comes to the crucial
issue of knowledge of God? Against both, must we not joyously assert
that God has in fact made himself fully known in Jesus Christ: "For it
is the God who said, 'Let light shine out of darkness,' who has shone in
our hearts to give the light of the knowledge of the glory of God in the
face of Jesus Christ" (2 Cor. 4:6)?

Finally, though Lindbeck is to be applauded for his ecumenical concerns, I question whether his approach to doctrine can truly lead the
church forward in shaping a new doctrinal consensus. Church doctrine
allows for great variety and flexibility of expression. The fundamentalist
concern for a univocal system of true propositions is certainly pointing

36. Ibid., 106.
37. *First Letter to Serapion*, quoted in Quasten, 3:67.
38. Schleiermacher, 52.

in the wrong direction. However, church doctrine also traces boundaries, outside of which the gospel is not rightly preached. The church at large has never found it possible to make doctrinal affirmations without also making negations, however difficult that may at times be. Lindbeck's approach knows no boundaries. Even the older liberalism sought to make some kind of distinction between authentic and inauthentic expressions of the faith; even the older liberalism sought in some sense to defend Christianity as a true expression of the divine. Lindbeck's postliberalism absorbs everything and defends nothing. Is it really an advance? Or is it not rather the dissolution of dogmatic theology altogether?

Clearly, the future of dogmatic theology lies in a renewed search for the subject matter of the Bible. Modern natural theology, whether conservative or liberal, can only be pronounced a complete failure, unusable for the theology of the church. Moreover, despite the overwhelming brilliance of the classical tradition, a simple retreat into the past is not the answer. Dogmatic theology cannot carry out its genuine task of providing help to the contemporary church simply by a mechanism of retrieval. Despite the necessary role of tradition, dogmatic theology must search the scriptures afresh for the true reality of the living God. Nor can we be content today simply to approach the questions of theology from within the confines of a particular tradition, such as Reformed, Lutheran, Orthodox, or another. Certainly we all start from one such tradition. We all bring to the study of scripture our own set of concepts and questions, derived in part from our received tradition. However, our aim is not simply to confirm from scripture what we have brought to it; our aim rather is to penetrate to the living subject matter of scripture in order to grow in insight. We cannot do so as an exercise in natural theology; we can do so only insofar as God has graciously made himself known to us in Jesus Christ. We search only as those who have ourselves been searched. Nevertheless, in the shining light of the gospel we must search, with eagerness and anticipation. The only ultimate concern for all dogmatic theology is concern for truth, which is received in the sheer awe of faith.

6

Theological Interpretation

Theological interpretation of scripture is a ruled endeavor. Rules of theological interpretation do not bind interpretation to a narrow set of preconceived theological propositions. Theological interpretation is an act of genuine freedom; but it is a freedom based on the authority of scripture. The normative quality of scripture brings with it a set of rules governing its proper usage in the church. There are rules for the interpretation of scripture in nearly all of the major creeds and confessions of the church. There is likewise a tradition of theological reflection on those rules going back to Augustine, and even earlier to Origen. By proposing a set of rules for theological interpretation of scripture, we therefore enter a conversation that has guided the mainstream of Christian theology from the beginning. Nevertheless, though we must be guided by that tradition, it is not enough simply to rewrite it; Christian theology today has the contemporary responsibility of formulating rules of theological interpretation in light of the resources, challenges, and possibilities of the present.

Before we turn directly to a consideration of these rules, one issue in particular deserves special focus in any consideration of theological interpretation, and that is the relationship between scripture and tradition. The confession of canon brings with it a fresh articulation of the relationship between scripture and tradition. On the one hand, there is an element of absolute discontinuity between scripture and tradition. Scripture alone is the Word of God, not tradition; scripture alone is inspired by God, not tradition; scripture alone is the source of our knowledge of God, not tradition. By definition, canon implies a sacred text that is radically distinguished from all other texts, a text that functions as the exclusive critical norm for all Christian speech and action. Here it is impossible to insist too strongly upon the sheer distinction between scripture and every element of Christian postbiblical tradition, including exegesis, dogma, and proclamation. On the other hand, there is also an essential element of continuity between scripture and tradition. Canon also implies an ongoing community of faith that treasures the sacred text and that lives by its word in worship, mission, prayer, and care for the poor. The absolute distinction between scripture and tradition can never become a separation, for canon circumscribes both text and community in the light of God's living will. What ties scripture and tradition together is the church's encounter with the risen Lord, who shapes the church through the former, calling forth the response of the latter.

In order to clarify what is at stake theologically, it is essential, following Heiko Oberman, to distinguish between Tradition I and Tradition II. According to Oberman, Tradition I is the affirmation that there is a "history of obedient interpretation" in the church.[1] Tradition I upholds the sole authority of scripture as canon; scripture alone is the norm by which all church speech and action are to be judged. However, scripture is necessarily linked to the ongoing life of the faith community. Scripture is the one source of revealed truth, yet it is not to be contrasted with tradition, for there is a long history of faithful interpretation of scripture within the church by those committed to the task. Such interpretation is necessary given the role that scripture plays in the church's life. Scripture and Tradition I are both affirmed without in the least compromising the unique authority of scripture. Irenaeus and Tertullian are good example of Tradition I, as is perhaps also the famous principle of Vincent of Lerins in the *Commonitorium*: "Morever, in the Catholic Church itself, all possible care must be taken, that we hold that faith which has been believed everywhere, always, and by all."[2] On this reading of Vincent (which strikes me as persuasive), his concern was not to offset scripture with an ecclesiocentric magisterium but to preserve the teaching of scripture in the ongoing life of the faithful community against heresy.

Tradition II is very different, for it represents an affirmation of a secondary source of revelation in the oral tradition of the church. According to Tradition II, scripture is not sufficient, for Christ committed to his disciples oral tradition as a necessary supplement to biblical revelation. According to Oberman, Basil's treatise *On the Holy Spirit*

1. Oberman, 54.
2. Vincent of Lerins, 132.

can be seen as the originator of Tradition II in the East, while certain passages of Augustine at least were understood this way by medieval theology, especially his well-known statement "I would not believe the Gospel, unless the authority of the Catholic Church moved me."[3] Of course, Augustine himself often asserts the sole authority of scripture. His well-known statement, according to Oberman, is intended to affirm a "practical authority" of the church in relation to its scriptures. However, in medieval theology it was taken to imply a "metaphysical authority" of the church, in which oral tradition becomes a second source of revelation. This move represents Tradition II.

Certainly on the basis of canon it is necessary strongly to affirm Tradition I and equally strongly deny Tradition II. Any claim to an alternative source of revelation alongside Holy Scripture must be resisted at all costs. It is important, however, to observe that such a theological commitment is common not only to the Reformers but also to much of the Catholic and Orthodox tradition. It is also equally important to affirm Tradition I, for by its very nature canon implies a living community in which scripture is treasured for instruction and guidance and in which the truth of scripture is continuously defended against heresy. Indeed, scripture itself is the result of a traditioning process, in which the sacred text is shaped for the very purpose of addressing an ongoing community of faith. Denial of Tradition I is in fact denial of scripture itself.

Evangelicalism and liberalism err on opposite extremes of the relation of scripture and tradition. Hodge, in a misguided effort to defend a hyper-Protestant position over against Roman Catholicism, in fact ends up mired in pietistic biblicism. According to Hodge, there is no authentic visible church: "Christ certainly did not die for any external, visible, organized Society."[4] The true church has no visible organization but consists only of "the people of God as such in their personal and individual relation to Christ."[5] For Hodge, everything in the dispute with Rome rests on this crucial distinction between the visible and invisible church: "But the question is, whether the Church to which the attributes, prerogatives, and promises pertaining to the body of Christ belong, is in its nature a visible, organized community . . . or, whether it is a spiritual body consisting of true believers."[6] This separation of the invisible from the visible church brings with it the pietistic distinction between professed believers, or nominal Christians, and true believers. Given his understanding of the church, it is clear that Hodge will have nothing to do with tradition. Tradition cannot be part of the rule of faith in any way:

3. Quoted in Oberman, 56.
4. Hodge, 1:131.
5. Ibid.
6. Ibid., 1:137.

"Protestants object to tradition as part of the rule of faith, because it is not adapted to that purpose."[7] It can only be either/or when it comes to the relation between the two: "Making tradition a part of the rule of faith subverts the authority of the Scriptures."[8] Hodge clearly means to reject not only Tradition II but also Tradition I, and this rejection is of the essence of fundamentalism.

The problem with Hodge's view is that it is itself unscriptural. There is no such thing as an "invisible" church in the Bible. The distinction is foreign to any part of the biblical canon. Instead, the visible church is described in very different tones: "I am writing these instructions to you so that, if I am delayed, you may know how one ought to behave in the household of God, which is the church of the living God, the pillar and bulwark of the truth" (1 Tim. 3:14–15). The church is given the knowledge of the truth and guards that knowledge with every fiber of its being. It also lives to communicate the gospel to the surrounding world in love. The visible church has an astonishing role to play on earth: "so that through the church the wisdom of God in its rich variety might now be made known" (Eph. 3:10). The church exists as a visible sign on earth of God's eternal plan of redemption of all creation. Through the witness of the church, the truth of the gospel is sounded forth in every new generation. Indeed, the church constitutes a new humanity, the firstfruits of God's Spirit in the world. Of course, nowhere does scripture reverse the relation between ecclesiology and Christology; the role of the church is grounded in the absolute priority of Jesus Christ over its very being. It lives from him, and to him, and preaches only Christ to the world. He is the true measure of its speech and action, the source and guide of its very life. Nevertheless, there is a visible church, with a necessary role to play.

Moreover, the role that the church plays results in tradition. Every new generation of the church must learn the language of faith afresh in the world in which it lives. It is not enough simply to repeat biblical sayings by rote; the church of each new age must penetrate to the true subject matter of which the scriptures speak, under the guidance of the Spirit. This process of handing on the faith is tradition: "And what you have heard from me through many witnesses entrust to faithful people who will be able to teach others as well" (2 Tim. 2:2). For Hodge and evangelicalism to assume that they can simply "return" to scripture without any genuine engagement with church tradition is self-delusion, for the counterweight of correction by the community of faith through the ages is missing, leaving only the voice of the present interpreter. In

7. Ibid., 1:127.
8. Ibid., 1:128.

other words, without tradition, scripture is simply subsumed under the spirit of the age, yielding error and misinterpretation. Hodge represents a massive confusion of Tradition I and Tradition II; thinking to reject the latter, he also rejects the former and in the process rejects the role of scripture in the church.

Liberalism by contrast errs in collapsing the authority of scripture into an ongoing process of tradition. This is clear in David Kelsey's proposal. According to Kelsey, tradition is a process embracing both the church's use of scripture and the presence of God, which interrelate dialectically to form the church's self-identity. Jesus Christ is present among the faithful through tradition, that is, through the act of handing on the gospel. Tradition comprises a variety of activities in which scripture is the mode of God's presence for the shaping of the church's self-identity. This yields Kelsey's characteristic definition of scripture: "'Scripture is used to name, not something the church is, but something she must *use* . . . to preserve self-identity.'"[9] *Tradition* is the name for the dialectical relation of scripture and the gracious presence of God in the church's ongoing effort of self-identification. For that reason, there can be no absolute distinction between scripture and tradition, as proposed in my presentation of canon above. Why? According to Kelsey, since tradition describes the ongoing use of scripture in the church, the two must be seen as complementary and mutually reinforcing: "It is misleading to contrast them as alternative and competing authorities for the church's forms of speech and action."[10] No more than Hodge does Kelsey make a distinction between Tradition I and Tradition II, though in fact Oberman's work predates Kelsey's by several years. On the contrary, clearly Kelsey affirms Tradition II as normative; he believes that the churchly act of self-identification is logically prior to scripture, and therefore constitutes a mode of divine self-manifestation distinct from scripture. Indeed, he goes much further even than Tradition II, for he sees the church's act of self-identification as the theological context for the church's use of scripture. Yet he interprets all criticism of Tradition II as simultaneously criticism of Tradition I. Hodge contains an all or nothing rejection of Tradition; Kelsey contains an all or nothing acceptance of Tradition. Neither recognizes the careful theological distinction necessary to bring clarity to the issue.

Kelsey makes several serious theological errors in his proposal, errors that are characteristic of Protestant liberalism since Schleiermacher. First of all, the church's use of scripture and the presence of God are not in dialectical relationship—that is the heresy of Pelagianism. It is

9. Kelsey, *Uses of Scripture*, 96.
10. Ibid.

through scripture alone that the church hears the living voice of Jesus Christ. There is no partnership or dialectic involved; there is only the speaking Lord and the obedient church. The knowledge of Christ is a gracious gift, not the exercise of any human capacity. The voice from heaven said to Peter, James, and John on the mountain of transfiguration: "This is my Son, the Beloved; with him I am well pleased; listen to him!" (Matt. 17:5). The fine formulation of Calvin remains forceful and true: "God alone is a fit witness of himself in his Word."[11] Kelsey's proposal involves a disastrous reversal of ecclesiology and Christology under the guise of "theological neutrality."

Second, while it is certainly true that the process of tradition flows from scripture and must be included in the concept of canon, that is very different from saying that scripture is defined by its use within that process. That has never been the confession of the church. Such an error openly invites the domestication of scripture by captivity to church tradition. The church appeals to scripture as a *text* possessing inherent authority to guide its life and guard it from error, not to a *process* in which that text is embedded. The true interpreter of scripture is not the process in which it is embedded but Christ the living Lord, who through the Spirit continually evokes from the church an ever-fresh response to the Word.

Third, the risen Lord is present to his church not through tradition but solely through scripture: "Were not our hearts burning within us while he was talking to us on the road, while he was opening the scriptures to us?" (Luke 24:32). Tradition is the written record of that encounter, a record that must be gratefully acknowledged by every new generation of the church. Indeed, we are all embedded in that very tradition. Tradition is not, however, the means for that encounter on a par with scripture. Canon implies an essential distinction between the sacred text and every effort to interpret it. Tradition thus has the role of an essential aid in understanding the true content of scripture.

Finally, it is simply false to describe the church in terms of an effort at self-identification. The goal of the church in reading scripture is not to wrestle with its identity; the goal is to be transformed into the image of Christ. The church's growth in understanding has nothing to do with a self-grounded struggle for identity but everything to do with genuine obedience to Christ: "But speaking the truth in love, we must grow up in every way into him who is the head, into Christ" (Eph. 4:15). To use the fine distinction of Karl Barth, we are responsible, but we are not autonomous.[12] The golden calf stands as the perpetual reminder of what

11. Calvin, 1.79.
12. *CD*, 1/2, 693.

happens when the church turns its rightful search for the living God into a crisis of identity. Aaron's excuse was lame then, and it is lame now: "So I said to them, 'Whoever has gold, take it off': so they gave it to me, and I threw it into the fire, and out came this calf!" (Exod. 32:24).

Once again extremes meet. Hodge and Kelsey are joined in one profound error: neither can make sense of the *mishearing* of scripture in the church. Hodge separates scripture from tradition and thus eliminates the possibility of a necessary correction of the individual interpreter by the confessing heritage of the church. Hodge's personal, individual reader is put outside any accountability to the church's tradition in a way foreign to the Reformers. For Kelsey, on the other hand, there is a kind of "prestabilized harmony" between scripture and the church (the phrase is used by Bernhard Lohse to describe the similar logic of Johann Eck's position, against which Luther protested so vehemently).[13] The church cannot meaningfully mishear scripture on Kelsey's view; one can speak only of a variety of uses. But in fact the church can and does all too often mishear scripture. Pelagianism misheard Paul; donatism misheard the Gospels; the German Christians misheard the Old Testament; liberation theology mishears Exodus; fundamentalism mishears the radically new quality of the gospel. Scripture can and must be used to criticize the church when it goes astray. A view that eliminates even the logical possibility of such criticism—such as Eck's or Kelsey's—must be stoutly resisted.

This reflection on the relation of scripture and tradition in the light of canon is a modern echo of the early church, especially the view of Irenaeus. According to Irenaeus in *Against Heresies*, the rule of faith circumscribes both scripture and tradition. The rule of faith is nothing other than the comprehensive teaching of the apostles and prophets handed on to succeeding generations in the form of a summary. Its content is not identical to the witness of the Old and New Testaments; however, it is the true subject matter of which scripture speaks. The rule of faith is scripture rightly understood and interpreted according to the inner harmony of its substance: "The entire Scriptures, the prophets, and the Gospels, can be clearly understood by all, although all do not believe them."[14] It is not merely an ecclesiastical perspective on scripture but the objective content of the Bible that can be shown without any ambiguity or distortion and used as the critical norm by which to defeat heresy. The error of Gnosticism is precisely that they base their system on a secret tradition not derived from scripture. Scripture contains the truth whole and entire, without need of added explanation; and yet the

13. Lohse, *Martin Luther's Theology*, 188.
14. Irenaeus, 398.

preaching of the truth is the living voice of Christ throughout creation: "But as the sun, that creature of God, is one and the same throughout the whole world, so also the preaching of the truth shineth everywhere, and enlightens all men that are willing to come to a knowledge of the truth."[15] When Irenaeus refers to the unbroken line of succession that ties the church of the present to the apostolic witness, his focus is on the continuity of theological substance over time. Bengt Haegglund rightly states: "Irenaeus, after all, was primarily concerned about doctrinal content and not about ordination."[16] Irenaeus is also deeply concerned to assert the continuity of the gospel message over space: "It is within the power of all, therefore, in every Church, who may wish to see the truth, to contemplate the tradition of the apostles manifested throughout the whole world."[17] Tradition is thus the spatial and temporal extension of the one biblical gospel throughout creation. Jesus Christ is the true reality of whom both scripture and tradition faithfully speak.

It is of course well known that the dynamic conception of scripture and tradition in the early church, which held them in unity without collapsing them into each other, was torn apart during the period of the Reformation. Protestants unanimously insisted upon the ultimate authority of scripture alone, apart from any appeal to church approval. Roman Catholics and Eastern Orthodox countered by emphasizing the necessary role of tradition in preserving the truth of scripture over the ages. It is not my concern here to rehearse the details of this controversy, which are widely available in studies of church history. It is, however, essential to ask: is there not now, in our time, the possibility for convergence of Protestants, Catholics, and Orthodox around canon, as a genuine solution to this longstanding problem? Two points must be made before attempting to address this question.

First, the extreme positions of evangelicalism and liberalism fail to meet the necessary canonical affirmation of scripture and tradition. The evangelical separation of scripture from tradition is not an option for the church of today. Likewise, the liberal appeal to self-identity, in which scripture is locked as a "religious classic" into an ongoing dialogue of the church with itself, is simply false. Second, it is important to recognize the signs of convergence already present in all three historic communions. Did not the reformed Second Helvetic Confession include a warm affirmation of the "interpretations of the holy Greek and Latin fathers"?[18] Did not the Lutheran Smalcald Articles admit that there are certain matters of church tradition—namely, the continuing truthfulness of the ancient

15. Ibid., 331.
16. Haegglund, 45.
17. Irenaeus, 415.
18. Leith, 135.

creeds—that are shared by "both parties" in the dispute?[19] Did not the great Eastern theologian John of Damascus speak of scripture as a "very fair garden," a "spiritual vineyard" that leads us through Christ to the "Father of lights," and warmly assert that "to search the Scriptures is a work most fair and most profitable for souls"?[20] Does not the official contemporary Roman Catholic position openly assert that the "study of the sacred page" is the "very soul of theology"?[21] It is impossible to deny a certain movement of mutual understanding; it is likewise too soon to speak of final agreement.

What are we to say of this conflict from the standpoint of our theological confession of canon? On the one hand, in a cultural era that has largely lost its historical memory, it is essential for the community of faith to protect and preserve its theological heritage. Our connection with the creeds and confessions does not involve simply historical influence; we today continue to retain an authentic theological connection to the same subject matter that was held as sacred in the grand tradition of the church. We are not the first generation of Christians to worship the one true God; it is therefore the height of ignorance and arrogance to turn our backs upon the church fathers, the medieval scholastics, and the Reformers as if we had somehow invented the gospel. They clearly saw through theological errors that continue to be repeated in the present, and we need their help and guidance in order to find our way. We cannot live without tradition. It is the great strength of the Roman Catholic and Eastern Orthodox communions to insist on the preservation of that memory.

On the other hand, the role of tradition is not to mediate biblical truth to the present. Scripture does not contain a deposit of doctrine that must be filtered through the successive development of ecclesial application. Scripture is shaped to address every new generation of the church with the living Word of God, and the role of the Spirit is to lift our gaze in the time-conditioned reality of the present to encounter the risen Lord of all times and ages, including our contemporary age. It is the great strength of the Reformation to insist that scripture alone serves as the vehicle by which the risen Christ constitutes, gathers, guides, corrects, and comforts his church. This Reformation insight must never be compromised, even for the sake of ecumenical mutuality. Church history amply testifies to the destructive role that tradition, contemporary church practice, and above all pious spirituality can play in obscuring the gospel message. It was not against unbelievers but against the spiritual elite that Jesus

19. *BC*, 292.
20. John of Damascus, 89.
21. *Cat*, 37, quoting from *Dei Verbum*.

unleashed his harsh condemnation: "You have a fine way of rejecting the commandment of God in order to keep your tradition! . . . thus making void the word of God through your tradition that you have handed on" (Mark 7:9–13).

So what is the role of tradition in relation to scripture? I would suggest that the dogmatic relation reverses the relation of historical dependency. In other words, though it is true that tradition flows historically from scripture, the proper conclusion is not to proceed from scripture through tradition. Rather, theologically, we must proceed from tradition to scripture. Necessarily prepared by the memory of our historic heritage—here Augustine's statement concerning the role of the church in moving the individual believer to search the scriptures is fully in order—we ourselves must now turn afresh to scripture in the contemporary world. Chastened by the wisdom of our ancestors in the faith, we today must nevertheless search the scriptures anew for the living will of God. Scripture is not a preparation for tradition, though historically the trajectory moves forward in that way; theologically, tradition is a preparation for the study of scripture, to which the church of today turns for the bread of life without which it cannot live. We cannot simply repeat the theology of the past, however impressive and important; we must bear witness to Christ in our own contemporary culture. We in our time must sing a new song, whose melody we draw directly from the full range of notes found in scripture itself. In the end, the critical norm for all speech and action in the church is the true content of the biblical witness, which is Jesus Christ himself.

It is now our task to consider the basic hermeneutical question of dogmatic theology: how do we interpret scripture in the light of its subject matter, which is Jesus Christ, the risen Lord of all creation? The same Spirit who guides the church from the witness of the text to the true reality to which it refers also guides the church from the true reality to which it refers back to the text, in order to lead the church from faith to faith in the full knowledge of God. What rules guide the church's theological interpretation of scripture? I propose the following set of rules of theological interpretation, whose validity is ultimately confirmed only in the actual content of dogmatics. These rules are not steps or stages of reflection; they are rather various dimensions of the church's manifold response to the living God made known through scripture.

1. *Dogmatic theology begins with the confession of Jesus Christ as Lord of all reality and turns to scripture in the light of that confession.* Faith in Jesus Christ is shared by the labor of dogmatic theology with the rest of the community of faith. That faith is simply a miracle, through the gracious gift of the Holy Spirit. The question for dogmatics is not whether Jesus Christ rules the entire universe in exalted glory, for the

reality of his rule is already joyfully acknowledged and affirmed with the church's very profession of faith, a faith that the church theologian also professes. Jesus Christ is Lord of the entire universe; all things in creation serve his gracious purpose of love for humankind. Dogmatic theology does not ground the ontological reference of scripture on any other basis than that which is gratefully received in the miracle of faith. Proceeding from faith, it reflects ontologically upon the true reality of Christ's rule. The question for dogmatics is thus how to understand the rule of Christ over all reality in the light of the scriptural witness. Since it is true that all things serve Jesus Christ, what does that mean for our understanding of creation, reconciliation, and redemption? Thus we do not proceed from the possibility of Christ's rule to its reality; we proceed from the true reality of Christ's rule to its meaning for our understanding of human existence.

2. *Dogmatic theology is based on the historical witness of the text, which it learns from biblical theology.* It is now necessary to insist upon the cooperative division of labor between the various fields of theology. While we share the exact same faith of the early, medieval, and Reformation church and share with them the task of reading scripture in the light of the subject matter, we now have an opportunity for precision that they lacked. The tools of modern historical criticism, despite their widespread misuse, are to be fully accepted. Here the dogmatic theologian must rely on the biblical theologian, who has mastered those tools and deployed them in a way that carefully renders the discrete voice of each pericope and unit according to its canonical shape and intentionality. In other words, dogmatic theology does not begin immediately with scripture; it begins with biblical theology and then returns to scripture in completion of the hermeneutical circle. This is our version today of the role of the literal sense at the time of the Reformation, which sought to liberate the living word of the text from domestication to the medieval allegorical system. The rich concern of allegory for multiple meanings is not to be denied; rather, it is a matter of introducing a disciplined basis for theological reflection that frees the Bible to gain a full hearing in the church. Dogmatic theology is not simply a repetition of biblical theology. It turns to scripture with a different set of problems, a different range of questions, and a different aim of reflection. It is free to hear the biblical text in a wide variety of metaphorical figures as it searches the scriptures to know the truth of the gospel. Nevertheless, its freedom is grounded in the historical witness, which is faithfully rendered by the discipline of biblical theology.

3. *Dogmatic theology assumes the unity of scripture and yet preserves the variety.* There is one voice in all of scripture, for all scripture is inspired by the Spirit of God, who is the Spirit of Jesus Christ the living

Lord. It is the voice of Christ the living Lord that we hear in the pages of scripture. The entire canon of scripture is the direct existential address of the risen Christ to the church, and through the church to the surrounding world. It is not therefore the role of dogmatics to achieve the unity of scripture. Rather, the unity of scripture is everywhere assumed. The role of dogmatic theology is to make that unity visible in our world today. Guided by the past labors of dogmatic theologians, we today must engage in the challenging endeavor of making manifest the unity of scripture through a grasp of the whole. Constructions of the subject matter that fragment the whole are to be rejected. And yet in seeking to make the unity manifest, we must not lose in the slightest way the splendor of variety in the scriptural witness. Constructions of the subject matter of scripture that silence whole parts or dimensions of the biblical witness are likewise to be rejected. The unity of scripture is fully transparent only where the variety is most fully maintained. The great need in the church today is for a holistic interpretation of the Bible in language that is appropriate to our contemporary world. Given the widespread biblical illiteracy of the church, including often enough the clergy, it is essential for the church today to learn once again to speak the language of faith drawn from scripture.

4. *Dogmatic reflection searches for the pattern of truth that it discerns in the biblical text in light of the subject matter.* In returning to the witness of scripture in light of the subject matter, the role of dogmatics is to trace the contours of divine truth as these are revealed in the manifold witness of the biblical text. Here I must introduce a note of caution. We are not prophets or apostles; while their access to the divine reality was immediate, ours is not but is mediated through their testimony. That is why dogmatic theology is dependent upon biblical theology for its basic orientation, because the basic theological shape of scripture is the only reliable guide to knowledge of the divine reality. Moreover, given the economy of disciplines in contemporary theological study, dogmatics is in a position to search for the pattern of truth only after it has learned from biblical theology to move from the witness to the reality to which it refers. A pattern is not a proof-text; a proof-text ignores the hermeneutical circle by seeking to move directly from the reality to the witness, without having first learned from those more qualified in historical criticism to move from the witness to the reality. Nevertheless, with this caution in mind, the role of dogmatic theology is to reflect upon the fullness of divine being as reflected in the intertextual ordering of truth in the biblical witness. Dogmatic reflection is an ontological interpretation of the subject matter of scripture. We not only learn of God by being led by the Spirit from the pages of scripture to the reality of which it speaks; we also grow in our understanding by being led by the same Spirit back to the

same scriptures toward a deeper understanding of the living God, which comes only as a gracious divine gift. The pattern of truth in scripture is not organized around a theological or ethical idea, even a doctrinally "correct" one, but is rather a transparency to the living divine being. In the end, the reality of Christ himself is the only objective measure of the truth of dogmatic reflection.

5. *Dogmatic theology must protect and defend the boundaries of truth in scripture, while at the same time preserving the flexible variety.* On certain issues, scripture of both Testaments speaks without ambiguity; it sets down parameters within which the genuine truth of God is to be found. One role of dogmatics is to trace the outlines of those boundaries. In this effort, the guidance and confirmation of the creeds and confessions of the church are essential, for they are themselves a clear echo of those same boundaries. Nevertheless, dogmatic theology has the additional task of showing how those boundaries offer correction to the contemporary church; it must ask the question whether lines beyond which the gospel is not rightly preached are being crossed in contemporary proclamation, and if so in what way. It is likewise the role of dogmatic theology to insist upon and savor the flexibility of biblical truth within those lines of right doctrine. Often scripture gives no right or wrong answer to a given question; it gives outer markers yet leaves the inquirer free to wrestle with the substance of the faith with unrestrained creativity. On these issues, the church theologian must preserve the flexibility of scripture and carefully guard against an unwarranted rigidity. The trial-and-error historical experience of the church is crucial in this endeavor. Of course the error of liberalism is to deny the existence of those boundaries, while the error of fundamentalism is to draw boundaries where none exist in scripture. Dogmatics must preserve both truthfulness and flexibility in order to serve the church. In so doing, it recognizes that there is not one right theology, for there are often several legitimate ways of approaching many of the basic issues of dogmatic theology, and none must be granted a privileged or exclusive position. The aim is illumination, not exclusive correctness.

6. *Dogmatic theology uses the tools of rational analysis to unfold the inner logic of the subject matter of scripture; the inner logic of the subject matter determines the proper use of those tools, and never the reverse.* In my condemnation of natural theology I have spoken harsh words against the idolization of human reason and experience. Those words are necessary and true, and the condemnation of natural theology is essential. However, we must think dialectically; we must condemn human reason and experience and yet must also realize that we are no nearer to God by abandoning or canceling out rational human response. Mysticism is no nearer the truth than natural theology but is in fact a form of it.

Rather, rigorous reflection is part of the obedience we owe to the majesty of divine truth, and all resources of human culture are available for this purpose. The key to their proper use is to orient reason and experience toward the inner logic of divine truth grasped in faith; natural theology, including all forms of mediating theology, moves in the opposite direction, by seeking to orient divine truth to the intrinsic claims of reason and experience. The canons of critical analysis must yield to the inner logic of the subject matter, even when those canons are shattered and reformed. Natural theology can lead only to heresy, but the proper use of rational analysis not only is allowable but is in fact an indispensable dimension of dogmatic theology. Here there are no limits to the tools that may be used, including various concepts of philosophy, history, literary analysis, political science, and other disciplines. We all approach the Bible with such concepts; there is no *tabula rasa*. The issue is not the presence or absence of such concepts but the direction of interpretation. Natural theology bends the truth to meet the inner exigencies of human thought; faith seeking understanding molds human thought to the inner demands of the divine substance. Dogmatic theology is therefore systematically unsystematic, as befits the miraculous paradox of grace.

7. *Through the guidance of the Spirit, dogmatic theology must apply the truth of scripture to the contemporary world with creative imagination.* Scripture is shaped for the very purpose of addressing every new generation of the church with the living Word of God. However, the movement from past to present is not accomplished by scripture itself; rather, Jesus Christ the risen Lord continues to address the church of each new age with the living imperative of his eternal rule. Through the gift of the Spirit, fresh application of the message of scripture serves to guide the church in its direct, existential encounter with the risen Lord. The initiative of that encounter lies with Christ himself, who sends forth the truth of his word with absolute authority and overwhelming power. His Word cannot and will not fail. The role of dogmatic theology is to search for the living Word of Christ through the use of human imagination. Once again, natural theology must be condemned; human imagination is in itself held captive to the sinful abyss of distorted ideology. The supposed liberation of self-grounded imagination is in fact a vain lie, leading only to idolatry: "The LORD saw that the wickedness of humankind was great in the earth, and that every inclination of the thoughts of their hearts was only evil continually" (Gen. 6:5). Nevertheless, through the gracious presence of the Spirit, the dogmatic theologian, despite human frailty, is led to a creative and energetic exercise of imagination in applying the biblical message to the contemporary world for the sake of the gospel. Such use of the imagination is not self-grounded but is shaped by the form of the biblical witness; yet it is free to use whatever resources are

available in seeking the living command of Christ. There is no hermeneutical system for appropriate application; the ultimate measure of Christ's living command for the world of today is Jesus Christ himself.

8. *The purpose of dogmatic reflection on scripture is the transformation of the whole world.* There is of course a place for dogmatic theology in the academy. The study of dogmatics is an essential ingredient in the preparation for ordained ministry, and there is likewise no reason that the same study might not be undertaken elsewhere in the university. The great dogmatic theologians of the church, from Augustine to Barth, have often gained a readership beyond the walls of the church. Nevertheless, dogmatic reflection is anything but an "academic" exercise in which ideas about God are discussed. The language of faith can never be curious talk about God; it is always talking to God himself, a process in which the absolute claim of God upon human life takes hold with compelling power. The aim of dogmatic reflection is the total and radical transformation of human existence in all aspects: mind, body, will, and emotions. The fruit of genuine dogmatic labor is nothing less than the Spirit's sublime gift of peace, joy, and love. Therefore, the individual human response—including the profound struggle of faith that dogmatic reflection entails—is necessary for all who undertake the task in the obedience of faith. The individual struggle does not take place apart from but within the community of faith; "rugged individualism" has no place in the church. Nevertheless, there is always an ultimate individual response that cannot be erased by an ideology of "community." In the end, the goal of dogmatic theology is discipleship. It is not talk about God but talking to God in the journey of faith. Dogmatic theology begins and ends in prayer, in which human speech is submitted to the gracious testing of the living God. As Augustine states in the concluding words of his treatise *On the Trinity*: "O Lord the one God, God the Trinity, whatever I have said in these books that is of Thine, may they acknowledge who are Thine; if anything of my own, may it be pardoned both by Thee and by those who are Thine. Amen."[22]

---

22. Augustine, *On the Trinity*, 228.

Part III ✻

Proclamation

7

The Word of God

Jesus Christ is known in the world today. The voice of the living Lord is heard with simplicity and clarity in the contemporary world. The task of theological reflection does not begin with the well-meaning but ultimately fatuous cynicism of modern theology. Nor does it begin with the equally well-meaning and equally fatuous defensiveness of conservative "apologetics." The current crisis of dogmatic theology is not the self-serving pseudo-crisis of the skeptic. On the contrary, the true crisis of contemporary dogmatics, and indeed of the contemporary church, comes from a very different direction. The true crisis is created by the fact that Jesus Christ is indeed present, that the voice of the living Lord does indeed declare himself to all creation. The great struggle of current church life is created by the living Word of God, not by the ultimately harmless sideshow of philosophical critique and countercritique. "I was ready to be sought out by those who did not ask, to be found by those who did not seek me" (Isa. 65:1): such is the genuine crisis of the church. But such also is the true promise of contemporary church life, and with it the promise of dogmatic reflection as well. The true reality of God's living Word is profound judgment of the church; but it is likewise the even more profound hope for the future of the church and therefore for the world as well: "I will bring forth descendants from Jacob, and from Judah inheritors of my mountains; my chosen shall inherit it, and my servants shall settle there" (Isa. 65:9).

The proper question for dogmatics is not whether Christ is known in the world of today. The proper question rather is this: Given the reality of God's self-manifestation in Jesus Christ for all humanity, how is he manifest? How is Jesus Christ known in the world today? How is the voice of Christ heard by humankind throughout the earth? How does the risen Lord lay claim on the life of the contemporary community of faith, including the individual disciple? The answer to these questions is the proclamation of the Word of God. The essence of canon is the shaping of scripture for the purpose of serving as the instrument by which the living Lord continues to govern his church in every new age and for every new generation. Of course, scripture serves a variety of functions in the church in fulfilling its role: the faithful reading of scripture by the individual Christian, the gathering around scripture for study and reflection by the community of faith, the profound influence of scripture on the liturgy of the church, the guidance of scripture for the church's life and mission, pastoral care of the weak and vulnerable, and so forth. However, the primary application of scripture to the ongoing life of the community is through the proclamation of the Word of God. As the book of Acts stresses, the history of the church is the history of the Word of God, the history of preaching: "The word of God continued to spread; the number of the disciples increased greatly in Jerusalem, and a great many of the priests became obedient to the faith" (Acts 6:7). Through the preaching of the Word, the living voice of Christ is heard throughout the whole of creation. Indeed, through the miraculous presence of the Spirit, the preaching of the Word is the voice of Christ sounded forth to all humanity. John Donne correctly states concerning the call of the gospel: "Now, this *calling*, implies a voice, as well as a Word; it is by the Word; but not by the Word read at home, though that be a pious exercise; nor by the word submitted to private interpretation; but *by the word preached*, according to his Ordinance, and under the Great Seal, of his blessing upon his ordinance."[1] Dogmatic theology must take up in earnest the theology of proclamation.

Perhaps the clearest statement of the theology of proclamation comes in the Second Helvetic Confession: "The Preaching of the Word of God is the Word of God"[2] (C.1). Through the miraculous presence of the Holy Spirit, the words of the preacher become in reality the living voice of Jesus Christ the risen Lord. Through the work of the Spirit, the simple, ordinary Sunday sermon is the conduit through which the eternal power and wisdom of Christ the exalted Lord of the entire cosmos are made manifest to every new age of the church. What the preacher says on

1. Donne, 212.
2. Leith, 133.

Sunday morning, however fearfully and inadequately put into words, Jesus Christ himself now says in the church and for the world of today. This is not a vague metaphor but a literal truth; this is not a poetic exaggeration but a true description of the eternal Now of Christ's living presence encountered in the weekly sermon. It does not matter that the sermon may be delivered by anxious or faltering voice; it does not matter that the one who speaks is hardly the most impressive figure in contemporary society. Impressive or not, the office of preacher is constituted by Christ himself for the purpose of serving as his voice for every new generation of the church. There is no other means so constituted, for in the good pleasure of Christ the minister of the Word serves in his or her unique role not because of self-endowed importance but because of the command of Christ: "You shall be my witnesses" (cf. Acts 1:8). There is thus only one source of faith in all creation: faith comes from hearing the preaching of Christ (cf. Rom. 10:17).

The preached word is the power of God for the redemption of all humankind. The preached word is the free gift of God's embrace to all humanity. The preaching of the Word renders people whole, guides them in the crucial decisions of life, comforts them in the moments of deepest darkness, challenges them to wondrous newness of life, heals their every distress, transforms and sets them free for passionate love for life under the rule of Christ. It is through preaching that the community of faith is gathered and built up for mutual love and active service in the world. Those who receive and act upon the preached word receive and act upon the command of Christ; those who reject the preached word reject Christ himself (cf. Matt. 10:40). The ultimate crisis of faith is thus the decision that comes in hearing the weekly sermon on the lips of the ordinary minister of the Word, for here, and here alone, every human being on this earth comes face to face with the one Lord of all reality. Affirmation of canon today fully embraces the Reformation view of the centrality of the proclaimed word, no matter how foreign it may sound in a modern context.

Before I chart the full range of issues involved in the theology of proclamation, it is essential to grasp the inadequacy of both liberalism and evangelicalism in regard to preaching. The theological errors of both are deep seated and ineradicable, but nowhere is the final lack of theological depth and biblical connection of both so crystal clear than in their failure to affirm the true nature of preaching. The failure is not recent and scattered; the failure rather is fundamental and endemic in both factions. According to Friedrich Schleiermacher, the Christian fellowship is divided up between those whose aptitude for piety is primarily receptive and those whose aptitude is primarily "spontaneous"—i.e., active and expressive. That is to say, some members of the community formed around a common determination of religious piety are more apt to be listeners, while others are more apt to be speakers. Indeed, this distinction is common within every kind of social organization. Preaching is an activity of the spontaneous members of the church; thus, for Schleiermacher, the ministry of preaching is ultimately grounded ecclesiologically, not christologically. It is a secondary result of the nature of Christian community, which includes the fact that some are naturally speakers and others are naturally hearers; it is not the primary result of the commission of Christ. Schleiermacher's conception of the nature of the office of preaching of course has massive influence on his understanding of the content of what is preached. For the substance of Christian preaching is in fact the spontaneous self-communication of piety. Preaching is a form of "self-presentation."[3] The content of the sermon must of course reflect back upon the "view of Christ" that is contained in scripture.[4] However, this is in the manner of historical influence; there is in Schleiermacher's view no recognition whatsoever of the sovereign act of the risen Christ in commissioning the Christian ministry. It is no surprise therefore that the liberal tradition of Christian preaching that flows from Schleiermacher is ultimately a matter of communicating the personality of the preacher. That is what it should be in his view. Indeed, according to Scheiermacher, the very distinction between ordained and non-ordained persons in the church is destined ultimately to fade away. Because the distinction is grounded ecclesiologically, rather than christologically, it is merely a relative one, and the trajectory is toward the disappearance of preaching as the Christian community evolves over time.

Schleiermacher and the liberal tradition have simply lost sight of the theology of proclamation that guided the Reformers and that in fact is grounded in scripture itself. Nothing less is at stake than the very future of the ministry of the Word. According to scripture, the preaching of the Word is the living voice of Jesus Christ himself: "Whoever listens to you listens to me" (Luke 10:16). This theological insight may have been recovered in a powerful way at the time of the Reformation, but it was in fact always preserved in the church from the beginning. Already in the *Didache*, the essential point is firmly grasped and asserted: "My child, him that speaketh to thee the word of God remember night and day; and thou shalt honour him as the Lord; for [in the place] whence lordly rule is uttered, there is the Lord."[5] The preaching of the Word is christologically constituted and ordered, as recognized and acknowl-

3. Schleiermacher, 612.
4. Ibid., 613.
5. *Teaching of the Twelve*, 378.

edged everywhere in the universal church. Yet here liberalism radically breaks off from the faith of the church. For liberalism, the preaching of the Word is not an act of Christ's presence and rule over the church; it is an act rather of one set of members within the church in reference to another set of members. What determines the fact of the ministry, as well as the content of what is preached, is the nature of human personality in community. Preaching is an act of self-display, even if in the tones of piety and spirituality. And that is why we must reject the liberal theology of proclamation; for in it human beings dignify human personality with the attributes of self-imposed divinity. Human beings turn themselves into idols by preaching whatever their own personality suggests—whatever cultural agenda, political cause, social ideal, or personal aim happens to be conceived. Liberal preaching is the church talking to itself; it is not the church listening to and obeying the voice of Jesus Christ. Liberal preaching is a manifestation of the tyranny of self-validating human experience; despite its best intentions, it has lost contact with the service of the Word that in fact shapes the Christian ministry wherever it goes throughout the entire creation.

We do not gather on Sunday morning to hear the pious utterances of the strong as over against the weak, the talkative over against the passive; we gather to hear and obey the one voice of the one Lord of heaven and earth: "Understand, O dullest of the people; fools, when will you be wise? He who planted the ear, does he not hear? He who formed the eye, does he not see? He who disciplines the nations, he who teaches knowledge to humankind, does he not chastise?" (Ps. 94:8–10). God is an active God, a God who speaks his living Word to each new generation of the church. God intervenes in the direction of his church through his Word, shaping his people according to his eternal purpose of love. We do not believe that the Christian ministry will simply fade away into insignificance as the nature of religious community evolves; we believe that there is nothing more important on this earth than the training of ministers of the gospel of Christ for excellence in their calling. The liberal conception of preaching is a distortion of the biblical call to ministry and undercuts the christological basis of the Christian ministry.

And so likewise, and with equal force, must the dogmatics of the Christian church reject the evangelical conception of proclamation. What is the meaning and purpose of preaching according to the great architect of evangelical theology, Charles Hodge? In the three hefty volumes of the *Systematic Theology*, one hears of Christian preaching exactly—nothing. There is a chapter on the means of grace (pt. 3, chap. 20), which Hodge defines as the ordinary channels through which the grace of God is poured out. Hodge lists three such means of grace: the Word of God, sacraments, and prayer. So far, one is at least in the general realm of Reformation doctrine. But the opening line of the section on the Word makes clear just how far evangelicalism has strayed from the Reformers, under the influence of rationalism and pietism. According to Hodge, "The word of God, as here understood, is the Bible"[6]: the Bible is the means of grace; there is no mention whatsoever of preaching. Just as evangelicalism (rightly) stresses the inspiration of scripture but (wrongly) separates it from the illumination of the Spirit, so also does it separate scripture from Christ's own commission to preach the gospel to the nations. For evangelical theology, apologetics, not the biblical call to proclaim the name of Christ far and near, is the true form of missionary outreach. This is so because of the thoroughly modern (and erroneous) idea that the truths contained in scripture are manifest in the interior human psyche, which can therefore serve as a point of correlation with apologetic endeavor. As Hodge puts it, "These [the teachings of Scripture] are facts of consciousness, as well as doctrines of the Bible."[7] There is lacking in evangelicalism the need urgently to proclaim what no human being can see or understand; rather, there is only a desire to provide private religious instruction in what every human being can also see and confirm from the contents of their own self-based experience. Conservative evangelicalism has no theology of proclamation—or rather, it has substituted in its place a false theology of apologetic argumentation completely foreign to the good news of the gospel.

Where there is a theological vacuum, the voices of error will rush in, as indeed they have. Evangelicalism has lost its grasp of the fact that the voice of preaching is, through the miraculous gift of the Spirit, the voice of Christ himself. Christian preaching therefore becomes in evangelical practice one among several ways in which religious instruction is provided concerning the content of scripture. There is no commission to preach, no call to ministry; there is no service of the divine Word through the work of the Spirit. There is only the freelance opportunity to teach the contents of the Bible. Nowhere is this absence of a biblical understanding of preaching clearer than in the explosion of "televangelism," which has clearly become the primary mechanism of propaganda on the religious right. I do not for a moment question the good intentions of the various televangelists; I have no doubt of their sincere endeavor to preach the gospel of Christ to the whole world. Nevertheless, despite the sincerity of their desire, they are not preaching the gospel. Instead, a wide variety of cultural and personal agenda provide the motive force

6. Hodge, 3:466.
7. Ibid., 3:471.

for their various "ministries." Televangelism, and with it the rest of evangelicalism, has sought to engraft the gospel onto a conservative cultural agenda heralding a national and global "return" to conservative cultural values. It is time, we are told, to turn the cultural clock back to a previous era in our society, when Christian faith provided the primary religious background to the structure of society as a whole. One way or another, this conservative cultural agenda pervades the message of the religious right; one way or another, the various personalities of the religious right sell themselves as purveyors of this cultural Christianity. The conservative cultural agenda is the broad scope of the movement; the gospel of Christ is brought forward as the way to attain that agenda. What is our response to this televangelist explosion and its widespread proliferation of imitators at the level of the local church?

Our response can only be serious and uncompromising. Televangelism, and together with it the entire religious right, is a form of false prophecy. I speak globally and widely of the movement as a whole. Dogmatic theology does not name heretics; that is the concern only of the gathered community of faith. Nevertheless, dogmatic theology does have the role of criticizing ideas when they have become pervasive in their influence on church life. Who can deny that the flowering of televangelism has had massive influence on the very shape of church life among conservative evangelicals? When false ideas are widely proclaimed and gain massive influence to the destruction of the church, it is the necessary role of dogmatic theology to draw lines of right doctrine, no matter how influential those may be who are indirectly criticized.

The Bible is well aware of the sad reality of false prophecy. According to Jeremiah (23:23–32), God is not unaware of the various voices of those who claim to be prophets. "Am I a God near by, says the Lord, and not a God far off? Who can hide in secret places so that I cannot see them? says the Lord. Do I not fill heaven and earth? says the Lord." There are those who claim to speak in the name of the Lord, using for their message their own personal and cultural agenda: "I have heard what the prophets have said who prophesy lies in my name, saying, 'I have dreamed, I have dreamed!'" Yet the dreams of the false prophets have nothing to do with the true divine Word: "They plan to make my people forget my name by their dreams that they tell one another, just as their ancestors forgot my name for Baal. Let the prophet who has a dream tell the dream, but let the one who has my word speak my word faithfully." The essence of false prophecy is not outright rejection of God's Word but rather the perfidious assumption that God's Word can be used for an alien cultural agenda: "What has straw in common with wheat? says the Lord. Is not my word like fire, says the Lord, and like a hammer that breaks a rock in pieces?" For that reason, the false prophets, though they claim to speak in the name of God, are in fact rejected by God himself: "See, I am against the prophets, says the LORD, who use their own tongues and say, 'Says the LORD." See, I am against those . . . who lead my people astray by their lies and their recklessness, when I did not send them or appoint them; so they do not profit this people at all, says the LORD."

Televangelism as a whole—the issue is not the technological medium, which is perfectly fine, but the erroneous message that has taken it captive—is false prophecy. The televangelists do not build up the church of Jesus Christ but create only a cult of personality profoundly alien to the community of faith. They are not preaching the gospel of Christ but a strange gospel of success through self-improvement utterly foreign to the cross of Christ. Yet what is televangelism but the symptom of the global error of the religious right as a whole? Just as there is no way forward in the church on the religious left, so is there likewise no way forward on the religious right; both are transcended and set aside by the simple call to proclaim Jesus Christ to all humanity.

The preaching of the Word of God is the only true crisis for the church and the world: "Do you think that I have come to bring peace to the earth? No, I tell you, but rather division!" (Luke 12:51). But even more important, the Word of God is also the one great promise of God's redeeming love for church and society. What does it mean for us in the contemporary world to make the basic confession "The preaching of the Word of God is the Word of God"? It is essential to recognize the christological basis for proclamation. In the book of Acts, Jesus Christ the risen Lord sends forth his disciples as his witnesses to the ends of creation. The unfolding drama of the book surrounds the ever-increasing reach of the Word of God throughout the earth: "The word of God continued to spread" (Acts 6:7). We today live by the same commission of the same Lord to preach the same gospel to the whole of creation. The proclamation of the gospel is the living voice of Jesus Christ for all creation. The exalted Lord speaks; Christ the ruler of the entire cosmos addresses humanity. But how and where? The Sunday sermon is the voice of Jesus Christ. Here, and here alone, the will of the living Lord of all humanity is made known to all who hear and obey. To those in the world who seek Christ, the answer of the church is clear and simple: he is encountered in the preaching of the Word. It is precisely for this reason that dogmatics and the church at large are zealous to defend the proclaimed Word against liberal and conservative ideology. For our proclamation to the world is not conservative or liberal ideology; our proclamation is Jesus Christ, and him alone, for the redemption of the world. Christ alone is the one content of proclamation, because Christ alone is the true agent of proclamation. Those who preach are his ministers, his ambassadors, whose calling is the faithful delivery of his message to the listening ears of the world.

No one is adequate for such a calling; no one is able in their own strength to carry it out. The issue is not the persons who deliver the word; the focus rather is upon the living claim of the One whom they proclaim. The power does not belong to the person who preaches; the power belongs to God alone. God alone builds his eternal kingdom, not the minister of the gospel; all responsibility for God's miraculous rule can only be left in his hands. The preaching of the Word is the Word of God not because of the special insights or particular religious genius of those who speak, but rather because of the miraculous presence of the Holy Spirit. It is through the presence of the Spirit that the words of the minister on Sunday morning are rendered the very Word of God to the specific congregation that hears them. The miraculous work of the Spirit renders the words of the preacher, however faltering and frail, the very Word of God to a specific place and at a specific time.

The work of the Spirit began with the forming and shaping of the canon of scripture; it is completed in the application of the biblical word to the contemporary world in which we live. The distance between the biblical word and the world of today is not overcome by any act of human capacity, such as reason, experience, or imagination. The distance is overcome solely by the mystery of God's Spirit, who seals on our hearts and minds today the true content of God's eternal will. The Spirit of God is the sole teacher of the church; the scriptures are the sole means he uses to instruct each new generation in the one faith of the gospel. Application therefore is not a matter of human capacity in any form whatsoever; application rather is carried out according to the analogy of faith, which is itself the gift of the Spirit. The Spirit alone provides the bridge from the biblical world to the contemporary world and guides the church in the living will of God. Through the work of the Spirit it becomes crystal clear that there is no distance at all, that the new world of God attested in scripture is in fact the real world in which we live and work in everyday life today. The Spirit acts not according to human whim and prejudice but according to the sovereign rule of Christ over all reality. The Holy Spirit is the Spirit of Christ, who alone teaches the church the true content of the gospel. The work of the Spirit undercuts every human attempt to evade the living claim of Christ, especially through forms of human piety and spirituality.

The grave danger of the church is not the outright rejection of the Word; the grave danger rather is adding to God's Word on the basis of human religiosity, which is the ultimate folly. "You must neither add anything to what I command you nor take away anything from it, but keep the commandments of the LORD your God with which I am charging you" (Deut. 4:2). Both evangelicalism and liberalism add to the Word of God out of (well-intended) human piety and are therefore false doctrine. The great challenge of Christian proclamation in our time is to recover our understanding of the work of the Spirit, who guides the preaching of the Word not according to human judgment but according to the gracious purpose of God for all humanity.

The great promise of proclamation is the transformation of the church and the entire world. God's Word formed the universe from nothing; God's living Word fashions a new creation as a gracious divine gift grounded solely in God's good will for his people and for his world. God's living Word guides our steps in the way of justice and peace when the confusion of our times threatens to lead us astray. God's living Word alone makes a person whole, reaching into the core of human existence where no power on earth can truly reach, changing human life from the inside out. God's living Word not only lays before us a message, to which we adjust our lives; God's living Word is the true power of change in the universe, making all things new. God's living Word shapes history, remakes human life according to God's gracious intent, brings into reality the divine purpose of redemptive love for all things living.

There is nothing more important to the very future of the church than excellence in the ordained clergy. Everything concerning the future welfare of God's flock rests on the development of a new generation of well-trained, devoted, imaginative, energetic, and compassionate ministers sent forth by Christ into the world. Where will they come from? Unless they come, faith in the gospel is not possible: "But how are they to call on one in whom they have not believed? And how are they to believe in one of whom they have never heard? And how are they to hear without someone to proclaim him?" (Rom. 10:14). The excellence of Christian ministry cannot be the concern of a few; the need for a new generation of dedicated pastors cannot be the province of only "professional" Christians; the entire church of Jesus Christ is deeply involved in and deeply concerned for the Christian ministry. The world is waiting to hear the message of the gospel; who will proclaim that message? Humankind lies under the burden of their own sin; who will announce to them the only relief from that horrible burden? Christ has died and risen again for the sake of all humanity; who will go to tell the nations the good news of redemption? Of course that is not to deny the vital role of the laity in the life of the church. Without the laity there is no church, for we are all one body in Christ. However, the Christian church of all ages, and in all historic communions, has set aside certain individuals called by God to the specific duty of ministry of the Word of God. "The harvest is plentiful, but the laborers are few; therefore ask the Lord of the harvest to send out laborers into his harvest" (Matt. 9:37–38). We need ministers of the

Word of God who give their entire being to this special service of Christ. We need ministers who are well educated for their task, who function as spiritual, moral, and intellectual leaders to the flock they serve. We need a church willing to support these ministers and their families fully, so that their ministry can be what it has always been when the church thrives: a full-time devotion to preaching and pastoral care. The need is as great now as it has ever been.

Every denomination has specific traditions for recognizing, confirming, educating, and commissioning those who have been called. That is as it should be, for Christian ministers do not call themselves nor ordain themselves. The Pauline injunction certainly applies here: "All things should be done decently and in order" (1 Cor. 14:40). Nevertheless, the stress of dogmatics must be on the fact that the call comes from God himself. God calls ministers, teaches them the glory of his will, sends them forth into the world to love and serve the Lord as ministers of his Word. There is no more important calling on this earth. Of course every calling is equally essential in the eyes of God; such is the priesthood of all believers as taught by the Reformers. However, let it not be forgotten that the same Reformers also stressed without any ambiguity the astonishing reality of being called by God to preach the Word and pastor the flock. Indeed, those same Reformers were profoundly distressed at the failures of the church—even especially the newly formed Protestant churches—to generate able and consistent labor in the ordained ministry. Luther spoke of the bitter laziness of the clergy, which kept them from learning, and therefore from teaching, the truth about God. Through a false sense of security, they had forgotten the very rudiments of the faith, with disastrous consequences for the whole people of God: "These dainty, fastidious fellows would like quickly, with one reading, to become doctors above all doctors, to know all there is to be known. Well, this, too, is a sure sign that they despise both their office and the people's souls, yes, even God and his Word. They need not fear a fall, for they have already fallen all too horribly. What they need is to become children and begin learning their ABC's, which they think they have outgrown long ago."[8] The issue is not only old but new; Karl Barth stressed that those who proclaim are ultimately responsible to God alone and that such responsibility has direct consequences for the substance of preaching: "Church proclamation, as regards its content, cannot let itself be questioned as to whether it is in harmony with the distinctive features and interests of a race, people, nation, or state. . . . A proclamation which accepts responsibilities along these or similar

8. *BC*, 359.

lines spells treachery to the Church and to Christ Himself."[9] The call to
ministry means direct responsibility and accountability to Christ the
risen Lord for the witness of the minister in word and deed. Yet despite
the church's failures, then and now, the fact remains that the calling of
God to the Christian ministry contains in itself the very future of the
church and therefore the very future of the world. There is nothing more
important in the entire universe than the preaching of the gospel; there
is no greater joy and fulfillment under heaven than faithful service to
Christ in the ministry of his Word. Let the challenge go forth to a new
generation to give their lives, their all, to this wondrous task.

The Christian church believes in an educated clergy. Every minister
must come to the task with a solid theological education and must continue that education as long as he or she lives. Who ever outgrows the
need to learn the mysteries of God's marvelous purpose in the universe
that he made good? Every minister must receive a thorough education
in the basic knowledge required to preach and teach the Word of God,
pastor the congregation, celebrate the sacraments, lead the worship of
God, and administer the people of God. That education must include full
proficiency in Greek and Hebrew; a complete grasp of church history in
its setting in world history; comprehensive training in the canonical shape
of both Testaments of scripture; firm grounding in biblical and dogmatic
theology; wide exposure to the history and contemporary work of biblical exegesis; practical training in the art of pastoral care; and genuine
understanding of the mission of the church to the world. These topics
take time and effort, and it is therefore essential that ministers receive
an advanced theological education. The universal church has everything
at stake in supporting those institutions that provide that education,
and those who teach future Christian ministers these disciplines have
on their shoulders a serious yet marvelous responsibility before the living God. The answer to the church's need for ministers is not at all to
lower the standards of the Christian ministry in order to attract more
candidates; this is a short-term solution that in the end leads to miserable failure. The long-term solution in fact is to guard those standards,
to keep them high, and then to do everything in the church's power to
support those who respond. Without that support the church itself will
only suffer; with it, the church itself, and indeed the surrounding world,
will receive the benefits.

Who is eligible to serve as an ordained minister of the gospel of Jesus
Christ? The short answer is, whoever is called by God and approved by
the church. But that answer needs further elaboration. In the past, and
still in the present in some Christian circles, ordination to the Christian

9. *CD*, 1/1, 72.

ministry has been restricted to men. Only in the twentieth century were women in significant numbers ordained to the regular office of parish minister. Is restriction of the Christian ministry to men legitimate? I am convinced that the consensus of the faithful embraces the ministry of men and women equally in the church. Valid Christian ministry is equally open to women and men. Of course there are biblical passages that point in a different direction. Chief among them is the prescription of 1 Timothy that women should "learn in silence with full submission" (see 1 Tim. 2:8–15). For some this passage, and a few others like it, is enough to ensure that no woman can become a minister of the gospel. That is still the case in circles of Protestant fundamentalism, as well as in the Roman Catholic communion. What is the answer?

The answer is not to try to wrest a different meaning from such passages as these. They are in fact rather clear. The answer, rather, is to recognize that on some issues scripture presents a wide range of options for the church. Thus, while there are passages that forbid women's leadership in the church, there are others that equally strongly commend the role of women as leaders of God's people. One thinks, for example, of the prophet Deborah (Judges 4–5), or of the impressive figure of Esther, or of the stunning loyalty and creativity of Ruth, or the celebration of the wise and courageous woman that concludes the book of Proverbs and that certainly includes high praises of her public role as a teacher (Prov. 31:10–31; cf. v. 26: "She opens her mouth with wisdom, and the teaching of kindness is on her tongue."), or of the crucial role of women in the earthly life of Jesus, singled out especially by the Gospel of Luke (cf. 8:1–3), or of the commendation of Phoebe and other women by the apostle Paul (Rom. 16:1). The issue cannot be solved by biblicistic appeal to isolated proof-texts, for in this instance scripture presents a range of witnesses. Such a range is not in any way a violation of scriptural authority. Rather, it is of the essence of canon at times to make clear that the church must struggle to find the will of God within a considerable spectrum of possibility. The role of the Spirit is to guide the church in that endeavor through the instrument of scripture.

The Spirit of God is clearly moving the church at large to see in a new light scriptural passages that represent women with equal authority and legitimacy, as coequal leaders of the church with men. I am convinced that the way forward is for all historic traditions to admit women to the Christian ministry, to encourage them in the use of their gifts according to their own insight and experience, to promote them for positions of ministry and teaching, and to enjoy and appreciate their accomplishments and service. The church needs women leaders in every segment of its life, now more than ever. Without the role of women as leaders in the church, do we not deprive ourselves of essential and irreplaceable

gifts and talents? Here we must declare with the apostle Paul: in Christ
"there is no longer male and female" (cf. Gal. 3:28).

On the other hand, we must likewise recognize a necessary restriction
of the Christian ministry for the sake of the gospel. Approval of Christian ministers by the church of Jesus Christ is given only to those whose
lives reflect the highest standards of Christian discipleship. In particular,
ordination to the Christian ministry requires fidelity within the covenant
of marriage between a man and a woman, or chastity in singleness.
Let us be crystal clear about an issue that is now well known for its
controversial role: the church cannot and must not ordain self-avowed
homosexuals who do not repent and change their behavior. Indeed, the
confessing faith of the gospel of Jesus Christ rests upon this point. I am
convinced that the consensus of the faithful in the universal church is
to sustain the validity of this restriction, despite enormous pressure to
relax or abandon it.

Why is the matter so clear cut and so terribly important? On this issue,
canon illustrates the other possibility of scriptural authority; that is to
say, on some issues scripture does not present a wide range of options.
Indeed, here its answer is simply no. In all parts of the canon homosexuality is condemned, not simply as a sin but as sin symbolic of the
profound distortion of self-worshiping humanity (e.g., Rom. 1:18–27).
In both Testaments, and in all of the different parts of the canon, the
censure of homosexuality is severe and unanimous. As Paul Gagnon has
shown in his comprehensive treatment, there is simply no room whatsoever for theological maneuvering on this issue, wherever the authority of
scripture is retained (see his definitive study *The Bible and Homosexual
Practice*). On this issue the Spirit of God leaves the church no room for
"opinions" and "options." On this issue, to follow the guidance of the
Holy Spirit is to hold firm to the biblical requirement for fidelity and to
insist that the line drawn against ordination of self-avowed, unrepentant
homosexuals be retained. We wholeheartedly affirm the civil rights of
homosexuals, as of all people; but ordination to the Christian ministry
is not a civil right. We welcome homosexuals into the life and practice of
the church. But the issue is ordination, not church membership. Again,
I think it is significant that numerous mainstream denominations in
the global church, such as the Presbyterian Church (USA), the United
Methodist Church, and the Roman Catholic Church, have drawn a clear
line in relation to this issue, for this represents recognition of a boundary in scripture that should not be crossed.

The confessing church must also do everything in its power to protect
the Christian ministry from any form of clergy sexual abuse of the weak
and innocent. While due process must be observed, surely a policy of
no tolerance toward clergy who abuse the trust of parishioners is ap-

propriate to the high calling of the Christian ministry. Those accused
and found guilty ought to be banished from Christian ministry. They
must be offered the forgiveness of the gospel, if they repent of their
sins, but no repentance, however sincere, should allow them back into
active or passive ordained ministry. Sexual abuse of parishioners is ipso
facto automatic and inviolable grounds for permanent removal from
the Christian ministry, with no second chances and no room for ecclesiastical maneuver. The credibility of the gospel itself is at stake in this
deeply troubling issue in contemporary church life. "If any of you put
a stumbling block before one of these little ones who believe in me, it
would be better for you if a great millstone were fastened around your
neck and you were drowned in the depth of the sea" (Matt. 18:6).

Despite the need for caution, we must end not on the negative but
on the positive. There are in fact countless faithful ministers of Jesus
Christ serving the church today, women and men; their work is to be
commended heartily, for they serve in the company of faithful witnesses
extending back to the eleven disciples sent forth by Christ into all the
world (Matt. 28:16–20). There is likewise great need for a new generation
of ministers who put the priorities of God's gracious rule above their
personal well-being and convenience; who lead the church not by the
arrogant exercise of dominating power but by the wise form of eager
service in love; who care nothing for the trappings of status and rank
and glory only in the common good of the church; who understand fully
the sublime beauty of ordinary life and the exalted challenge of concrete
obedience; who are engaged and involved in the contemporary world,
yet who cherish in memory the grand tradition of the church that binds
its children together in all times and places; who preach the Word with
courage when it is popular but also when it is unpopular; who live with
awe and wonder at the truth of God's love; who exercise every last ounce
of their intellect and imagination to sound forth the subtle complexity of
God's overwhelming wisdom; who love God above all things and revere
and respect the world of creation that comes from him; whose one aim
in life is to please Christ, who sends them forth into the world. May the
Lord of the harvest send forth such workers into the harvest!

8

The Shape of Proclamation

Canon means that scripture is shaped to serve as the instrument by which every new generation hears the living Word of God. The sermon is the means by which Christ the risen Lord speaks in the world of today, through the presence of the Spirit. What does that mean for the shaping of the Sunday sermon? Our concern here is not with the details of homiletics, which belong to practical theology. Our concern rather is the overall purpose of preaching and the effect that purpose has on the form and function of proclamation,

We begin with a crucial question: what is the relation of proclamation to the authority of scripture? Two answers must be rejected, one from the religious left, the other from the religious right. According to the standard view of theological liberalism, preaching is in an analogous relation to the biblical text. Just as the prophets and apostles once heard the Word of God vertically from above and so declared what they heard, so the minister today stands in the same vertical relation to God. There is, in other words, an immediate analogy between the offices of prophet and apostle and the office of minister. Pastors function as prophets and apostles in the contemporary world and learn from scripture how to fulfill their divinely appointed role. Certainly this view of the preaching office has massive appeal and is widely held. Countless pastors view their work in this way and are taught to do so by equally countless seminary professors.

For example, such is the view of a popular book of Walter Brueggemann, *The Prophetic Imagination*, first published in 1978. A whole generation of proclamation on the religious left in the latter decades of the twentieth century has seen its task in the light of this book and the ideas it contains. According to Brueggemann, Moses began a radical movement establishing an "alternative community,"[1] which necessarily clashed with the old views of Pharaoh. The kings of Israel and Judah tried their best to silence the "movement" but were themselves attacked by the prophets for their misguided "royal community." Jesus of Nazareth then came along to practice the "prophetic ministry."[2] Moreover, today we are engaged in the very same prophetic ministry of protest and energizing the movement of the alternative community against the "royal community" of our time. The prophetic ministry takes place in congregations that are "bourgeois," in fact "downright obdurate."[3] Brueggemann's approach is reproduced in countless imitations, using a myriad set of concepts, yet all tending to the same point: the Bible is about a radical social movement whose prophetic agents continue in the form of the contemporary minister. How are we to respond to this widely represented and well-known view?

On the basis of canon, we must reject the view of preaching dominant on the religious left. Canon, by definition, sets limits and boundaries. The apostolic and prophetic writings are gathered together as authoritative scripture for every new generation of the church. They and they alone are the standard, the critical norm, by which all proclamation in the church is to be weighed and tested. They and they alone are the source from which all valid proclamation in the church derives. There is therefore an absolute distinction between scripture and proclamation; they are not primary and secondary forms of the same reality, nor is the act of proclamation in any way an analogy to the apostolic and prophetic testimony. We must be perfectly clear: there are no prophets and apostles in the world today. Holy Scripture is not being written anywhere in the contemporary world. As ministers of the Word, we treasure the same authoritative scriptures of every previous generation, and our living proclamation today turns to the same treasure of knowledge that they contain. Those who claim to be prophets and apostles in the world today are telling a lie.

Once again, just as with televangelism on the religious right, the question of false prophecy must be raised. Once again, my concern is not with the criticism of individuals, however influential they may be. My criticism

1. Brueggemann, 109.
2. Ibid., 110.
3. Ibid.

is with a set of ideas that has taken hold in large segments of the church, with destructive consequences. We must say to the religious left what Jeremiah once said to the false prophet Hananiah: "Listen, Hananiah, the LORD has not sent you, and you made this people trust in a lie" (Jer. 28:15). And with the apostle Paul we must say: "For such boasters are false apostles, deceitful workers, disguising themselves as apostles of Christ" (2 Cor. 11:13). That is not to deny that there is a vertical dimension to Christian proclamation, for there clearly is; the point is that the vertical dimension cannot be severed from the horizontal continuity grounded in the sole authority of scripture. Brueggemann's claim to be engaged in the ministry of a prophet causes him to read into scripture a social ideology that is not in the least new; in fact it is the well-known Marxist idea of a classless society. There is nothing whatsoever new in Marxism, which cannot in any way echo the marvelously new reality of God's eternal rule over his universe. Nor is capitalism the new reality of which scripture bears prophetic witness and which the church today proclaims to all the earth. Just as the Reformers were forced to reject the false claims of prophetic authority among the radical left; just as Karl Barth and Reinhold Niebuhr attacked the easy prophetism of the social gospel, so we today must point out that no human starting point, whether Marxist or capitalist, ever leads to the new world of God. All human promises are false, whether on the left or the right. Jesus Christ is the only true Prophet, who alone proclaims the *radically new* world of God, which by his gracious gift enters our world and our everyday lives. The new world of God is not an "alternative community" known only by the spiritual elite through an exercise of imagination; the new world of God is Immanuel, God with us. The issue that separates Brueggemann's position from the living gospel proclaimed by the church is not the use of imagination. The issue rather is the purpose for which imagination is used: whether the proclamation of God's utterly new and living will, made real in our midst solely through his gracious and miraculous act of divine transformation and in no sense through human "partnership," or, in the case of the religious left, social agitation for an all-too-well-known political cause. There is a sharp prophetic edge to all genuine preaching, but this edge is defined in a very different way from the edge of the religious left.

On the other hand, we must just as decisively reject the common view of preaching on the religious right. Preaching is not an analogy to the biblical text, but nor is it simply a mode of private religious instruction in the content of the biblical witness. For the religious right, preaching is a matter of mere repetition of the biblical word. The horizontal relation is certainly preserved, but at the cost of denying the genuine vertical dimension of true biblical proclamation. For the religious right, preaching is simply one way among others in which the scriptures are taught to the individual Christian. There are Bible studies, personal devotional study, evangelistic witness, and also sermons; all function together indifferently as modes of instruction in which the individual believer is taught the content of scripture. Where liberalism severs the vertical dimension of preaching from its horizontal axis, thus separating the content of the proclaimed word from its dependence on the biblical norm, conservative evangelicalism simply collapses the vertical into the horizontal dimension, thus seriously underestimating the significance of proclamation. The religious right has no real understanding of the role of preaching as the living Word of God; in that error, evangelicalism shows its roots in pietism and not in the Reformation.

Typical of the religious right is the popular volume of J. I. Packer, *Fundamentalism and the Word of God*. The problem can be seen most clearly in his section called "The Holy Spirit as Interpreter."[4] First, Packer stresses the need for "spiritual insight" and "spiritual receptiveness" among readers of the Bible. Such "spiritual enlightenment" is a "supernatural gift" from God. The role of the Holy Spirit is thus precisely to give "spiritual perception" to the church. Second, the work of the Spirit is tied exclusively to the apostolic word: "And 'he that is spiritual'—he in whom the Spirit abides to give understanding—discerns the meaning of the message and receives it as the testimony of God."[5] And third, the Spirit in no sense adds to the internal meaning of the Bible: "The only meaning to which He bears witness is that which each text actually has in the organism of Scripture; such witness as is borne to other meanings is borne by other spirits."[6]

Against Packer's view it must be asserted, first, that the role of the Spirit cannot be transferred to a human capacity but always remains the free work of the sovereign God. The mystery of the Spirit is secured in the freedom of God's unrestrained rule and unmeasured wisdom. Second, though Packer is right to underscore the connection between the Spirit and scripture, he fails to see the canonical insistence upon the relation between scripture and proclamation. The scriptures are given as a rule of faith for every new generation of the church. The Reformers' cry of *sola Scriptura* never meant to isolate scripture from the living Word of preaching. Indeed, the whole point of the authority of Scripture is the freedom it gives to preach the divine Word with confidence and imagination. Third, just as Brueggemann collapses the horizontal dimension of scripture into the vertical, so Packer just as clearly collapses the verti-

4. Packer, 110–14.
5. Ibid., 111–12.
6. Ibid., 112.

cal dimension into the horizontal. The role of the Spirit is precisely to generate ever new, ever fresh, ever powerful senses of scripture in the changing world.

Preaching is not the same as Bible study or Sunday school, however vitally important these might be. While preaching certainly contains a didactic element, it is not one among other forms of private religious instruction. Through the gracious presence of the Holy Spirit, preaching is the Word of God. Proclamation is an encounter between the risen Lord and the gathered congregation. Preaching is not a humanly designed mechanism of instruction that can be changed at will; preaching is chosen and established by Christ himself as the one form of witness by which his voice is sent forth to all creation. The proclamation of the Word of God is an event in which the risen Lord addresses a specific congregation in a specific time and place. Genuine preaching takes place in the local church and nowhere else on this earth. In it, Christ himself, at his own initiative, speaks his sovereign word of grace to our world today, not to the world of yesterday. Preaching has no obligation whatsoever to retain the moral values of the past; on the contrary, it is both free and obligated to attack those values at the root, however cherished they may be, as contradictions of the absolute imperative of the gospel. Preaching is not a form of nostalgia; it seeks to uncover the hideous unbelief concealed in hallowed forms of human piety. Preaching is not a form of conservation, or confirmation, seeking to reaffirm what believers already know so well. "Do not say, 'Why were the former days better than these?' For it is not from wisdom that you ask this" (Eccles. 7:10). Rather, the preaching of God's Word is the herald of God's revolutionary transformation of the entire universe through the cross and resurrection of Jesus Christ. While the Bible is the one authority for the life of the church, its authority is functional; that is, its purpose is fully realized only when the minister of today proclaims God's living Word on the basis of scripture to the needs of the modern world. Just as the world changes from one generation to the next, so too does the content of Christian preaching, for Jesus Christ is a living Lord who addresses each new generation of the church with words of wonder and surprise. In its preaching the church never looks backward but always forward in anticipation of God's new word of gift and claim upon all human life: "Sing to the LORD a new song, his praise in the assembly of the faithful" (Ps. 149:1).

The true relation of proclamation to scripture is not analogical as in liberalism, nor is it merely repetitive and instructional as in evangelicalism. The true relation is one of *figuration*: the proclaimed word is a figurative application of the inspired Word. Figuration means first of all that the direction of authority is all one way; scripture alone has absolute authority, and the authority of the preached word is derived from the authority of scripture. We are not prophets or apostles; we are entirely dependent upon the true prophets and apostles for our understanding of God's living will. On the other hand, figuration means that the transfer of authority is in fact a real one, for both scripture and proclamation are alike grounded in the authority of Jesus Christ. It is the will of Christ, who once gathered scripture to serve as his authoritative witness, now to send forth his ministers bearing the same authoritative Word to his gathered community in each new age. "O rider in the heavens; listen, he sends out his voice, his mighty voice" (Ps. 68:33). If we must insist, against liberalism, that the preached word is different from scripture in terms of the office that it represents, we must likewise insist, against evangelicalism, that the preached word bears the full authority of the risen Christ. God not only once spoke through the prophets and the apostles; the living God now speaks in a fresh way through the words of the Christian sermon. The God who once revealed himself there and then even today continues to reveal himself in the contemporary world, and that revelation is through the divinely chosen instrument of proclamation. Despite the frailty of the Christian minister, the sermon always begins with the words "Hear the Word of God," and these words are literally true. Those who received the preached word in faith receive Christ; those who reject the preached word in unbelief reject Christ. The message of the preached word encounters the hearer with the self-validating authority of Jesus Christ himself, for it is the living voice of the exalted Lord. Figuration means that the specific content of the weekly reading from scripture becomes the means through which the risen Christ lays claim to the hearts and minds of his people in the contemporary world. The new world of God in scripture becomes the instrument through which the risen Lord enters our present world as wondrous gift for all humanity.

The horizontal and vertical dimensions of Christian proclamation are held together best in the expository sermon. In his comprehensive history of preaching, *The Reading and Preaching of the Scriptures in the Worship of the Christian Church*, Hughes Oliphant Old has sought to recover the brilliance and excitement of the grand tradition of Christian proclamation. His multivolume survey clearly lays before the contemporary reader the vast range of powerful and exciting voices from the Christian past, with the corresponding challenge that those voices present for the future. Old has done the universal church an enormous service. Above all, his endeavor to show the magnificent reach of proclamation in every time and place across the face of the globe sets a high standard for the work of the coming generations. In his introduction, Old charts what he sees as the primary forms of proclamation that ebb and flow across the years: the expository sermon, evangelistic preaching, catechetical preaching, festal preaching, and prophetic preaching.[7] There is no doubt that Old has accurately captured the wide range of preaching in this classification. Throughout the volumes, he is able to show the various forms shaped and reshaped according to the changing resources of the church. Furthermore, every working minister knows that the form and function of sermons occasionally differ according to changing circumstance. Surely any real progress in contemporary proclamation will depend upon a fresh recovery of the grand tradition that Old describes.

Nevertheless, despite the need to describe the literature of preaching with historical accuracy, I would argue that the sermonic tradition must not only be recounted but also weighed theologically. In the light of the authority of scripture as canon, it must now be said that in fact the expository sermon is the main current that runs through the whole history of preaching. If there is to be a renaissance of Christian preaching in our time, it will come in the form of renewed vigor for the expository sermon. Given the current illiteracy of biblical knowledge on the part of both laity and clergy, there is nothing more challenging than a renewed effort of genuine expository preaching. False politicizing on the left and false moralizing on the right require no deep engagement with the theologically shaped reality of the canonical text; at best the text provides useful warrants for an already self-designated message. Expository preaching requires an open-minded encounter with the biblical Word on the part of both hearers and preacher. The messenger may begin with an idea of what the text is about, but the true messenger allows the text itself to shape the idea, never the reverse. Expository preaching is at the same time profoundly traditional, for it insists that the biblical gospel alone is worthy of a hearing in the church, and utterly revolutionary, for it concedes to the gospel alone, and not to any form of human piety or morality, the right to guide human life in the presence of God.

But canon not only yields fresh perspective on the past; even more important, canon is the horizon of the future. We must today recover the full power of the expository sermon, but we cannot do so simply by reviving and repeating models from the past, however powerful they may once have been. We must learn anew the meaning of expository preaching in our world today. The horizontal dimension appears in the expository sermon in the form of explication; the vertical dimension appears in the form of application. Together, explication and application in expository preaching are the living dynamic of the Word of God for the particular time and place of each new age of the church.

Explication of the text in the expository sermon is grounded in direct study of the Greek and Hebrew text by the working pastor. All preach-

7. Old, 1:1–18.

ing in the contemporary world should take place on the basis of close familiarity with the biblical text in the original languages. Needless to say, ministers of the gospel therefore need to be carefully trained in Greek and Hebrew. In my judgment, this ought to be a universal requirement that can and should be met wherever the gospel is sounded forth with the serious purpose of Christ. Of course, a loud objection will be quickly forthcoming: what about great preachers from the past who knew only Greek, or neither language at all? Surely the most famous example is Augustine, who knew no Hebrew, and there is no doubt whatsoever of his greatness as a preacher. What did Augustine himself say about the issue? In *On Christian Doctrine*, Augustine states plainly: "Against unknown literal signs the sovereign remedy is a knowledge of languages. And Latin-speaking men . . . need two others for a knowledge of the Divine Scriptures, Hebrew and Greek."[8] He goes on to contrast the many ambiguities contained in the numerous translations that can be cleared up only through direct knowledge of the original. Augustine himself was apparently not able to reach the high standard that he set. Indeed, very few were able in antiquity, fewer still in the Middle Ages. It was not until Johannes Reuchlin published his *De Rudimentis Hebracis* in 1506, a millennium after Augustine, that the standard he set was first beginning to be reached. But the crucial point is this: even though a great preacher like Augustine was unable to reach the standard, he set it in exactly the right place. Moreover, knowledge of Greek and Hebrew has jumped forward in massive leaps and bounds since the Reformation. Expert grammars in both languages are now universally available, including on CD-ROM. Lexical aids abound. Solid teachers of both languages reside wherever the Christian ministry is studied. The standard has not changed since Augustine; what has changed are the virtually endless resources by which to reach it. In short, there is simply no excuse not to hold the Christian ministry in the world today accountable to the highest standards of excellence.

This is not an arbitrary standard, for there are in fact nuances in the original text that do not appear in any translation, however well done. Those nuances are often important in leading the minister in the direction of the canonical intentionality of the text. Moreover, some nuances in English and other modern languages are highly misleading if carried over to the biblical text, where they may not appear at all. The ordinary reader is extremely well served by the fine translations that are now available; they are reliable and should be wholeheartedly recommended. However, for the preaching of the Word by the ordained minister of the gospel, Hebrew and Greek are essential and should be used on a regular basis.

8. Augustine, *On Christian Doctrine*, 43.

Greek alone—the common practice in certain circles—is not enough. Both Old and New Testament are the Word of God and together form the one source of proclamation. Old Testament scholar Ellen Davis rightly states: "Study that is practical for ministry includes advanced Hebrew syntax."[9] Preaching must explore the wide range of pericopes from all parts of both Testaments. Knowledge of both original biblical languages is therefore essential for the modern minister of the gospel and should be the standard everywhere in the community of faith today.

Expository preaching based on the canonical text moves from explication to application. It includes both, but there is a directional flow from the one to the other. Wherever that directional flow is reversed, preaching suffers immeasurably. Ministers of the Word do not come to the biblical text with their own moral system, looking for theological support; such moralism is a pagan outgrowth of the Enlightenment, not the gospel of Jesus Christ. Ministers of the Word do not come with their own cultural or social agenda, whether conservative or liberal, looking for biblical backing; such "proof-texting" from the pulpit is a perversion of the living challenge of the new world of God. The biblical text sets the agenda for preaching, for the biblical text itself is the instrument of Jesus Christ, the risen and exalted ruler of all creation. Through the proclamation of the Word, the ever new and surprising reality of God's realm impinges directly upon the hearer. As Luther in particular clearly saw, preaching is an eschatological event in which the living Christ speaks and acts through the proclaimed word. For that reason, it is the scriptures that shape the contemporary church, and not the reverse.

Here we can only lament the widespread biblical illiteracy that has resulted from the practical disregard for the genuine authority of scripture on both the religious left and the religious right, for both factions treat the biblical text as "backing" or "warrant" for religious "values" derived elsewhere. But Christian preaching is not the communication of religious "values." It was Immanuel Kant who spoke of moral values, not Martin Luther or John Calvin, or before them Augustine or Athanasius. It was the liberal Protestant theologian Albrecht Ritschl who sanctioned the language of "values" in theology, and one is constantly shocked at the ignorance of the religious right concerning the liberal origin of their own dearest cause. The preaching of Christian "values" is antithetical to expository preaching, because it insists that the text of scripture accord with the moral commitments of the hearer. Preaching the Word of God from scripture has no interest whatsoever in finding common ground with the moral commitments of the hearer. The whole point of

9. Davis, *Imagination Shaped*, 261.

preaching is radically to transform the moral commitments of the hearer, indeed to effect a total change of the very person of the hearer, including moral life. As Jesus told Nicodemus, "No one can see the kingdom of God without being born from above. . . . What is born of the flesh is flesh, and what is born of the Spirit is spirit" (cf. John 3:3–6). Genuine expository preaching recognizes that the divine perspective on human life radically overturns and sets aside all human values and abolishes all human piety and spirituality, for the Spirit of God renders us a new creation. Careful explication of the canonical witness is the true foundation for all expository preaching.

The divine purpose for human life is communicated through the theological shaping of Holy Scripture. Canon means that through the work of the Spirit, the sacred text of scripture is shaped theologically according to the divine rule of truth. Conservative "grammatical-historical" reading will not find that rule, for it is limited to the verbal sense in abstraction from its theological content; liberal historical reconstruction will likewise not find that rule, for it seeks the content through ostensive reference rather than through the living witness of scripture. The divine rule of truth is found only in the text of scripture as theologically shaped. Explication in the expository sermon means laying out the text for the congregation according to its canonical shape. How that is done differs according to the genre of the text, for the canon leaves biblical forms relatively intact. Narrative must be retold with dramatic power; prophecy must be declaimed with life-or-death urgency; Pauline dialectic must be unfolded with the profound paradox of the gospel; the emotional world of the Psalms must be painted with all the subtle shades of human feeling; the sayings of Jesus must be presented with the self-validating authority of the sovereign Lord; parables must be told with the full exercise of vivid imagination. Theological shaping leaves great variety in the form of the scriptural word, and that variety must be carried over into proclamation.

Nevertheless, despite the necessary preservation of variety, expository preaching must retain the serious focus of canon as well. There is one, and only one, purpose for all of scripture: service of God's living will embodied in Jesus Christ himself. It is essential that expository preaching maintain its exclusive focus on that divine purpose. Here the highest degree of theological skill is necessary, indeed vital. It takes deep concentration and effort to preach expository sermons that reflect the divine purpose of scripture. Distractions are almost endless; finding, and then communicating with accuracy, the genuine purpose of the weekly lesson for a specific congregation is a momentous challenge, requiring every gift and talent that one can summon. The same requirement applies whether one uses *lectio selecta* (individually selected texts) or *lectio continua* (a series of sermons over an extended text or entire book). The aid provided by the field of biblical studies is essential; the working pastor must rely on such works as the two introductions by Brevard Childs to find his or her way. The working pastor also desperately needs help from exegesis that is focused upon the same divine purpose and not distracted by conservative apologetics or liberal reconstruction.

Finally, the role of dogmatics is essential for explication, for expository preaching is not simply the explanation of words but the communication of the reality of which those words speak. Preaching is never biblicistic; it moves from the text to the true reality to which it refers and presents the full glory of that reality to the listening ears of the congregation in the light of the biblical witness. Augustine states: "It is a mark of good and distinguished minds to love the truth within words and not the words."[10] Just as dogmatics focuses on the inner logic of the reality of which scripture speaks, so must the valid expository sermon lay bare before the congregation that same inner logic with clarity and precision. The issue is not a "popular" version of academic theology; condescension has no part in proclamation. Rather, just as the preacher has been helped by dogmatics to recognize the inner ordering of divine truth in scripture, the preacher must now proclaim the clarity and beauty of that truth to those gathered to hear. Intertextuality is often a necessary means of expanding the full lesson of the text toward appropriate and precise comprehension by the congregation. In short, the highest degree of theological training and concentration are required in order to expound the text of the Bible in words that are appropriate to the congregation living in today's world; yet nothing less than that challenge can count as valid proclamation in the Christian community.

God's word is not given for curious admiration; it is given in order to be obeyed. Expository preaching must include earnest and timely application. What now passes for application on the religious left and the religious right fails to meet the strenuous biblical challenge of figurative application. To put it even more bluntly: the common practice of "illustrations" in sermons falls far short of the theological requirement of application. Good expository preaching contains no "illustrations" whatsoever. Of course, it will immediately be retorted that the purpose of illustrations is to make the Word of God practical for the life of today. And no doubt those who use them are genuinely seeking to fulfill the requirement for contemporaneity. However, attractive anecdotes have nothing whatsoever to do with the ultimate decision with which the hearer of God's Word is encountered in today's world. Biblical truth is not measured in terms of correspondence to an object; biblical truth is

10. Augustine, *On Christian Doctrine*, 236.

measured in terms of the transforming effect that it brings about. According to the prophet Isaiah: "For as the rain and the snow come down from heaven, and do not return there until they have watered the earth, making it bring forth and sprout, giving seed to the sower and bread to the eater, so shall my word be that goes out from my mouth; it shall not return to me empty, but it shall accomplish that which I purpose, and succeed in the thing for which I sent it" (Isa. 55:10–11). In the words of the great Anglican preacher Joseph Hall: "Thy will is thy word, and thy word is thy deed."[11] The pleasant fluff of illustrations provides no aid at all in applying the inspired Word; on the contrary, such inanities only empty the divine Word of transforming power and majesty. Illustrations trivialize the splendor of truth; a contemporary renaissance of proclamation can only look elsewhere for the task of application.

Am I here being too rigid? In his study of Calvin's proclamation, T. H. L. Parker makes the straightforward observation: "But one thing that is totally lacking is the use of anecdotes. We have already heard him saying that they are out of place in the pulpit."[12] Or again, in his volume on Reformation preaching, Old reports on the three major abuses of worship that Luther saw prevalent in the medieval church. The second is this: "mixed in with the Word of God are many fables and fabrications." Old explains further: "By this Luther had in mind not only the legends of the saints that were read at the daily office, often side by side with the canonical Scriptures, but, perhaps even more, the exempla which had become part of the late medieval preacher's stock-in-trade. These exempla about which so many Reformers complained were in many ways similar to the sermon illustrations to which modern American preaching is so addicted."[13] Reform of the church means reform of preaching; reform of the church comes through reform of preaching; vigorous reform of preaching in our time is not possible without doing away with the prevalence of illustrations, which make a mockery of the divine Word and in fact add nothing to genuine understanding or Christian practice in the modern world.

The issue is not merely a matter of techniques of communication but is in fact theological in nature. Illustrations are the natural theology of preaching; despite the good intentions of those who use them to augment the truth of the divine Word, they inevitably become a second sphere of interest side by side with the Word. And then, as all natural theology inevitably does, illustrations seek to replace the divine Word with a human truth. True proclamation avoids the distraction of illustrations,

11. Hall, 1:9.
12. Parker, 148.
13. Old, 4:29.

for the Word of God is self-confirming: "Now when Jesus had finished saying these things, the crowds were astounded at his teaching, for he taught them as one having authority, and not as their scribes" (Matt. 7:28).[14] It will take hard work for the Christian ministry of today to preach sermons without falling back on the pabulum of illustrations. It will take proclamation that is venturous enough to counter the expectations of the hearers, in a generation grown accustomed to the low level of challenge contained in the "interesting." It will take persistence to retrain the church at large to a form of hearing to which the ear has grown exceedingly dull and a form of seeing to which the eye has grown exceedingly dim. But it can and must be done for the sake of the gospel. Let all illustrations be cast into the wastebasket of fruitless distraction; let the modern preacher of the Word suddenly discover what is infinitely more challenging and rewarding: the figurative application of scripture to the contemporary world.

Figurative application—the second essential component of expository preaching, flowing from explication—is the drawing of connections between the Word of scripture and the contemporary world. Drawing those connections is an exercise in what Davis aptly calls "imagination shaped"—she draws the phrase from a quotation by Frederick Robertson, and it is the title of her excellent study of Old Testament preaching in the Anglican tradition. Imagination involves the whole person—mind, will, emotions, even the body—and the use of the imagination in proclamation is shaped by the sacred text of scripture itself. Imaginative application requires hard work on the part of the pastor, and yet in the end, the mystery of the Spirit gives relevance to the biblical text according to his own sovereign purpose. The Holy Spirit opens up the text of scripture to its immediate relevance for faithful life in our world today, and the presence of the Spirit is a miraculous divine gift. "I will pour out my spirit on all flesh; your sons and your daughters shall prophesy, your old men shall dream dreams, and your young men shall see visions" (cf. Joel 2:28). There is no hermeneutical system for application; there is no convenient recipe for theologically legitimate application. However, it is both legitimate and necessary to speak of concerns that are always present where figurative application achieves the desired goal. How are we in the church today to use imagination in the service of proclamation?

First, preaching of the Word of God must be couched in language suitable for the contemporary world. We do not live in the fourth century, or the sixteenth century, or even the twentieth century; the words of

14. It should be noted that the theological function of the parables of Jesus within the biblical canon is very different from a typical modern sermon illustration. And besides, the parables of Jesus are in a class by themselves, precisely because they are the parables of *Jesus*.

proclamation today must be framed to strike the ears of our contemporary age. In the paradox of faith, only timely preaching is truly timeless. Through the preached word, the living Christ speaks to contemporary human beings; every sermon must therefore address the congregation in language appropriate to the present day world. This certainly means that the minister of the gospel must be fully at home in the world of today. Preaching is not an invitation to withdraw from the world; preaching is the entrance of God's new world into present day time and space. Even the best preaching of previous generations, however useful as a model, is no substitute for the hard effort of speaking the truth in words that matter in the world today. Every pastor must be fully alive to the present, fully involved in the world, and fully engaged in the issues that concern our present day in order to preach the living gospel of Christ.

Second, preaching must address the practical concerns of everyday life. The Word of God does not hover above the human condition in the realm of ethereal ideas but directly enters the ordinary features of human existence in order to transform them completely from the inside. All genuine application is concrete and challenges the hearer to practical changes of life grounded in the gospel. It is not enough to hear the Word; it is essential to do the Word: "Therefore, whoever breaks one of the least of these commandments, and teaches others to do the same, will be called least in the kingdom of heaven; but whoever does them and teaches them will be called great in the kingdom of heaven" (Matt. 5:19). The proclaimed word must set before the congregation the practical consequences of obedience that redirects the focus of human life and brings about specific change in human behavior. The issue is not isolated acts; the issue rather is a total reorientation of one's existence in every dimension. God's Word always brings practical change, involving the full expression of human existence on earth.

Third, preaching must speak to the whole range of human life and emotion: from the depths of agonizing despair, to the struggle against disappointment and doubt, to the elevation of life through the precious gift of joy. The preacher must derive from scripture itself a full appreciation of the human condition in all its threat and promise and must offer the Word as a mirror in which the contemporary human struggle is perfectly reflected and refined according to the divine will. God himself, according to scripture, is directly involved in human emotion. Indeed, God himself, according to the biblical picture, passionately feels the joys and pains of his world, far beyond all human imagination. For that reason, genuine Christian preaching must seek to master the grammar of human emotion as richly displayed in all forms of the biblical witness, radiating outward from the Psalms. If we live in a time in which emotional intelligence is a rare commodity, should not the Christian church be the first to celebrate the full range of human emotion in its preaching and life? Forget the pagan notions of "positive thinking" and "liberated consciousness"; surely today the proclamation of the gospel must once again seek to instruct the faithful in the language of genuine emotion in the presence of God, for the sake of the church and the human community.

Fourth, application draws connections that are unexpected. It has no desire to confirm moral prejudice or established piety; on the contrary, it seeks precisely to break through such moralism and pseudospirituality in order to lead the hearer to genuine discovery of the living Lord. Here the gospel always cuts both ways: it cuts against the piety and spirituality of the religious right, which offers the world a safe haven of self-righteousness; it likewise cuts against the piety and spirituality of the religious left, which likewise offers the world the self-righteous spirituality of the "alternative community." The gospel is not an extension of established culture, nor it an extension of established counterculture; the gospel is the new world of God that comes only in wonder and awe. It gives blessing to the poor in spirit, comfort to those who mourn, perfect fulfillment to the morally hungry, overwhelming joy to those rejected by established religious opinion for the sake of the gospel. God's inbreaking rule overturns the present order, not by offering the escape of an alternative but by directly entering that order, making all things new.

Fifth, application brings home the direct responsibility for faithful Christians in church and society today. It leaves no doubt that the ordinary Christian in the congregation is in fact responsible to the risen Lord himself for faithful service in church and world. As Jesus said, "As the Father has sent me, so I send you" (John 20:21). Application always focuses upon the role of the ordinary Christian, who is in fact the salt of the earth, the light of the world. It presents to the congregation not the escape of nostalgia, nor the dreams of lofty idealism, but the present claim of the gospel engaging one's whole being in the tasks of discipleship. The service of Christ with one's whole existence is the claim of the gospel, and true application always leaves the hearers with tasks to do in everyday life. It never appeals to a spiritual or moral elite; such elitism—found on both left and right—is surely the modern equivalent of works-righteousness. The gospel is pragmatic and practical for ordinary people, and yet practice flows from the truth, which is grounded in God's self-manifestation in Jesus Christ.

Sixth, true application never leaves the people in the congregation confirmed in their established ways; it meets them where they are, but for the sake of challenging them to radical transformation that comes from the surprising work of God. The comprehensive transformation of human life at its very core is in fact the true measure of successful preaching; all other "achievements" will perish in the fire of divine judgment (cf. 1 Cor. 2:10–15). There is room in the preaching of transforming grace for the theme of judgment; indeed, no genuine application can leave aside the persistent threat that comes from abusing God's compassion. Nevertheless, the heart of the gospel is the positive message of God's abiding love, which rules and overrules human folly. Application constantly lays before the hearer the sheer delight of obedience, for it never comes as a burden but always as the joy of freedom.

Seventh, application should be suggestive in nature.[15] It should never use the Bible to illustrate moral values drawn from elsewhere; that is the essence of heresy. Rather, it should draw from scripture genuine illumination for the ethical problems of today, and yet in such a way as to leave the Spirit room to work in the individual Christian life. "The kingdom of heaven is like yeast that a woman took and mixed in with three measures of flour until all of it was leavened" (Matt. 13:33). The gospel is literal truth, but its power is also metaphorical. It works its way into the hidden corners of human life, making vision clearer despite blind spots, making lives purer despite the brokenness of sin. Genuine application tolerates the ambiguities of the biblical witness. It leaves in the background issues that seem clear yet are foreign to the text, and it allows for flexibility in those issues that scripture itself leaves open to the wrestling of conscience.

And finally, genuine application never trivializes the claim of Christ upon human life. It never degenerates into the how-to fads and gimmicks of moral self-improvement, nor does it take up the predictable rant of liberating self-discovery. Genuine application presents the daily Christian life in the contemporary world as a source of profound wonder for which we can only be utterly grateful. Preaching the rule of Christ is "like treasure hidden in a field, which someone found and hid; then in his joy he goes and sells all that he has and buys that field" (Matt. 13:44). All of life is presented in its relationship to the living God. The call of the gospel presents before the gathered congregation as well as the individual Christian matters of life and death, in the presence of God; for the hearing of the Word is in fact a living encounter with God himself. The gospel always requires ultimate decision.

The minister is called to figurative application of the biblical Word under the guidance of the Spirit. It is in fact a stunning calling, requiring every last ounce of learning and full use of endless creativity. The proper attitude is eager anticipation for the unfolding will of God, for the gracious reality of truth is granted only to those who cherish the joy of discovery. Yet here a note of caution must be entered. The presence

15. See Davis, *Imagination Shaped*, 170.

of the Spirit is a miraculous gift, never a human possession. According to Acts 8:9–24, heresy begins with the attempt of Simon the magician to purchase the Spirit from the apostles for his own schemes. Both the religious right and the religious left are equally guilty of the sin of Simon in modern church life. Both attempt to coerce the Spirit for the various cultural, social, and personal agendas of conservative and liberal ideology. Needless to say, the preaching of both factions follows the lead of their theology. The result of course is the cultural Christianity of the religious right and the countercultural Christianity of the religious left, both equally distant from the new world of God brought into reality through the gospel of Christ. How are we today to distinguish the proper work of the Spirit from the human perversions of God's Word derived from very different sources? To be sure, the Spirit is sovereign and free; he guides the church according to the utter freedom of his own intention. Yet the Holy Spirit is not the human spirit; what then are the marks of the *Spirit of God* in leading the church?

First, the Holy Spirit is the Spirit of holiness. In scripture, holiness is not an abstract moral norm by which human behavior is judged—though it certainly involves the total transformation of life, including all ethical aspects. Holiness rather is the condition of being set apart wholly and completely unto the service of God. The Spirit never calls the church to leave behind the exclusive loyalty we owe to Jesus Christ, the one Head of the church. We are not the moral conscience of society, as on the religious right; we are not the agents of social revolution, as on the religious left. "For those who live according to the flesh set their minds on the things of the flesh, but those who live according to the Spirit set their minds on the things of the Spirit" (Rom. 8:5). We are children of God, freed by the Spirit to new life in joyful obedience to Christ in the world today. All preaching must conform to this central concern. Put in positive terms, we must strongly affirm the life-giving freedom of proclamation. Precisely because it is service (*ministerium*) of the Word, it is perfectly free in relation to all other forces and claims.

Second, the Spirit is the Spirit of truth (John 14:17). It is not the duty of the Christian ministry to pass along the moral prejudices and good causes of the minister. It is not the prerogative of the minister to draw the content of proclamation from the inner resources of human personality, as if every minister had their own equally valid "version" of the faith. Scripture sets boundaries outside of which the gospel is not rightly preached, and every minister is obliged by sacred oath to honor those boundaries. Appeals to charity are false appeals wherever scriptural norms are cast aside. Augustine carefully argues, "Charity itself, which is the end and fulfillment of the Law, cannot be right if those things which are loved are not true but false."[16] Similarly, no minister is permitted to draw boundaries not contained in scripture, for such legalistic rigidity is in fact a denial of truth in exactly the same way as a libertine disregard for those boundaries. Either way—by disregarding the boundaries or by drawing new ones not contained in scripture itself—preaching becomes another gospel. Against the religious left we say: "Every word of God proves true; he is a shield to those who take refuge in him." Against the religious right we say: "Do not add to his words, or else he will rebuke you, and you will be found a liar" (cf. Prov. 30:5–6). In contrast to all ideology, the proclaimed word breathes the fresh air of flexibility where that is needed yet also evinces a steely determination where circumstances require it.

Third, the Holy Spirit is the Spirit of Christ. According to John's Gospel, Jesus "breathed" on the disciples and then gave the gift of the Spirit (cf. 20:22). The Spirit is given by Christ; the Spirit bears witness to Christ; indeed, the Lord is the Spirit (2 Cor. 3:17). Proclamation is always service of Jesus Christ; the relation is never one of balance or partnership, and still less can it ever be reversed. Ministers are sent by Christ himself as his ambassadors, bearing his name to the nations of the earth. With unspeakable awe, through the gift of the Spirit human thoughts are filled with the mind of Christ, and human words are his voice in the contemporary world. Such service to Christ radically excludes all forms of self-defined piety and spirituality. Exclusive attachment to Christ is betrayed not primarily by unbelief but by well-intended attempts to yoke belief with religiosity. We preach Christ crucified and risen; all else is sheer folly.

16. Augustine, *On Christian Doctrine*, 166.

Part IV

The Trinity

9

The Triune God

What is the true subject matter of Holy Scripture? Whose name do we proclaim to the nations of the world when we proclaim the gospel? To whom do we owe our worship, our service, our gratitude, and our every endeavor in life, indeed life itself? We turn now to the Christian doctrine of the Trinity, which provides the answer to these questions and is the focal point of the Christian understanding of God. It was the special theological genius of Karl Barth to recognize that the doctrine of the Trinity belongs in the prolegomena of dogmatics, directing the church's attention from the outset to the true reality of God by which all valid proclamation is measured. The church fathers, the medieval scholastics, and the Reformers all give the doctrine of the Trinity the same emphatic role; the entire Christian tradition, East and West, agrees that the Trinity is the heart of our message about God and his will for the world. But it was the special contribution of Barth to see the implications of the weight of the doctrine of the Trinity for the very shape of dogmatic reflection.

The place of the doctrine of the Trinity in the unfolding of dogmatic truth sharply distinguishes the core of the Christian confession from the errors on the religious left and on the religious right. Both liberalism and evangelicalism construct a doctrine of God from natural theology logically and materially prior to the doctrine of the Trinity and then at best strive to add the Trinity on at the end; both therefore, despite good intentions, fail to achieve the radiant splendor of God that shines in the biblical witness. If the Trinity does not guide our witness concerning the reality of the living God from the very beginning, nothing good can be expected from the results. Careful and thoughtful reflection on the doctrine of the Trinity is at the center of church dogmatics and constitutes a sure rule of faith by which all Christian language and action in the contemporary world are measured. We here enter the life-or-death struggle of the church in our time to maintain faithfulness to the living God whom we joyfully serve with all our being.

Jesus Christ the risen Lord commissions the church to go forth into the nations of the world, teaching his commands and baptizing new disciples in the triune name of God. His commission rests on the self-grounded basis of his universal authority over all reality. His commission is thus self-evidential and flows directly from his unrestricted power and unrestrained rule over the entire creation. He promises his presence to every new generation of the church as it seeks to fulfill the one great commission by which the church lives in every new age (Matt. 28:16–20). Every Christian is baptized "in the name of the Father, and of the Son, and of the Holy Spirit." Valid baptism in the universal church is baptism in the triune name of God. It has long been recognized in the dogmatic tradition that the name of God is singular: we are not baptized in the "names" of the Father, etc., but in the name of the Father, and of the Son, and of the Holy Spirit (εισ το ονομα του πατρος και του υιου και του αγιου πνευματος). Thus baptism, the visible sign of the unity of every Christian with Christ the risen Lord and therefore the foundation for the entirety of the Christian life, is trinitarian. The name of God is one, yet the One is realized in the Three. John Calvin correctly states: "For this means precisely to be baptized into the name of the one God who has shown himself with complete clarity in the Father, the Son, and the Spirit. Hence it is quite clear that in God's essence reside three persons in whom one God is known."[1]

The unity and diversity of God that constitutes the doctrine of the Trinity is not a peripheral concern of speculative theology; every Christian is baptized in the name of the Trinity, and all Christian discipleship unfolds only on the basis of God's triune name. It is thus simply false and profoundly misleading to speak of the "simple" gospel alongside of which the doctrine of the Trinity is placed as a supporting scholastic exercise. On the contrary, the triune reality of God is made known in God's very name, and every Christian is baptized in the faith of the gospel only and exclusively in that name. The doctrine of the Trinity thus tells us whom we serve and worship in songs of adoration and whom we obey with every fiber of our being. The doctrine of the Trinity is a burning issue

1. Calvin, 1.140.

for the everyday life of every Christian, for whom baptism is the visible sign of unity with Christ.

The one source for the church doctrine of the Trinity is Holy Scripture. Of course the church has long recognized that scripture does not contain the full doctrine of the Trinity; but it does contain the roots of the doctrine, which do nothing but grasp in the language of faith the true reality of which scripture speaks. The Trinity is not a separate, philosophically derived addition to the witness of scripture. In a well-known thesis, Adolf von Harnack once argued that Christian dogma is a "work of the Hellenic spirit on the Gospel soil."[2] He speaks of the loss of the "simple gospel" to the inroads of "Greek speculation." According to Harnack, church dogma "drew into the domain of cosmology and religious philosophy a person who had appeared in space and time."[3] It is now quite clear that Harnack's thesis, however popular at one time, is exactly opposite the truth of the matter. From the very beginning, the Christian understanding of God, disclosed in God's very name, speaks of the unity and diversity of God. It took time for the Christian understanding to become elaborated in the form of established dogmatic formula, in a process that is now only partially understood historically. But what is clear is that the doctrine of the Trinity *protects* the special Christian understanding of God from the inroads of Greek, especially Neoplatonic, philosophy. Indeed, the early heretics who rejected the church doctrine of the Trinity were themselves captivated by a speculative philosophical view by which they sought to measure the Christian confession, and the church rightly reacted by insisting ever more forcefully and ever more carefully on the doctrine of the Trinity. The doctrine of the Trinity is not a philosophical incursion into pure biblical theology; quite the opposite, the doctrine of the Trinity is a Christian articulation and defense—certainly using philosophical concepts—of the biblical witness to the reality of God against the incursion of alien rationalistic philosophy. In the summary statement of Bernhard Lohse: "Does [the doctrine of the Trinity] imply, as has been so often asserted, a falling away of the church from the Christianity of the New Testament? If the development of the doctrine of the Trinity from its beginnings to the end of the fourth century is seen in its totality, it becomes difficult to make such an accusation. In fact, it is more correct to insist upon the opposite, namely, that by means of this dogma the church erected a barrier against the onslaught of the tidal wave of Hellenism, which threatened to inundate the Christian faith."[4]

2. Harnack, *Outlines of the History*, 4.
3. Harnack, *What Is Christianity?* 204.
4. Lohse, *Short History*, 65.

Dogmatic theology must thus turn to the one source of Holy Scripture for its reflection on the doctrine of the Trinity. In doing so, it is guided by biblical theology; it takes up the text of scripture only after it has learned from biblical theology where to look, and what to look for, in moving from the witness of scripture to the true subject matter. Nevertheless, complementing biblical theology, church dogma returns to scripture in the light of the subject matter, according to the method of faith seeking understanding. Our concern now is not so much the movement from witness to divine reality as it is serious and rigorous reflection on the inner logic of the divine reality, as reflected in the scriptural testimony. The various features of the biblical witness are essential for understanding the Christian doctrine of the Trinity; contrariwise, the Christian doctrine of the Trinity is essential if we are rightly to understand the various features of the biblical witness.

God is known by the giving of his name; he is not discovered by the analysis of a general concept of deity. God's name is God's very identity, which is disclosed in the event of divine self-manifestation. In his encounter with Israel, God declares his identity by announcing his name: Moses "rose early in the morning and went up on Mount Sinai, as the Lord had commanded him, and took in his hand the two tablets of stone. The Lord descended in the cloud and stood with him there, and proclaimed the name, 'The Lord'" (Exod. 34:4–5). The content of God's name is filled out not by rational analysis based on human consciousness but by God's own action of self-manifestation: "The Lord, the Lord, a God merciful and gracious, slow to anger, and abounding in steadfast love and faithfulness, keeping steadfast love for the thousandth generation, forgiving iniquity and transgression and sin, yet by no means clearing the guilty" (Exod. 34:6–7). God's name is disclosed in the context of the covenant that God establishes with his people.

The name of God is the most treasured possession of God's people, to be celebrated in worship: "Let them praise his name with dancing, making melody to him with tambourine and lyre" (Ps. 149:3). The worst conceivable disaster for the life of the community is to act in such a way that the name of God is defamed or abused. For example, Jeremiah announces a severe divine accusation against Israel for its treacherous mistreatment of slaves. The issue upon which the accusation turns is the destructive perversion of the covenant and the profanation of God's name: "You yourselves recently repented and did what was right in my sight by proclaiming liberty to one another, and you made a covenant before me in the house that is called by my name; but then you turned around and profaned my name when each of you took back your male and female slaves, whom you had set free according to their desire, and you brought them again into subjection to be your slaves" (Jer. 34:15–16).

God's name is a matter of life and death for one simple reason: by means of his name God discloses his very identity. In giving us his name, God tells us who he is. God's name is given in a divine act of self-revelation; it is not discovered in a human act of creative imagination. As John of Damascus rightly observes: "And this also it behooves us to know, that the names Fatherhood, Sonship, and Procession, were not applied to the Holy Godhead by us: on the contrary, they were communicated to us by the Godhead."[5]

What is at stake in the doctrine of the Trinity is the reality of divine self-revelation, and what is at stake in the reality of divine self-revelation is the very identity of the God we worship. In the ongoing history of the community of faith we have come full circle, for the burning issues at the forefront in the early church have once again come forward to challenge the church to new affirmation and therefore to new defense. We come to the crossroads: either we proclaim the divine name of the triune God into which we are all baptized and orient our speech and action accordingly, or we replace the Christian proclamation with another message. For the church of Jesus Christ, there can be only one true direction to take; from the beginning of our journey of faith to the very end our understanding of God is strictly bound to the triune name. Who is God? God is the Trinity. What is God's name? God's name is Father, Son, and Holy Spirit. From this critical standpoint we can in no wise stray and still remain the church of Jesus Christ.

At stake in the doctrine of the Trinity is the reality of God's self-revelation in Jesus Christ. The doctrine of the Trinity, both historically and materially, is derived from the full humanity and divinity of Jesus Christ. God has made known the reality of his very being in Jesus Christ; that is the astonishing declaration of the gospel, treasured by the church at all times and places. "For in him all the fullness of God was pleased to dwell" (Col. 1:19). God's self-revelation is not based on divine need; he does not need to make himself known in order to be God. His self-revelation is based rather on the freedom of divine love, grounded in the mystery of God's eternal will. For his own gracious purpose, God has declared the true reality of his nature and will through Jesus Christ. God's self-revelation is in no way whatsoever coordinated with any human capacity to receive it. Herein lies the massive error of both liberalism and evangelicalism. On the contrary, God's self-revelation in Jesus Christ creates anew those who receive it as a miraculous divine gift, through the presence of the Spirit.

God remains free in his self-revelation. His self-disclosure is a gift that can never be taken for granted, twisted or perverted by human

5. John of Damascus, 8.

agenda, nor manipulated for the sake of personal or cultural ideology. God's self-revelation is received only by the childlike wonder of joyful celebration. However, the point must be stressed that God exercises his freedom not by withholding knowledge of himself from his people but by freely granting it through Jesus Christ. The skeptic vainly declares that the world is in crisis because God is ultimately unknowable; the church responds rather that the world is indeed in crisis precisely because God has made himself known for all humanity in Jesus Christ. Both Testaments of scripture agree that God has made himself fully known. When Moses asks God to make clear who is sending him, what is God's name, God responds: "I AM WHO I AM" (cf. Exod. 3:14). God has a name, and in giving his name he manifests himself, making a direct claim upon human life. Similarly, Jesus tells the disciples: "In a little while the world will no longer see me, but you will see me" (John 14:19). Scripture leaves no doubt that God makes himself known and in so doing binds his people unto himself. Here we must declare in no uncertain terms: The Trinity is God. There is no other God but the Trinity. There is no "true" God behind the Trinity, for God himself, in his inmost reality, is revealed in Jesus Christ. The doctrine of the Trinity is therefore an absolute rejection of modern pluralism. There is only one true God, whose name is Father, Son, and Holy Spirit. All other so-called gods are idols. There is only one way to the knowledge of God, who has made known his glory only in the face of Jesus Christ. God's very being is made known in his act of self-revelation. On this issue the church can never yield a single inch, for at stake is the first commandment: "You shall have no other gods before me." We affirm ecumenism with all our hearts, for confession of the Trinity is the basis for the one, universal church and a call to the peace, unity, and purity of the church; but we renounce pluralism as a pagan myth.

The validity of God's self-revelation in Christ cannot rightly be compromised on the basis of the abstract notion of divine freedom. It is asked: Are we not restricting God's freedom to act any way he desires if we limit his self-revelation to one particular form? Are we not overstepping the limits of human capacity if we Christians so boldly and confidently assert the exclusivity of God's revelation in Christ? Of course these questions are not new; they were posed already during the period of the Enlightenment and clearly flow from the rationalistic assumptions of modernity. The issue was put forcefully in the famous query of Gotthold Lessing: "If on historical grounds I have no objection to the statement that Christ raised to life a dead man; must I therefore accept it as true that God has a Son who is of the same essence as himself? . . . That, then, is the ugly, broad ditch which I cannot get across, however often and however earnestly I have tried to make the leap."[6] There is, according to Lessing, an unbridgeable gap between historical fact and eternal truth. What is our answer to Lessing and his many recent followers?

First, our knowledge of Christ does not in the least rest on historical grounds; Christ the risen Lord is known through the proclaimed Word heard in faith. Christian faith is based on the resurrection of Christ, not on historical access to the "historical Jesus." The mystery of the incarnation is completely overlooked in the rationalism of the Enlightenment. On the one hand, God is fully known in Jesus Christ, for Christ himself is truly God and truly human in the unity of his person. Yet the true identity of Christ is concealed from unbelief; he is known only by faith, which is grounded in the proclaimed Word.

Second of all, faith is not a human leap from historical particularity to eternal truth. It is God alone who bridges the chasm that separates us from him. Faith is not an exercise of human piety or spirituality; faith is a miraculous divine gift, not an exercise in human capacity. Thus the movement across the ugly ditch of which Lessing speaks is a movement that God himself has already enacted for us in Jesus Christ. Not only is Jesus of Nazareth truly divine; so also is he truly human, in every sense of the word. In Christ, God has fully entered human time and space, becoming one with his creature. God himself has become fully involved with human history by entering the real world that we daily experience. Human thought does not accomplish a leap; the chasm has already been overcome. Human thought recognizes and confesses what God himself has already done on our behalf.

Third, the truth of the gospel is grounded in the sovereign divine will, as taught by the Spirit of God. The Spirit is the truth; the Spirit teaches the truth to human persons. The truth of God's self-revelation is therefore in no way subject to the strictures of human reason; rather, human persons are taught by God himself how to understand the inner logic of his true reality. The use of critical reason in dogmatic theology is completely legitimate within the bounds of faith seeking understanding. For Lessing and his many followers, reason stands by contrast as a self-grounded test of truth by which God's will is to be criticized and judged. To such an absurd imposition of frail humanity the answer of the church can only be the answer of scripture: "But who indeed are you, a human being, to argue with God . . . ?" (Rom. 9:20).

And fourth, it is essential to distinguish, as Barth does, between divine freedom as *potestas* and *potentia*. *Potestas* is the divine freedom to act according to his own gracious purpose without any external constraint whatsoever. Even in his self-revelation, God remains free; even in giv-

---

6. Lessing, 54–55.

ing himself to human understanding, he does not give away the free
mystery of his wondrous reality. Nothing restricts his free accomplishment of his design, even in ways that forever remain hidden to believer
and unbeliever alike. *Potentia*, by contrast, is the abstract philosophical
notion of sheer undetermined ability. It is power in itself, unrestrained
by proper order. Power in itself is chaos, which is the exact opposite of
who God is. As Barth observes, "Where 'power in itself' is honoured and
worshipped, where 'power in itself' wishes to be authority and wishes
to impose law, we are dealing with 'the revolution of nihilism.'"[7] God
exercises *potestas*; he is free to do as he pleases and even in his doing
remains unrestricted by any obstacle outside himself. God does not
exercise *potentia*; he does not retain for himself a supposed right to be
different from his self-revelation in Christ. The issue here is the truth
of divine self-commitment in the incarnation. Denial of the divine self-
commitment in Jesus Christ is denial of the truthfulness of God, than
which there is no greater error. "Those who believe in the Son of God
have the testimony in their hearts. Those who do not believe in God have
made him a liar by not believing in the testimony that God has given
concerning his Son" (1 John 5:10). Does the scandal of particularity
create an offense to modern rationalism? Of course it does, but so be
it; for it is the offense of the gospel itself, which can never be removed,
apart from faith.

God reveals himself.[8] God is the Revealer; he graciously manifests himself
according to his own sovereign design. God is the Revelation; he makes
himself known by entering human space and time and becoming a human
being, yet in such a way that he remains no less God. His entrance into
human life is an exercise of full divine power, not a limitation of that power.
God is the One Revealed; through the miracle of his own presence, God
creates a human response, which in no way is based on any form of human
ability or worth. God is Revealer, Revelation, and Revealed; he is the Subject
of Revelation, the Object of Revelation, and the Predicate of Revelation. And
yet there is one God, not three; there is one God in the threefold movement
of divine self-revelation. God's self-revelation is the act of God by which he
establishes relationship to humanity. There is no such relationship prior to
this act, nor does God's self-revelation ever become a permanent human
condition. God's act is always a miracle and is never converted into a human
possession. Under no circumstances can it ever be treated with presumption or domesticated by human stratagem or neglect.

The doctrine of the Trinity recognizes and confesses the triune act of
God in self-manifestation. The economic Trinity is the threefold form

7. Barth, *Dogmatics in Outline*, 48.
8. Barth, *CD* I/1, 295–333.

of divine act in the world. But the church doctrine goes farther than the economic Trinity, though it is the basis for what follows. The doctrine of the Trinity asserts that the threefold act of God in self-revelation is in fact the replication in time of the divine being in eternity. God acts in the threefold form of Revealer, Revelation, and Revealed, because God in eternity is one God in three eternal modes of being: Father, Son, and Holy Spirit. This is the immanent or ontological Trinity. Both the economic and the ontological Trinity are essential to Christian confession, which always lapses into sheer idolatry wherever the triune God is ignored or displaced by an idol of human manufacture.

There is a dialectical relation of being and act in the divine life. Both sides of the dialectic must be stressed. On the one hand, God's being is known only through his act of self-revelation. Human beings have no access to God whatsoever through self-reflection or reflection on the world around. God's being cannot be known through rational reflection on the structure of the universe, moving from cause to effect, nor from rational reflection on the nature of human experience, moving from self-consciousness to transcendent source. God's being is known only in the event of divine self-disclosure, which is accomplished according to the eternal purpose of God. On the other hand, God's very being is known through his act of self-revelation. God himself takes on the form of his creation, becoming a human being, for the sake of his redeeming love for all humanity. It is only in this dialectic of being and act that God's self-revelation is truly confessed.

Here two errors must be avoided: an ontological interpretation in abstraction from God's act and an exclusive focus on God's act while refusing a full ontological affirmation. Despite his clear endeavor to remain true to the inner logic of the biblical witness, Thomas Aquinas represents the former error. He argues repeatedly that God's nature is not known to us but that God is known as cause from his effects in the world. Both sides of his argument need correction in the light of the biblical witness. On the one hand, God's very nature *is* disclosed to us in Jesus Christ, and on the other hand, we can know *nothing* whatsoever about God by observing ourselves and the world around us as effects of God's creativity, for we are sinners and in no position to assess rightly what we see. Thomas fails to see fully the implications of his own clear commitment to the Trinity for the Christian understanding of God. God is fully known in Jesus Christ; God is fully known only in Jesus Christ, and in no form of human ability to observe the surrounding world: "All things have been handed over to me by my Father; and no one knows the Son except the Father, and no one knows the Father except the Son and anyone to whom the Son chooses to reveal him" (Matt. 11:27). God's being is known only in God's act; God's very being is known in God's act.

The contrary error is clearly represented by a figure such as Albrecht Ritschl, who denies that the ontological understanding of God flows from his act of self-revelation. According to Ritschl, there is no movement from God's act in Jesus Christ to God's being. He states: "To the degree that a man wants to be a Christian, he has this datum which he must acknowledge as given: the relationship to God which is expressed by Christ and sustained by him through his death and resurrection. One must avoid all attempts *to go behind this datum*, that is, to determine in detail how it has come into being and empirically how it has come to be what it is."[9] The historical Trinity yields no understanding of the inner life of God. Ritschl confuses two very different issues. It is one thing to argue that the economic Trinity yields understanding of the ontological Trinity only on the grounds of faith seeking understanding. It is quite another to argue, as Ritschl does, that every movement from the economic to the ontological Trinity must necessarily employ a previously derived philosophical ontology. He states: "Therefore the substance and worth of Christ should be understood in the beneficent actions upon us Christians, in the gift of the blessedness which we sought in vain under the law—not in a previously held general concept of his divinity."[10] Under the influence of Kant's philosophy, Ritschl elides two very different issues. The church roundly denies that the doctrine of the Trinity ever employs a previously derived philosophical ontology. It does not; the whole point of the Trinity is to ward off such philosophical incursions. However, not as natural theology but as faithful confession, the church absolutely insists on an ontological Trinity. God's act in Christ guides us to a true understanding of God's very being. Such an assertion is not optional; it is a necessary dimension of faith in the gospel.

I must complete the dialectical point with a final statement: God's being is active. The ontological Trinity is not a different God from the economic Trinity. It is not as though God were a lifeless, unchanging substance in eternity to which action is then added as a secondary characteristic in his temporal relations. Rather, God himself is supremely active and alive in the eternal reality of his being. God's movement in time is the direct result of God's eternally active life, which constitutes the majesty of his supreme act of being. As Ezekiel 1 makes fully clear, God's reality unfolds in ceaseless energy that moves in all directions simultaneously: "When the living creatures moved, the wheels moved beside them; and when the living creatures rose from the earth, the wheels rose. Wherever the spirit would go, they went, and the wheels rose along with them; for the spirit of the living creatures was in the wheels. When they moved,

9. Ritschl, 178.
10. Ibid., 204.

the others moved; when they stopped, the others stopped; the wheels rose along with them; for the spirit of the living creatures was in the wheels" (Ezek. 1:19–21). God is a God of ceaseless motion: "He will not let your foot be moved; he who keeps you will not slumber. He who keeps Israel will neither slumber nor sleep" (Ps. 121:3–4). Thus, God's act is not foreign to his being but in fact is grounded in it.

The Trinity is not a lifeless proposition or idea; the Trinity is the living God. God dwells in the freedom of his eternal reality; yet God enters human space and time to encounter human beings with the surprise and wonder of his earthly form. God acts according to his own unrestrained initiative and in his own good time; yet God's movement into the world is overwhelming in force and radically transforms the whole creation. God is fully revealed in the face of Jesus Christ; yet God is concealed in his revelation and cannot be seen apart from the eye of faith. There is one triune God; yet God is not a changeless thing but a living reality who constantly leads his people forward to fresh discovery of new dimensions of his wondrous identity. God has no need of making himself known to humankind; yet it is precisely God who seeks us out, long before we ever seek him. God is known only in Jesus Christ; yet his coming is always full of stunning surprise in the sheer variety of his ways of encountering human beings. God is transcendent over all reality, which he governs according to the eternal wisdom of his self-determined will; yet God is profoundly immanent in the world. He enters directly into human history and experiences life in our world from the inside, knowing for himself the life of creaturely existence by becoming a creature. God makes himself fully known; and yet the more we know, the more we realize there is much yet to learn, for God can never be fully comprehended in the splendor of his being. God always acts according to the gracious purpose of his love, which is the redemption of all humanity and the restoration of the whole creation; and yet he allows for human spontaneity and protects the sheer contingency of human occurrence. God binds himself in covenant to his people; yet God rules all the nations of the earth and acts with compassion for the sake of all humanity. This entire dynamic of the Christian understanding of God is possible only where the Trinity is honored.

The Trinity must not be seen as the final chapter of the Christian doctrine of God, which is otherwise essentially based on a philosophically derived ontology. Quite the opposite: the Trinity is the essential moment of identification of the Christian God. The doctrine of the Trinity is the necessary introduction to the full grandeur of God disclosed in scripture. Theological reflection on God in dogmatics begins with the Trinity not in order to close off fruitful discussion of God's true identity; rather, dogmatics begins with the doctrine of the Trinity in order to orient dogmatic reflection to the God of the biblical witness from the outset and there to discover a God of glorious life and unconditional love beyond all human imagination. The purpose of doctrine is to protect the church from error, but it does not stifle resourcefulness and vision. Doctrine rightly understood leaves plenty of room for human discovery and exploration; indeed it alone shows where exploration can find what it is looking for. Genuine doctrine is an invitation to human creativity in the search for God, not a condemnation of it. Nevertheless, doctrine also recognizes that the living God is not a projection of human consciousness in any form. The truth of God's identity is primary; human response to God is secondary. Faith is in no way an attempt to mold God into human conception, which is blasphemy. Genuine faith is to know God as he gives himself to be known, to know God therefore as he is in reality. Toward this end, the church wrestles with God. Or better said, the living God wrestles with the church (cf. Gen. 32:22–32), directing its attention and its worship away from the idols of human making toward the supreme wonder of his own eternal being.

The present reflection on the Christian doctrine of the Trinity begins with the self-revelation of God. That is to say, the threefold act of divine self-manifestation shown forth in the economic Trinity is the basis for our affirmation of the ontological Trinity. Noetically, the act of God is the only basis for our knowledge of the being of God. But now we must proceed a step further, in a theological movement of thought that is just as legitimate and necessary. Ontically, the being of God is the only basis for the redemptive act of God for the sake of humanity. God acts for our salvation in Jesus Christ in a way that reflects who he is in his eternal being. Based on the threefold form of divine self-revelation—the Father reveals himself by means of the Son through the Holy Spirit—we now seek to reflect theologically on the being of God. Our aim is to discover the answer to two broad questions: who is God, and what is the purpose of his ways with humankind? Of course the entire content of dogmatic theology is an elaboration of the answer we find. In a sense, we are here getting our initial bearings for the entire journey of Christian discovery. The attempt at understanding God and his purpose for human life is placed in the prolegomena on canon precisely in order to highlight the guiding role it plays in all Christian doctrine. Dogmatics is not a rationalistic system of true propositions; dogmatics is a discipline of the Christian church, which lives by its encounter with a living Lord. Any initial attempt to articulate the true subject matter of scripture—God and his gracious purpose for humanity made known in Christ—is in the end measured not by any form of human piety or rationality but by the One of whom it speaks.

God is a relationship of love. That is the stunning truth contained in the doctrine of the Trinity in its rightful place at the head of dogmatic reflection. God is not a lifeless, solitary "thing." God is not an incomplete, single monad in search of an "other" in order to fulfill his identity. For that reason, the language of Christian "monotheism" must be abandoned as an unfortunate accommodation to modern philosophical theism. Just as the ancient church sought to understand the Trinity as a check against philosophical speculation, so we too must ground the language of faith in the triune God, not in the various modern philosophical options. God is not an impersonal force or process; God is not an unknown X standing behind the realm of human experience. God is a relationship, a communion of love: Father, Son, and Holy Spirit.

God is supremely fulfilled in the eternal reality of his own being, for God is himself a relationship of love. He does not *have* a relationship, as if it were external or accidental to his otherwise isolated existence. Rather, God *is* a relationship. We mean that in the full sense of the word; we are speaking not metaphorically but quite literally when we say that God is, in his eternal being, a relationship of love.

That is my initial attempt to answer the first question: who is God?—an answer to which we shall shortly return. My initial attempt to answer the second question, concerning God's purpose for humanity, is this: God's redemptive purpose is to establish a relationship of love with the creatures he has made for himself. All that we know, or think we know, about the world around us and about ourselves must be reoriented to the realization that God's purpose for all that exists independently of himself is to be in relationship of love to him. God himself is a communion of love; God made a world independent of himself in order that he might enter into a communion of love with it. As Jesus states: "I know my own and my own know me, just as the Father knows me and I know the Father" (John 10:14–15).

Once again, a final point is necessary in order to tie these two answers dialectically together. God is a relationship of love; God's purpose is to establish a relationship of love with humanity; and finally, God's purpose is constitutive of God's very being. Freely, without necessity or coercion, external or internal, the eternal God in the mystery of his sovereign will binds his very existence, his being, to his redemptive love for humankind. God's love for the world is, by his own free decision, at the heart of who he is. We know this to be true not through wishful thinking or hopeful optimism; we know this because we know Jesus Christ, in whom the eternal purpose of God is embodied. God's sovereign purpose of love, to which he commits his very being, is the reconciliation of the whole creation through Jesus Christ. In speaking about the being of God, the purpose of God, and the unity between the two, we have before our eyes nothing but the glory of Jesus Christ himself, "in whom are hidden all the treasures of wisdom and knowledge" (Col. 2:3).

The church's answer to the question "Who is God?" is the ontological Trinity. God is the ontological Trinity. God is a relationship, an eternal communion of love between the Father, the Son, and the Holy Spirit. God is one in the diversity of three modes of being; God is threefold in the unity of his one essence. Both the unity of God and the diversity of his three modes of being must be clearly affirmed and protected. It is not that the three modes of being, Father, Son, and Holy Spirit, are mere appearances of a unitary Subject that somehow lies behind them. That is the heresy of modalism, which the early church rightly rejected. The Christian church joins with the Jewish synagogue in maintaining the absolute confession: God is one. There are not three gods but one God. But the one God is not somehow behind the three, through whom he appears. Rather, there is one God in threefold form; one God in three coeternal modes of being that together constitute his true unity; one God now as Father, now as Son, now as Holy Spirit, one in threefold unity.

There is real otherness, real difference, in God; for the Father is not the Son, and the Father and the Son are not the Spirit. And yet there are not three gods; there is only one God. We worship the Father, we worship the Son, we worship the Spirit; and yet we do not worship three gods, but one God. The early church rightly also rejected tritheism as heresy. The otherness in God is not separation; the togetherness in God is not confusion. God is a communion of love, in such a way that his unity is in no way compromised by the diversity of his modes of being; nor is the distinction of his modes of being erased by the majesty of his eternal unity. God has one essence, one nature—not three essences or three natures. Yet his nature or essence is not an abstraction from, or universal common to, his diverse modes of being. Rather, his essence is realized in the genuine differentiation of his triune existence. The three modes of being are not parts of God, which somehow added up make a single divine being. God's absolute unity is in fact constituted by the threefold form of his eternal reality. God's unity is defined in diversity; God's diversity is grounded in unity. For that reason, to speak of God as relationship is not to describe a capacity of which he subsequently makes use but to recognize the splendor of his own self-constituting reality. To speak of God as a relationship is not to put God in a class, even a class of which he is the primary member. The absolute rule that governs all proper speech about God is this: God is not in any class (*Deus non est in genere*). Rather, to speak of God as relationship is to assert that God, and God alone, defines what is meant by relationship. We use the word *relationship* not in such a way as to bend God to human categories; we use the word in such a way that human language is drawn, through encounter with the living God, to truthful witness to his eternal reality and joyful celebration of his amazing radiance.

There is a difference of emphasis between the Western and Eastern traditions of reflection on the communion of love that constitutes God's reality. The West, following the magnificent treatise of Augustine *On the Holy Trinity*, starts with the unity of essence and proceeds to the distinction of persons. The East, following the Cappadocian fathers, starts from the distinction of persons and proceeds to the unity of nature. I think it is now best for the universal church to recognize and appreciate the validity of both approaches, for they are surely complementary, not contradictory.

On the one hand, relationship in God flows from his absolute unity. God has one essence or nature. The entire essence of God is in the Father; the entire essence of God is in the Son; the entire essence of God is in the Holy Spirit; and yet there are not three essences but one divine essence. God's self-relation is not a coming together of what is separated; there is no internal opposition or estrangement in the Godhead which must somehow be overcome. The diversity in God is not a threat to his unity but is in fact directly derived from it. There is one God; there is only one God. The unity of God is not threatened by the diversity; rather, the unity of God is confirmed in the diverse modes of being. There is no ground to the charge that the Western approach leaves God impersonal; the unity of God is in fact supremely personal, for the unity of essence is realized only in the diversity of persons.

On the other hand, it is both proper and necessary to speak of otherness in God. The divine unity is realized only in eternal diversity. Father, Son, and Holy Spirit do not spring forth as secondary characteristics of abstract primary unity. There is no real unity somehow hiding behind the apparent diversity of the three modes of being. The unity of God is constituted by the relationship of love shared by the three modes of being. The unity of God is not a kind of abstract mathematical summation; the unity of God is love, a communion of love that flows from real difference in the Godhead. There is no divine unity without divine diversity. The threefold reality of God defines the nature of his unity. There is no ground to the charge that the Eastern conception leads to tritheism; in beginning with the three modes of being we do not compromise the unity but only discover its true nature. The diversity of persons is in fact the only true guarantee of divine unity. Therefore, with the Western church, we must find the diversity only in the one unity; with the Eastern church, we must achieve the unity only through affirmation of real diversity in love.

What then is the distinction between the three modes of being in the Godhead? If the full essence of God resides in each of the three, what distinguishes one mode of being from the other two? The answer is the mutual relations of the three persons of the Trinity—in particular, the relations of origin. The Father is distinguished from the Son, and from the Spirit, in terms of the different relations of origin that they sustain to one another. Origin is not cause; cause is a temporal category, and the mutual relations of the triune God are eternal, not temporal. The Father eternally *begets* the Son. The Son is begotten, not made. In no sense whatsoever is the Son created by the Father. The Son is not a creature; on the contrary, through him the entire creation came into being (cf. John 1:3). The Son is coequal and coeternal with the Father, of the same essence with the Father. The Son is consubstantial with the Father; all that the Father is the Son is, in dignity, majesty, and power. The only difference is that the Son is begotten of the Father and not the reverse. The Spirit eternally *proceeds* from the Father and the Son—that is, from the unity of essence which the Father and the Son alike share. The Spirit too is coequal in dignity, majesty, and power with the Father and the Son; the Spirit too is consubstantial with the Father and the Son. The Spirit is the bond of peace that unites Father and Son in love. The Spirit is the joy of God's inner life.

There is one essence of God; the same identical essence exists in three diverse modes of being, which are distinguished in reference to the relation of origin to one another. The Father eternally begets the Son; the Spirit eternally proceeds from the Father and the Son. These are ontologically true descriptions of the inner life of God in his eternal glory. Where do they come from? Noetically, they come from God's self-revelation. We know that the Father begets the Son eternally because he sent his Son into the temporal world for the sake of our salvation. We know that the Spirit eternally proceeds from the Father and the Son because of the outpouring of the Spirit on Pentecost. God's redemptive action in time is the sure and certain basis for our knowledge of God's eternal being. Ontically, however, the relation is reversed: God's sending of his Son for our salvation and the outpouring of the Holy Spirit are a replication in time of God's eternal self-identity. God's redemptive love for humanity is an expression of God's free decision to draw us into a relationship with himself, which is based on the relationship of love that he himself is. Redemption is not an afterthought or a side project of God; though an utterly free act, not based in any way on divine need, redemption is a pledge of divine self-dedication based on the reality of his own nature, which is eternal love. "With all wisdom and insight he has made known to us the mystery of his will, according to his good pleasure that he set forth in Christ, as a plan for the fullness of time, to gather up all things in him, things in heaven and things on earth" (Eph. 1:8–10).

Because of the coequality of the divine modes of being, all subordination in the Godhead is radically excluded. The differing relations of origin do not at all imply degrees of preeminence or gradations of being. The earliest church fathers often spoke in subordinationist terms, with the seeming implication that the inner ordering of the divine life demands a hierarchy or scale of being among the persons of the Godhead. The orthodox fathers did not mean to suggest a lessoning of the divinity of the Son or of the Spirit; rather, at an earlier time certain issues had not yet been raised and some language was used imprecisely. However, by the time of Arius, subordinationist language was seized on for very different purposes and clearly contributed to the corruption of the gospel message in Arianism. For that reason, Augustine in the West and the Cappadocians in the East carefully guarded against all subordinationist language. Church historian J. N. D. Kelly summarizes the mature trinitarian theology of Augustine as follows: "The unity of the Trinity is thus set squarely in the foreground, subordinationism of every kind being rigorously excluded."[11] Instead of subordinationist language, Athanasius speaks of the "coordination" (συστοιχια) of the three, based on the baptismal formula of Matthew's Gospel. Athanasius is followed in this by Basil: "And if the Spirit is coordinate with the Son, and the Son with the Father, it is obvious that the Spirit is also coordinate with the Father."[12] According to Jaroslav Pelikan, "Basil maintained that the relation of Spirit to Son was the same as that of the Son to the Father, and that this coordination expressly ruled out any notion of ranking."[13] Thus the eternal relations that constitute the inner life of God are not to be understood in terms of status or grade. The mutual relations of God's threefold unity are an expression of the coordinate energy of divine being. Biblical expressions that speak of the subservient role of Christ in relation to the Father ("the Father is greater than I," John 14:28) are references to the humility of Christ the incarnate Lord. As truly God and truly human, Jesus Christ in his earthly life serves the Father's will in all things for the sake of the redemption of all humanity. Christ "emptied himself, taking the form of a slave, being born in human likeness" (Phil. 2:7). There is no implication however that the eternal Son is less than the Father in any respect. On the contrary, the same Lord makes the clear confession "The Father and I are one" (John 10:30).

Indeed, not only must we speak of the coordination of the three modes of being of the divine reality, we must also speak of their coinherence (*perichoresis*). Human language must bend to its subject matter in ex-

11. Kelly, 272.
12. *On the Spirit*, 28, cited in Pelikan below.
13. Pelikan, 1:218.

pressing the marvel of divine unity. Jesus said, "The Father is in me and I am in the Father"(John 10:38). We must learn to allow the divine reality to define for us the very meaning of the terms we use to learn of him. When we speak of the relationship of love that God is, we do not refer to any kind of external linkage of the three persons of the Trinity. Rather, each divine person indwells the others; each mode of being completely fills the others while yet remaining itself. The diversity is not compromised by the coinherence of the three modes of being. The mystery of divine love is such that the diversity is truly confirmed and fulfilled only in the coinherence.

We approach here the startling statement of biblical faith: "God is love" (1 John 4:16). The point is not that God's chief characteristic is love or that God's primary act outside himself is love. These too may be true; but the point here is that God's being is his loving. Love is an internal relation to God; love is not something that God has or does for another, but simply who God is. The Trinity is love, for the triune reality is an eternal relationship of mutual fulfillment through mutual permeation, in which the diverse modes of divine being are not canceled out or lost but established by their concrete unity. Each person of the Trinity is defined in terms of the mutual relation sustained with the others. Individuality is defined by relationality; relationality is expressed in individuality. To understand the Father, you must know the Son and the Holy Spirit; to understand the Son, you must know the Father and the Holy Spirit; to understand the Holy Spirit, you must know the Father and the Son. The modes of divine being are not first defined and then brought into relation to one another; their individual expression is defined by their mutual indwelling.

One of the chief obstacles to understanding the triune God of love is the modern change in the notion of person. In the language of the fathers, person (*persona*, υποστασις) means independent, individual subsistence. In modern times, however, there is the additional quality of self-consciousness, which is entirely lacking in ancient usage. If we are to continue using the notion of person in relation to God, we must be careful to realize that no implication of self-consciousness is present in its theological expression. There are not three self-conscious personalities in God but one divine self-consciousness confirmed in God's threefold being. There are not three separate wills in God but one will. There are not three minds in God but one mind. One divine energy pervades the three modes of being or persons. I see no reason to eliminate the technical concept "person" as long as it is crystal clear that the modern idea of personality is not what is meant. There are not three personalities in God, though there are three "persons." One self-identical nature or essence exists in three individual persons. The word *person* is deeply embedded in much Christian liturgy and is certainly still usable. Nevertheless, in my judgment it is best in technical dogmatic theology to prefer the use of the Eastern "mode of being" (τροπος υπαρχεως).

While we must certainly stress the coinherence of the divine modes of being, we must also stress the distinction that is retained even in the unity. There remains, even in the complete unity of the Godhead, a diversity of divine function that is not canceled or set aside by the unity. The Father is neither the Son nor the Holy Spirit. The Father sent the Son into the world for the salvation of humanity; the relation between the two is never turned into its opposite. The Son, not the Father, died on the cross and was raised on the third day. The Holy Spirit, not the Father, was poured out into the early church. Dogmatic theology recognizes the genuine diversity by speaking of *appropriations*; different roles are appropriated to each of the three persons of the Trinity. Here again our language must yield to the substance. In the relationship that God is, the mutual indwelling of the divine modes of being does not diminish or withdraw their individual roles or functions. We confess, with the church of all ages, that the *opera Dei externa sunt indivisa*: the divine action in the world is the work of the undivided Godhead. The Father made the heavens and the earth, yet all things that exist came into existence through the Son, and the Spirit renews the face of the earth. Appropriation is not separation. However, the unity of divine action preserves the individual roles of the persons of the Trinity that must be observed in the language of faith. The Father sent the Son; the Son is our Savior and Lord; the Spirit sets us free to new life.

The Son of God is also the Word of God (cf. John 1:1–18). Jesus Christ is the eternal Word of the Father, with God in the beginning. The Word is God, through whom all things came into existence. All true knowledge of God comes through his self-manifestation in Christ, for Christ alone is God's act of self-declaration. In Christ, God declares his true identity for the blessing of all humankind. Our reflections now carry us back to the essential starting point of the doctrine of the Trinity. The doctrine of the Trinity asserts the true authenticity of God's act of self-manifestation in Jesus Christ. In Christ, God made himself known for the redemption of the world. Through Christ, God entered human space and time for the reconciliation of the cosmos. In confessing the triune God, the community of faith pledges itself to undying faithfulness to Christ alone, the one true source of our common life together. No ideology, no fad or custom, no claim to revelatory consciousness; no moral ideal, whether nostalgic or revolutionary; no attraction of human spirituality—nothing can displace the living Lord, the one Word of the Father. Christ alone is the way to the Father for all time, for every place, and for all peoples. Nothing less is at stake in affirming the ontological Trinity, without which the church ceases to be.

10

The Nicene Creed

In 325 the ecumenical church gathered at Nicaea in the midst of extreme theological crisis. The teaching of Arius was sweeping over wide segments of the church and threatened the unity of the faith. A creed was formulated to combat heresy and to clarify the true content of the faith. Again in 381 the ecumenical church gathered at Constantinople, as the crisis continued. The creed adopted in 381, now widely known as the Nicene Creed, brought to final maturity the trinitarian theology of the early church. The text is as follows:

> We believe in one God the Father Almighty, Maker of heaven and earth, and of all things visible and invisible.
>
> And in one Lord Jesus Christ, the only-begotten Son of God, begotten of the Father before all worlds, God of God, Light of Light, Very God of Very God, begotten, not made, being of one substance with the Father, by whom all things were made; who for us men, and for our salvation, came down from heaven, and was incarnate by the Holy Spirit of the Virgin Mary, and was made man, and was crucified also for us under Pontius Pilate. He suffered and was buried, and the third day he rose again according to the Scriptures, and ascended into heaven, and sits on the right hand of the Father. And he shall come again with glory to judge both the quick and the dead, whose kingdom shall have no end.
>
> And we believe in the Holy Spirit, the Lord and Giver of Life, who proceeds from the Father and the Son, who with the Father and the Son together is worshipped and glorified, who spoke by the prophets. And

we believe one holy catholic and apostolic Church. We acknowledge one
baptism for the remission of sins. And we look for the resurrection of the
dead, and the life of the world to come. Amen.

The Nicene Creed is an ecumenical creed, held universally where
Christians confess the triune God. In it, the crucial confession is made
that Christ is "of one substance" (ομοουσιον) with the Father. The *ho-moousion* became the hallmark of catholic Christianity in its ongoing
battle with heresy. Two broad errors were exposed and denounced by
the Nicene faith. On the one hand, Sabellianism taught a primordial
divine unity that lay behind the three persons of the Trinity. Against
the notion of an undifferentiated unity, the Nicene faith asserts the real
diversity of the three persons existing in the Godhead. On the other
hand, Arianism taught that Jesus is essentially a demigod, greater than
all other creatures but a creature nonetheless. Against Arianism, Nicene
faith taught the full divinity of Christ, without which Christian confession lapses into tritheism. Since its inception, the Nicene Creed has
commanded universal consent among faithful Christians wherever the
gospel has sounded forth. Dogmatic theology today can and must affirm
wholeheartedly the Nicene Creed.

Three objections are commonly made against the universal validity
of the creed. First, it is argued that the Nicene Creed was formulated
primarily to bring unity to a fragmented empire. Its origin and function
were primarily political and economic, rather than theological. Second,
because it came so late in Christian history it can hardly be considered a
valid expression of biblical faith. And third, the creed uses the technical
jargon of ancient philosophy and is thus foreign to the modern world
of thought.

In response, it is first of all necessary to concede that political dimensions were certainly present. The church of Jesus Christ is located in
history, and a purist mentality that denies all extraneous factors is clearly
unwarranted. Scripture itself makes no effort to conceal the very human
qualities of the apostles, who often act with misguided judgment. Nevertheless, nor does scripture ever deny their authority, nor the truthful
content of their testimony, despite their humanity. The Bible confesses
that the truth of the gospel shines through even the limitations of those
who profess it: "But we have this treasure in clay jars, so that it may be
made clear that this extraordinary power belongs to God and does not
come from us" (2 Cor. 4:7). There were doubtless political considerations
present in the early councils, some of which were not worthy of the exalted truth being formulated. Yet no one can doubt that the theological
issues were paramount and shine through these documents to the very
present day. The ancient creeds are not politics disguised as theology;

they are magnificent theology, unfortunately professed amidst often questionable politics. The Nicene Creed is a theological confession based on scripture, despite the human frailties of those who produced it; all who maintain a living connection with the early church must come to grips with the witness to Jesus Christ that it forthrightly professes, even if we are critical of the political motives of some of its supporters.

Second, there is no reason at all to be surprised or disturbed if the genuine content of biblical faith takes time to clarify and confess. Indeed, the process of clarification and confession continues into our own time. As canon, scripture is tied to an ongoing community of faith that develops over time and in varying circumstances. Scripture is not a set of timeless propositions but a living witness to a living Lord, who governs his church in the living world of change and growth. The truth of church confession is not measured by time and circumstance of discovery but by the illumination it brings to the subject matter of scripture. The universal consent of the church is that the Nicene Creed indeed sheds priceless and enduring light on the truth of the gospel.

And third, the oft-repeated cavil that ancient dogma was laced with philosophical concepts such as ουσια and υποστασις and is therefore unbiblical springs from a sophomoric biblicism. Canon comprises the witness of scripture and the reality to which it points. The church is challenged to move from witness to reality using whatever concepts are useful. Adhering to the Nicene Creed does not mean suddenly leaving modernity for antiquity, as if all that it offers us is the "Greek mentality." The creed offers us the gospel of Jesus Christ using concepts well deployed for that purpose. Of course the quibble of "philosophical concepts" employed in the doctrine of the Trinity is hardly new. The Reformers faced the same issue in combating the new antitrinitarian currents of the sixteenth century. For example, Calvin is aware of such criticism of the creed: "Now, although the heretics rail at the word 'person,' or certain squeamish men cry out against admitting a term fashioned by the human mind, they cannot shake our conviction that three are spoken of, each of which is entirely God, yet that there is not more than one God."[1] He responds with an aggressive defense: "But what prevents us from explaining in clearer words those matters in Scripture which perplex and hinder our understanding, yet which conscientiously and faithfully serve the truth of Scripture itself, and are made use of sparingly and modestly and on due occasion?"[2] The church's use of such words is not an arbitrary choice but a necessary clarification: "What is to be said, moreover, when it has been proved that the church is utterly compelled to make use of

1. Calvin, 1.123.
2. Ibid., 1.124.

the words 'Trinity' and 'Persons'?"[3] The fault, according to Calvin, does not lie in the church but in those who withdraw from it through unjust and destructive criticism: "If anyone, then, finds fault with the novelty of the words, does he not deserve to be judged as bearing the light of truth unworthily, since he is finding fault only with what renders the truth plain and clear?"[4] We can today hardly improve upon Calvin's fine defense of the use of technical concepts in trinitarian doctrine.

The crucial question thus arises: is the Nicene Creed binding on all Christians in the church today? The question is especially significant in the light of revolutionary changes now taking place in the church around the world. As is now widely recognized, the missionary churches of the past in the Third World are now established churches of the present. They are no longer dependent upon European and North American Christianity. They have a life of their own and have unique contributions to make to the universal community of faith, including the field of dogmatics. We cannot turn back the clock; these revolutionary changes are all for the good and must never be reversed through misguided political considerations. The churches of the Third World are free to find their own special place in the ecology of church life. The churches of Europe and North America are in no sense the center of Christianity; all are free to serve Christ in their own sphere of existence.

But where does that freedom come from? According to the gospel it comes from Jesus Christ himself: "I am the way, and the truth, and the life. No one comes to the Father except through me" (John 14:6). "You will know the truth, and the truth will make you free" (John 8:32). The new freedom of the churches of the Third World is not a self-conferred freedom, but a freedom to serve Jesus Christ in the world in a new way. Our answer therefore can only be yes: the Nicene Creed is binding upon all who profess faith in Jesus Christ as Lord and Savior. The role of the Creed is not to block imagination, nor halt fresh theological discussion, nor restrict freedom; its role is to bear faithful witness to the true source of freedom for all Christians of all times and places. The role of the Nicene Creed is to delimit and define the way of understanding along which fruitful theological discovery is possible. The true unity of the church preserves and protects the diversity; but the diversity is grounded only in the true unity, which is Jesus Christ himself, the one Head of the church. "Holy Father, protect them in your name . . . so that they may be one, as we are one" (John 17:11). "I have other sheep that do not belong to this fold. I must bring them also, and they will listen to my voice. So there will be one flock, one shepherd" (John 10:16). We

3. Ibid.
4. Ibid.

affirm the universality of the Nicene Creed under the authority of the risen Christ, who rules all nations.

Despite the universal consent of the faithful with which the Nicene Creed is embraced, one issue continues to divide East from West. According to the Eastern version, the Spirit proceeds from the Father; according to the Western version, the Spirit proceeds from the Father and the Son (*filioque*). The solution to the conflict is not to dismiss it as irrelevant detail, for the issue is in fact theologically weighty. Nor is the solution to seek a vantage point from which both can be true, for consensus is not always identical with the truth of the gospel. The Eastern tradition makes numerous objections to the *filioque*.[5] In my judgment, the most significant is the claim that the Western *filioque* empties the Spirit of independent personality. Such a deemphasis of the Spirit results in an arid institutionalism, including a misguided claim to papal infallibility. Can dogmatic theology clarify this disagreement?

I agree fully with the Eastern criticism of much Western church life; the threat of dead ecclesiastical self-satisfaction is ever present. Now more than ever we need a fresh outpouring of the Spirit for the renewal and rebirth of the church. And indeed, the way forward in the ecumenical church certainly lies in a Roman Catholic retreat from papal infallibility, which cannot be sustained on any biblical or theological grounds. The Eastern patriarch of Constantinople, Photius (c. 810–c. 895), is right; the papal claim to infallibility must be abandoned by the bishop of Rome, for it is in fact unworthy of such a distinguished leader of the church. However, I disagree with the Eastern diagnosis of the cause of the maladies. I believe Western errors are located in the heresy of natural theology, not in the *filioque*. It is the attempt to ground faith in human rational capacity that saps the life-giving energy of the Spirit's ever fresh presence.

Moreover, there is an essential reason for affirming the necessity of the *filioque*. In an age of rampant pseudospirituality, it is essential to recognize dogmatically the living connection between Christ the risen Lord and the Holy Spirit. The apostle Paul makes the necessary connection very clear: "The Lord is the Spirit" (2 Cor. 3:17). That is not to deny in any way the full divine majesty and power of the Spirit's work; the Holy Spirit is God, worshiped and glorified together with the Father and the Son. The *filioque* does not underemphasize the Spirit; on the contrary, by insisting on the association of the Spirit with the risen Christ the *filioque* celebrates the sovereign divine energy of the Holy Spirit's presence by protecting it from all human spirituality. Scripture enjoins us to test the spirits: "Beloved, do not believe every spirit, but test the spirits to see

5. Ware, 219–23.

whether they are from God; for many false prophets have gone out into the world" (1 John 4:1). The ultimate test is christological: "By this you know the Spirit of God: every spirit that confesses that Jesus Christ has come in the flesh is from God, and every spirit that does not confess Jesus is not from God" (1 John 4:2). The *filioque* is a truthful dogmatic assertion of the eternal ontological bond of the Spirit and the Son. The *filioque* therefore is a crucial element of Nicene faith and ought to be professed universally in the church. Just as the Roman Catholic Church should abandon papal infallibility for the sake of church unity, so Eastern Orthodoxy should affirm the *filioque*, not on the spurious grounds of papal infallibility but because it is a true and faithful dimension of Christian confession of the living God. It is to be confessed everywhere and by all because it is true. Surely the friendship of East and West can only be strengthened by such a compromise on both sides.

The Nicene Creed constitutes a reliable rule of faith by which the universal church tests the proclamation of those who profess the gospel of Christ. In the ancient church, it helped the church to identify and denounce the heresies of Sabellianism and Arianism. Are there such heresies in the world today, which our contemporary church must identify and denounce? The religious right and the religious left fail the test of Nicene trinitarianism. Both therefore fall outside the bounds of legitimate variety in the theological expressions of the Christian church.

The doctrine of God in evangelicalism is shaped by natural theology, not by the Trinity. According to Charles Hodge, human moral nature, religious nature, and above all self-consciousness provide the basic idea of God with which Christian theology must operate. God is defined as a "being," and the idea of being is derived from human nature: "We get this idea, in the first place, from consciousness."[6] God's being is then defined further as spirit, along the same philosophical grounds of self-analysis: "In saying, therefore, that God is a Spirit, our Lord authorizes us to believe that whatever is essential to the idea of a spirit, as learned from our own consciousness, is to be referred to God as determining his nature."[7] On this basis, Hodge constructs an understanding of God common to theism, from which the Christian doctrine of the Trinity is entirely absent. Only after some 250 pages of philosophical "theism" is there a final chapter on the Trinity in Hodge's system.

Now, there is no doubt whatsoever that Hodge intends to affirm the orthodox Christian doctrine of the Trinity that the Nicene Creed enshrines, and there is no doubt that he sincerely believes he has done so. Yet he makes it clear at the outset that he distinguishes clearly the bibli-

6. Hodge, 1:367.
7. Ibid., 1:377.

cal view of the Trinity from the Nicene faith and does not believe that the Nicene Creed is binding on all Christians: "It is only the doctrine as presented in the Bible, which binds the faith and conscience of the people of God."[8] The ecclesiastical form, including the creed, is not binding. Ordinary Christians must affirm only the biblical form, which presents all truths as related to religious consciousness. Furthermore, according to Hodge, subordinationism is essential to the doctrine of the Trinity. He of course does not mean subordination according to divine nature; Hodge thoroughly condemns Arianism and semi-Arianism and teaches forthrightly the full divinity of Christ. He means rather subordination according to the internal relations of the divine persons: "The subordination intended is only that which concerns the mode of subsistence and operation, implied in the Scriptural facts that the Son is of the Father, and the Spirit is of the Father and the Son, and that the Father operates through the Son, and the Father and the Son through the Spirit."[9] No inferiority is implied. Hodge makes a further distinction between the Nicene Creed and the theology of the Nicene fathers, who argued that the eternal generation of the Son from the Father involves a communication of essence. Hodge wants to leave this issue open, because the Nicene fathers went beyond the scriptural record: "The Nicene fathers, instead of leaving the matter where the scriptures leave it, undertake to explain what is meant by sonship, and teach that it means derivation of essence."[10] Hodge wants to leave what he considers biblical ambiguity intact, in which sonship may mean simply "equality and likeness."[11] In summary, "all that is contended for is, that we are not shut up to the admission that derivation of essence is essential to sonship."[12]

In response to Hodge, the following points must be made. First, his narrow biblicism shows a deep-rooted failure to grasp the true authority of scripture as canon. Certainly the doctrine of the Trinity is not taught expressly in scripture; nevertheless, the root of the doctrine is, and later church confession is a necessary affirmation of the true reality of God to which scripture testifies. By severing scripture from the community of faith that treasures it, Hodge cuts away the ground upon which church confession has always stood and stands today. It is inadequate to suggest that the biblical doctrine of the Trinity can be affirmed without necessarily affirming the Nicene Creed. The early church did not think so, as the Athanasian Creed makes clear in the binding statements of the opening line: "Whoever wills to be saved must, above all else, hold

8. Ibid., 1:443.
9. Ibid., 1:461.
10. Ibid., 1:468.
11. Ibid., 1:469.
12. Ibid., 1:470.

the true catholic faith."[13] Nor is the matter any different at the time of the Reformation. On the Lutheran side, the Smalcald Articles, after a brief summary of the doctrine of the Trinity taken from the early creeds, states without ambiguity: "These articles are not matters of dispute or contention, for both parties confess them"[14]—that is, the Roman and Lutheran parties share the same affirmation of the trinitarian formulas of the ancient creeds. Nor is the matter any different on the Reformed side, which Hodge mistakenly claims to represent. Calvin freely acknowledges the church's right to use nonbiblical terms in order to penetrate more closely to the substance of biblical teaching: "But what prevents us from explaining in clearer words those matters in Scripture which perplex and hinder our understanding, yet which conscientiously and faithfully serve the truth of Scripture itself, and are made use of sparingly and modestly and on due occasion?"[15] The evangelical distinction between the "biblical" form and the "ecclesiastical" form is a failure to understand the very nature of church confession, in which biblical truth is secured in the church for the sake of the gospel even when nonbiblical phrases may be used. Calvin was very careful to circumscribe the limits of authority for church councils within the limits of scripture. They do not have the right to coin new doctrine, and some councils have erred. However, this did not keep him from a forceful affirmation of the early creeds: "In this way, we willingly embrace and reverence as holy the early councils, such as those of Nicaea, Constantinople, Ephesus I, Chalcedon. . . . For they contain nothing but the pure and genuine exposition of Scripture."[16] Once again, it is clear that the true origins of Hodge's approach are not in the early Reformed theology of Calvin and his school but in rationalism and pietism. Against evangelicalism, it is necessary to assert that the Nicene Creed is binding on all Christians, not alongside the authority of scripture but precisely in necessary attestation of it.

Second, Hodge's method in theology starts with a philosophical definition of God that is foreign to the true God of scripture. For all his affirmation of the authority of scripture, it is remarkable how much authority Hodge gives to general human experience and insight. Scripture is trinitarian; it is not "theistic." There is no philosophical theism in the Bible; there is only the self-revelation of God in Jesus Christ. Hodge's "theism" is ultimately a rejection of the radical claim that God's self-revelation makes upon the speech, thought, and actions of Christian people everywhere. Hodge puts God in a class (spirit) with which human beings are all too familiar and then expects the biblical God to conform to

13. *BC*, 19.
14. Ibid., 292.
15. Calvin, 1.124.
16. Ibid., 2:1171–72.

his preconceptions of deity. Hodge is radically mistaken in this procedure, for the biblical God, the triune God, is not in any class: "for I am God and no mortal, the Holy One in your midst" (Hosea 11:9). Hodge is so captivated by the idol of theism that he loses his focus upon the biblical God who is, in his inmost eternal being, a relationship of love.

Third, it is not simply that Hodge has an unbiblical view of God (theism) to which he then attaches a biblical view at the end (trinitarian). In fact, his errors of method adversely affect his grasp of the Trinity, despite his own best intentions. His strong insistence on subordinationism, which he considers essential to trinitarian doctrine, is at best suspicious. Of course Hodge fully intends an orthodox witness concerning the person of Christ. However, his inability to distinguish between the verbal sense of scripture and the true reality of which it speaks makes it impossible for him to return to scripture in the light of the subject matter, which is the whole point of dogmatic or systematic theology. It is not a matter of going beyond scripture; it is a necessary matter of gaining clarity of understanding concerning the reality of God that the church encounters through the instrument of scripture. One can only marvel at the overwhelming distance between Augustine's *On the Trinity*, with its marvelous unfolding of the beauty of divine being as a communion of love, and the lifeless propositionalism of Hodge. Against the subordinationism of Hodge, we must wholeheartedly embrace the coequality of persons as taught in the (thoroughly Augustinian) Athanasian Creed: "And among these three persons none is before or after another, none is greater or less than another, but all three persons are coequal and coeternal."[17] The eternal divine life is a coordinate diversity, not a subordinate hierarchy.

How does the religious left measure up against the standard of trinitarian confession in the mainstream church? Once again, the pace is set early by Friedrich Schleiermacher. As is well known, Schleiermacher relegated the doctrine of the Trinity to a short appendix at the conclusion of his dogmatic volume. Thus it plays no part in the shaping of his doctrine of God, which relies upon the philosophical basis of the introduction. Nor does it play any role whatsoever in the remaining doctrines of creation, grace, redemption, and so on. He makes a strong distinction between the biblical form of the doctrine as grasped by piety and the church form of the doctrine. He explains the relative absence of the doctrine from his dogmatics with the argument that the traditional church doctrine of the Trinity cannot be considered an expression of self-consciousness, in which alone God-consciousness is present, and therefore is not truly dogmatic: "But this doctrine itself, as ecclesiasti-

17. *BC*, 20.

cally framed, is not an immediate utterance concerning the Christian self-consciousness, but only a combination of several such utterances."[18] According to Schleiermacher, the doctrine of the Trinity originally had the purpose of asserting the unity of divine essence with human personality, first as the divine essence is present in Christ and second as the divine essence is present in the church through the common Spirit. Thus, the Trinity asserts the divine work of creation, reconciliation, and redemption; in other words, the economic Trinity is the only genuinely dogmatic utterance. Schleiermacher expressly and forcefully rejects the ontological Trinity as an unwarranted introduction of speculation: "But the assumption of an eternal distinction in the Supreme Being is not an utterance concerning the religious consciousness, for there it never could emerge."[19] He comments on what he considers the inability of the traditional church confession to hold in proper tension the unity and diversity in God, which always end up coming unraveled. His solution is to eliminate entirely the ontological Trinity: "We have only to do with the God-consciousness given in our self-consciousness along with our consciousness of the world; hence we have no formula for the being of God in Himself as distinct from the being of God in the world."[20] He reintroduces the Sabellian view and while reaching no definitive conclusion clearly moves in the direction of embracing it against the "Athanasian hypothesis" of ecclesiastical doctrine.

The language and conceptuality of liberalism are transformed somewhat in the twentieth century, but the clear trend toward Sabellianism is, if anything, even strengthened further. According to Paul Tillich, the trinitarian persons (Father, Son, and Holy Spirit) are Christian symbols for what concerns human beings ultimately. Like Schleiermacher, Tillich rejects the church form of the doctrine and asserts his acceptance of the familiar criticism by Adolf von Harnack of the "philosophical speculation" intruded into the gospel. There is not, nor can there be, an ontological Trinity, for this would be to confuse the infinite with the finite: "Any non-symbolic interpretation of these symbols would introduce into the Logos a finite individuality with a particular life history, conditioned by the categories of finitude."[21] For Tillich, the divine Logos is manifest in Jesus as the Christ, but there can be no exclusive identification: "The God who is seen and adored in Trinitarian symbolism has not lost his freedom to manifest himself for other worlds in other ways."[22]

18. Schleiermacher, 738.
19. Ibid., 739.
20. Ibid., 748.
21. Tillich, 3:290.
22. Ibid.

How are we to respond to the religious left? Our answer can only be a decisive no, as decisive as the Nicene Creed's rejection of the heresies of the ancient church, for the same errors are at stake in modern form. First, the liberal objection that the Nicene faith is a philosophical incursion onto pure biblical thought is not only historically false, but exactly counter to the truth. The Nicene fathers used philosophical concepts, of course, but it was to protect and elaborate the biblical witness to God's dynamic reality from unwarranted Hellenistic philosophy. On the contrary, Arianism and Sabellianism are clearly captured by a philosophical idea of divine transcendence far removed from the mystery of the God of Israel and the early church. God is transcendent over all that exists: "Am I a God near by, says the LORD, and not a God far off? Who can hide in secret places so that I cannot see them? says the LORD. Do I not fill heaven and earth? says the LORD"(Jer. 23:23–24). Yet the same God is closer to us than we are to ourselves:

> Surely, this commandment that I am commanding you today is not too hard for you, nor is it too far away. It is not in heaven, that you should say, "Who will go up to heaven for us, and get it for us so that we may hear it and observe it?" Neither is it beyond the sea, that you should say, "Who will cross to the other side of the sea for us, and get it for us so that we may hear it and observe it?" No, the word is very near to you; it is in your mouth and in your heart for you to observe. (Deut. 30:11–4)

In the light of God's redemptive act in Jesus Christ Paul adds the essential New Testament witness: "(that is, the word of faith that we proclaim)" (Rom. 10:8). The church's affirmation of both the economic and ontological Trinity is not only essential to a true understanding of the biblical witness, it is essential to faith in the gospel. Who cannot see that it is Schleiermacher's idealistic philosophy and Tillich's existentialism that keep them from embracing the church's confession of the ontological Trinity, which is itself the proper protection of the truth of the scriptural witness?

Second, what is at issue is none other than the identity of Jesus Christ. The church's confession, based on scripture, is that God is wholly present and active in Jesus Christ; that Jesus Christ is the full and truthful self-manifestation of God to all humanity. Jesus Christ is not the teacher of a divine idea, nor is he the historical embodiment of divine-human unity, nor is he the one in whom divine essence is imparted to humanity. Jesus Christ is God, truly human and truly divine. In him, the eternal God directly entered the finite world under the conditions of finitude, while yet remaining the infinite God: "Though he was in the form of God, [Christ] did not regard equality with God as something to be exploited, but emptied himself, taking the form of a slave, being born in human likeness" (Phil. 2:6). The strident unwillingness of liberalism to receive this paradox with the joyous marvel of faith is nothing other than stubborn unbelief, which the church can only set aside.

And third, the denial of the ontological Trinity on the basis of an appeal to divine freedom is a basic misunderstanding of divine love. God's entry into the world for the sake of humanity is not an act of weakness, nor a restriction of divine freedom; rather is it an act of supreme divine power in which God freely establishes with humanity the relationship of love that he himself is in all eternity. In the divine life, love is not a limitation of freedom but its true expression: "For God so loved the world that he gave his only Son" (John 3:16). Only those who profess the Nicene Creed, including the ontological Trinity, truly understand the absolute sovereignty of divine freedom. God is free not only to be himself; God is free to enter our world as a human being while yet remaining God. God is free to commit his very identity, his very being, to the good of his creatures. God is not a captive of his own love; he is free to share that love with that which is not God. God's freedom is not the freedom to be other than he is; God's true freedom is the freedom to risk establishing with another the relationship of love that he himself is. God's freedom is expressed precisely by his faithfulness to his own self-commitment: "How can I give you up, Ephraim? How can I hand you over, O Israel? How can I make you like Admah? How can I treat you like Zeboiim? My heart recoils within me; my compassion grows warm and tender. I will not execute my fierce anger; I will not again destroy Ephraim; for I am God and no mortal, the Holy One in your midst, and I will not come in wrath" (Hos. 11:8–9).

One final issue commands our attention as we in the contemporary church confess our faith in the triune God. Flowing from theological liberalism, a vast movement known as "inclusive language" has swept through many areas of the mainline churches. Now almost universally mandatory in mainstream institutions of theological education, and continually making greater inroads in the communal practice of Christian denominations, inclusive language insists that the biblical example of referring to God as "he" must be strictly eliminated from Christian speech and life. Hymns must be rewritten, biblical translations must be redone, sermons must be altered accordingly, and all theological discourse must conform to the new rule. The ideological basis for inclusive language is unquestionably straight out of classic liberalism. Just as Tillich argues that all Christian language about God is symbolic and therefore interchangeable with other symbols, so modern feminists argue that male references to God must give way to gender-neutral language. All language about God is relative, and there are many different "paradigms" of divine-human relationship. As Sallie McFague argues: "To see Christianity as a paradigm acknowledges that all our ways of imagining and talking about God are inadequate and partial, but by that we are saved from worshipping the creation of our own minds."[23] Jesus of Nazareth is a paradigmatic figure, but he is certainly not the only one. Indeed, because he was male, there is need for new models of redemptive love. According to Rosemary Ruether, "Christ is not necessarily male. . . . Christ, as redemptive person and Word of God, is not to be encapsulated 'once-for-all' in the historical Jesus. . . . We can encounter Christ *in the form of our sister.*"[24] There is no true name for God; in the place of such a name comes the liberating encounter with God/ess: "The liberating encounter with God/ess is always an encounter with our authentic selves resurrected from underneath the alienated self. . . . We have no adequate name for the true God/ess. . . . Intimations of Her/His name will appear as we emerge from false naming of God/ess modeled on patriarchal alienation."[25] The common practice for "inclusive language" is to substitute for the triune name of God (Father, Son, and Holy Spirit) other words such as "Creator, Redeemer, Sanctifier." Notice the Tillichian rejection of the scandal of particularity in the incarnation; notice the coordination of God-consciousness and self-consciousness heralded by Schleiermacher; notice also the shift from the ontological Trinity to the economic Trinity. Despite the novelty of the practice, the ideology underpinning the "inclusive language" movement is squarely grounded in theological liberalism.

In response, the issue must first of all be precisely located. I see no reason whatsoever why contemporary Christians should not avoid masculine-centered language when referring to human beings of both genders. Indeed, the gospel does break down the walls that divide human beings, including lines of gender. Disciples are women and men and should be referred to accordingly; humankind includes male and female and should not be forced into the all-male domain of "man." We live in the modern world, not the ancient world, and in our time an increased sensitivity to language that needlessly wounds and alienates is welcome in the Christian church. Only an obstreperous conservatism can fail to see that a little extra effort in transforming the way we think and speak about human beings may go a long way toward welcoming all people into the family of faith and not needlessly putting up roadblocks to belief where they do not belong. This applies to the hymns we sing, the sermons we preach, the greetings we extend, even the Bible that we

23. Hodgson and King, 381.
24. Ruether, 138.
25. Ibid., 71.

read: the New Revised Standard Version is a clear and effective model for using inclusive language for human beings. On that score, I believe that the concerns of contemporary women not only are justified but yield greater insight into the substance of our faith.

The question remains, however, whether the same concerns apply to language referring to God. There is no doubt whatsoever that God is not male; we know that, not because of the advances of modern feminist consciousness but because of the authority of scripture. God is not male, because God is not human. But nor is God a projection of human consciousness, male or female. God is not the religious expression of male or female power. God is God and makes himself known in the majesty of his own self-declaration: "But the LORD is in his holy temple; let all the earth keep silence before him!" (Hab. 2:20). God is not a set of interchangeable symbols; God has a name, which he has graciously made known for the redemption of the world: "Blessed be the name of the LORD from this time on and forevermore. From the rising of the sun to its setting the name of the LORD is to be praised" (Ps. 113:2–3). We confess before the entire world that God has a name, Father, Son, and Holy Spirit, and into that name we are all baptized. Our one commission on this earth as disciples of Jesus Christ is to teach God's triune name to the nations of the world. To suggest that God's name can be eliminated for a substitute on the basis of ideological pressure is a grave trivialization of the human encounter with the living God. God's name is God's very identity; rejection of God's name is rejection of God himself. "Holy and awesome is his name" (Ps. 111:9). Attempts to replace the name of God must be resisted in the church of Jesus Christ at all costs.

Appeals to Creator, Redeemer, Sanctifier as a substitute for Father, Son, and Holy Spirit unavoidably slide over into the heresy of Sabellianism, which argues that the real God is somehow behind the forms of manifestation. Of course we believe in the economic Trinity; we believe that God creates, redeems, sanctifies; we affirm the historical activity of the triune God in the world. Nevertheless, it is not enough to confess the economic Trinity while leaving the question of God's real being open. Why? Because God himself has not left the question open. Even before we ask the question, God has already given the answer: "I was ready to be sought out by those who did not ask, to be found by those who did not seek me. I said, 'Here I am, here I am,' to a nation that did not call on my name. I held out my hands all day long to a rebellious people, who walk in a way that is not good, following their own devices" (Isa. 65:1–2). On his own initiative and for his own gracious purpose, God makes known his exalted identity: "In the year that King Uzziah died, I saw the Lord sitting on a throne, high and lofty; and the hem of his robe filled the temple. Seraphs were in attendance above him; each had six wings: with two they covered their faces, and with two they covered their feet, and with two they flew. And one called to another and said: 'Holy, holy, holy is the LORD of hosts; the whole earth is full of his glory'" (Isa. 6:1–3). There is no valid confession of the gospel without the ontological Trinity; there is no confession of the ontological Trinity without the triune name of God, Father, Son, and Holy Spirit. It is not for nothing that our very identity as Christians is sealed by baptism into God's holy name.

Furthermore, there are valid theological grounds for retaining as normative the biblical reference to God as *he*. How do we know the triune God? We know God because God has fully and completely made himself known in Jesus of Nazareth. Jesus of Nazareth is not one paradigm among others for the true reality of God, a paradigm in need of further completion in the light of unfolding history. For Jesus is not a mere paradigm; Jesus Christ is God himself in human form. He is the true God, beside whom there is no other; he is truly human, and from him alone we learn the very meaning of our humanity. We refer to God as *he* because Jesus, the male son of a carpenter from Nazareth, is God. Now that is not to deify masculinity, for the gospel is not about masculinity but about Jesus Christ the Son of God. Jesus is not Lord because he is male, for maleness is not in any sense divine. Nevertheless, Jesus is not less than Lord even though he is male. At stake is none other than the Nicene *homoousion*. We refer to God as *he* in hymns, scripture, and theology because Jesus Christ is the God to whom we refer. The very heart of the Nicene faith in the Trinity is at stake on this issue. That does not mean that women and men alike should not share in the task of theological reflection on the true reality of God. Indeed, women have a witness to make which may very well differ from men's, and that is not a loss to the church but a gain. The full and equal participation of women in the life of the church is absolutely essential, at every level of the church's life, including dogmatic theology. The point rather is that the scandal of particularity cannot simply be erased because of the internal requirements of modern ideology.

Once again, it is useful to test the struggles of dogmatic theology against the consent of the faithful. Where does the *consensus fidelium* lie on the issue of God's triune name? The church rightly tolerates a range of flexibility in referring to God in its hymns, prayers, and liturgy. Scripture itself shows an amazing and subtle variety of modes of speaking of God, and surely the church can do no less. Nevertheless, the confession of God's triune name by the church continues to stand, despite the enormous pressures of modern ideology. On the issue of baptism, the church speaks with one voice, as sounded in *Baptism, Eucharist and Ministry*, presented by the World Council of Churches: "Baptism is administered with water in the name of the Father, the Son, and the Holy Spirit" (B17). The Trinity is not a symbol, or a concept, or a paradigm, all of which can and should shift with the changing currents of the time; the Trinity is a name, God's name, the name into which we are baptized. Should we endeavor to change God's name in the light of modern consciousness? The very question rings false. "Arise, O Lord, and let thine enemies be confounded; let them flee from thy presence that hate thy godly Name. Give thy servants strength to speak thy Word with boldness, and let all nations cleave to the true knowledge of thee. Amen."[26]

---

26. Scots Confession 25; *Conf*, 26.

Part V

The Divine Imperative

11

The Will of God

We cannot even begin to speak of the glory of the triune God without at the same time speaking of the sovereign will of that same God. The God attested in Holy Scripture never reveals himself without making an absolute claim upon the totality of human life. Knowledge of God is therefore not possible without joyful service of God. To be sure, the contrary is also true: service of God is not possible without genuine knowledge of God. To stress the indispensable role of theological ethics is not to turn dogmatics into a mere reflex of ethical self-reflection. One can speak only of a paradoxical unity in diversity; valid dogmatics of the Christian church is not possible without including theological ethics, nor is valid theological ethics possible apart from its grounding in the dogmatics of the Christian church. Both are necessary; both are interrelated; the two are bound indissolubly together. Dogmatic theology alone provides the theological basis for Christian ethics, which can in no way be separated from it; yet Christian ethics alone shows the final goal of dogmatic theology, which is the comprehensive transformation of life.

Theological ethics falls into two parts: general and special. General ethics, which is treated in the present chapter, is included after the doctrine of the Trinity in the locus on canon. Just as I raised the question of the very identity of the God whom we worship in the introductory part on canon, so do I then immediately consider the majesty of the divine command. My effort in this section is to reflect upon the nature and content of God's command as it flows from the very identity of God: the way

God's command is communicated to his creatures, the radical obedience that is owed to God, the profound and comprehensive transformation of life that the claim of God works in human existence. Special ethics is the form of the divine command as it is refracted through the remaining parts of dogmatics: on God, creation, reconciliation, redemption. Once again, there is the paradox of unity in diversity, for though special ethics is necessary in order to reflect the detailed unfolding of the rule of faith and practice, the ultimate unity of God's command can never be splintered, for there is one true God. It is here in general ethics that we lay the proper theological basis for ethical reflection in all dimensions of the Christian life.

According to the Christian confession, God's will is not unknown, or unknowable, but fully known in God's self-revelation, for God himself actively communicates his will to his creatures. If there is moral confusion, the confusion does not lie in the lack of clarity in God's self-manifestation; the confusion lies rather in the human condition. The crisis of active faith has nothing to do with a purported difficulty in discerning the true will of God for human welfare; the crisis results rather from the fact that God actively lays claim upon human life by making his will known with absolute certainty and clarity. "He has told you, O mortal, what is good; and what does the Lord require of you but to do justice, and to love kindness, and to walk humbly with your God?" (Micah 6:8). Through the revelation of his will God lays a total claim upon human life in every dimension, calling for a response of glad and eager obedience. God teaches us his will; our only proper response is to follow his will with every fiber of our being out of love for him above all things.

The modern moral project after Kant depends upon a so-called turn-to-the-subject, in which the structures of human reason and experience actively shape all interaction with the world, including moral activity. The standard ethical project in liberal theology is thus to seek some form of moral justification for Christian norms within the limits of the Kantian universe, in which the ultimate reality of God's will is simply unknowable. At best, one can only "name" God's will for one's own life. The late-twentieth-century postmodern "turn-to-the-community" in some respects offers itself as a critique of the Kantian legacy, by turning away from disembodied self-consciousness to the moral self in community. Nevertheless, seen from the point of view of Christian ethics, the turn to the community is simply a logical extension of the turn to the subject; both lead exactly nowhere in the search for the divine will. Both in the end set preconditions for divine self-communication—a profoundly ludicrous endeavor from a biblical perspective—and fail completely to reflect upon the direct self-communication of God's will through scripture that is constitutive of Christian faith. Christians may disagree, often strongly, about the content of God's will made known through the pages of the Bible, but the language of faith always and everywhere turns to scripture, not with preconditions set by the subject or the community but with open anticipation of encountering the living God anew. The real crisis that faces humanity in our time is not the moral nihilism into which the liberal project has led it, though that is certainly a terrifying corruption of human life; the real crisis is in fact the active self-communication of God's will that confronts every human being with responsibility.

On the other hand, the standard ethical project of conservative evangelicalism is to debate the Kantian legacy and the communal extension of Kant on philosophical grounds, seeking in human reason and experience some capacity for discerning the divine will objectively. Liberal apologetic is replaced by conservative apologetic. A way is sought through human "values" to tie together human reason and experience on the one hand and the content of biblical faith on the other. The conservative evangelical procedure is equally contradictory of the very heart of the biblical testimony to the reality of God. The clarity and certainty of God's revealed will is not in the slightest degree grounded in the human capacity of reason and experience. On the contrary, God's free and active communication of his will is an astonishing miracle grounded solely in God's gracious purpose for the church and for the whole world.

We must be perfectly clear at the very outset of theological ethics, or we will never gain clarity as we proceed: Why is ethics inseparable from dogmatics? Why is knowledge of God always joined to the service of God? Why must the church ever reject preconditions for theological ethics, whether in the older or newer liberalism or the older or newer evangelicalism? The answer to all of these questions is the same: because Jesus Christ is the true measure of all theological ethics. Jesus Christ is the revelation of God's will for all human life. God's will is clear and certain because Jesus Christ is the will of God incarnate. Jesus said, "I am the way, and the truth, and the life" (John 14:6); he is therefore the true measure not only of Christian doctrine but also of Christian practice. God's will is not in the realm of Kantian noumena, disengaged from the phenomenal world of human perception, because in Jesus Christ the eternal God entered human space and time in order to transform the entire cosmos. God bridged the chasm that the human condition was utterly unable to bridge, showing forth in Christ the true claim of God upon every human being in all creation. Through Jesus Christ God defeated the "turn-to-the-subject," which is humanity turned in upon itself, showing its back to God rather than its face (cf. Jer. 2:27); through Christ God defeated the "turn-to-the-community," which is humanity gathered together in pious spirituality to make a golden calf of self-chosen worship (cf. Exodus 32); through Christ God defeated the attempt to find God through rationalistic

moral calculation based on human nature, which is in fact the essence
of the fall (cf. Genesis 3). Because Jesus Christ is the true will of God,
there is no knowledge of God apart from obedience, for to know Christ
is to follow him. There can be no separation of ethics from dogmatics
because knowing the truth and doing the truth are two sides of the same
reality: only those who know Christ obey God's will, yet only those who
obey God's will know Christ. There can be no preconditions for theological
ethics whatsoever—no natural theology of moral life—because the presence of Christ is a wondrous miracle, grounded solely in God's good will
for human redemption.

If we do not ground theological ethics exclusively in Jesus Christ himself, we will never find him no matter how hard we search. There will
be, as indeed there is on both the religious left and the religious right,
nothing but a confused longing for a Word of God that never comes: "The
time is surely coming, says the Lord God, when I will send a famine on
the land; not a famine of bread, or a thirst for water, but of hearing the
words of the Lord. They shall wander from sea to sea, and from north
to east; they shall run to and fro, seeking the word of the Lord, but they
shall not find it" (Amos 8:11–12). By sharp contrast, only if we begin
theological ethics squarely in Christology do we open the door to a fresh
season of ethical reflection in the church, in which piety and spirituality
are replaced by the shining light of God's true will: "Take away from me
the noise of your songs; I will not listen to the melody of your harps. But
let justice roll down like waters, and righteousness like an ever-flowing
stream" (Amos 5:23–24).

God's will is God's command. Precisely because theological ethics is
grounded exclusively in Christology, it takes the form of command. God
actively communicates his will by giving commands. Here we link up
with a theological tradition, begun in the twentieth century, of profound
brilliance and lasting significance for the church. In his revolutionary
lecture to the church at Lentwil in the autumn of 1916 "The Strange New
World within the Bible," Barth articulated a fresh point of departure for
theological ethics:

> It is not the right human thoughts about God which form the content of
> the Bible, but the right divine thoughts about men. The Bible tells us not
> how we should talk with God but what he says to us; not how we find the
> way to him, but how he has sought and found the way to us; not the right
> relation in which we must place ourselves to him, but the covenant which
> he has made with all who are Abraham's spiritual children and which he
> has sealed once and for all in Jesus Christ. It is this which is within the
> Bible. The word of God is within the Bible.[1]

1. Barth, "Strange New World," 43.

At a time in which pietistic orthodoxy reigned on the right and various streams of theological liberalism reigned on the left, Barth clearly saw a form of command ethics grounded not in the folly of human moral preconditions but in the sovereign claim of God upon all life. Barth's initial insight was developed in a first attempt at exploiting it by Emil Brunner in his 1932 book *The Divine Imperative*. It was then given brilliant treatment in the radiant masterpiece *The Cost of Discipleship* by Dietrich Bonhoeffer (published in 1937 when he was the astonishing age of twenty-eight). It was finally fully elaborated in the successive volumes of Barth's *Church Dogmatics*, although the ethical part of the doctrine of reconciliation is only a fragment and the doctrine of redemption was unfortunately never begun. Thus, theological ethics of the divine command of the sort I am here affirming stems from a twentieth-century stream of Christian tradition hammered out largely in the church struggle in Germany, against an ideology (Nazism) that plagued the entire world.

Did divine command ethics begin only in the twentieth century? Certainly not, for in some sense every major tradition of the mainstream of Christian thought embraces the divine command as the form of God's self-communication. Nevertheless, the radical clarity with which especially Barth and Bonhoeffer saw the issue is unique in the modern period, though not without precedent. At a time of equal stress and tension in church and world, the Protestant Reformers likewise firmly embraced theological ethics of the divine command. I think it is fair and accurate to say that Barth and Bonhoeffer recovered the moral vision of the Reformers in a new era of church life and that both derived that vision from a fresh hearing of scripture in a time of great crisis in the church and the surrounding world. As is often the case in church history, development of insight does not come in the form of an easy flow of natural progression from one stage to the next but in quantum leaps of life-or-death decision in situations of grave peril and distress. To do theological ethics based on scripture in our time is, without doubt, to seek to recover the same moral vision shared by the Reformers of the sixteenth and the twentieth centuries, which is the moral vision embraced by the new world of God attested in the Bible.

But here a crucial theological advance is necessary. We are not in the exact same situation as Calvin and Luther, or indeed as Barth and Bonhoeffer. We now live in a new century, indeed in a new millennium. We face a new set of crises, both in the confessing message of the church to the world and in the structures of society that we share with our fellow human beings around the world. The command of God has not changed from the sixteenth to the twentieth to the twenty-first century, and yet the living will of God is applied to a new situation of God's people. God's

command is not changed; yet God's command speaks in a new way to
a new generation. How is this to be understood?

It is essential at this point to recognize that a decisive theological
advance has been made and that it has come not from dogmatics but
from biblical theology. In his chapter on ethics in *Biblical Theology of
the Old and New Testaments* (6.10), Brevard Childs lays the groundwork
for a fresh grasp of the divine command by strengthening the living
theological connection between God's active communication of his will
and Holy Scripture, a connection that the church has always made in
principle but that Childs has seen more clearly in its full implication
than any scholar of the church before. Barth and Bonhoeffer clearly
recovered the vertical dimension of all true theological ethics, in which
humanity comes face to face with the living God. Genuine theological
ethics is an ethics of encounter, indeed an ethics of event in which the
living God directly seizes human life from above. God calls Abram:
"Now the LORD said to Abram, 'Go from your country and your kindred
. . . and I will bless you" (Gen. 12:1–2). Jesus says to Matthew the tax
collector, "Follow me," and he arises and follows him (Matt. 9:9). God's
command comes as God's word, without any preconditions and without any correlation with human reason and experience. The vertical
dimension of encounter with the living will of God directly undercuts
the spurious ethics of both the religious left and the religious right. Yet
Childs's work on canon is crucial and right at this point in the inner
ordering of dogmatic theology. The vertical dimension— the movement
of God's living will from one situation of human life to the next and
the direct encounter with God's absolute claim upon human life in the
immediacy of the living moment—intersects the horizontal dimension
of the biblical witness. God speaks only in the here and now; yet he
speaks only through the instrument of scripture, which is treasured as
the source of ethical instruction by each new generation of the church
of Jesus Christ. The essence of Childs's proposal on canon is to hold the
vertical and horizontal dimensions of scripture in creative, dialectical
tension. On the one hand, the living God directly encounters the church
through the Bible; biblicist proof-texts are shattered by the living voice
of God. On the other hand, scripture is shaped as the means by which
God continually addresses the church anew; God's living claim is always
through the word of scripture. Because of Childs's work on scripture as
canon, it is now essential to state without ambiguity: the moral vision
of the divine command is at the same time a new vision of the role of
scripture in the life of the church.

The obverse relation is also equally true: a new vision of the role of
scripture in the life of the church is at the same time a recovery of the
moral vision of the divine command. Thus we cannot simply return to

Calvin and Luther or to Barth and Bonhoeffer, despite the overwhelming insights they continue to teach us. It is ultimately through scripture
itself that Christ the risen Lord addresses the church of the present day,
and it is to scripture itself that we in the contemporary church must turn
seeking the will of God for our world. As Childs has convincingly shown,
scripture itself is shaped for the very purpose of playing the role it plays
in the household of faith. It is shaped, in detail and as a whole, for the
purpose of serving as the instrument by which the living Lord calls his
people to follow him in each new generation, facing the problems not of
the past but of the present. What is God's will for the world today? In the
end, that is the only serious question for theological ethics. Where do we
look in order to find our answer? Instructed by the moral vision of our
ancestors in the faith, we turn directly to sacred scripture with fear and
trembling, yet with unbreakable confidence that it unerringly points us
to the goodness of God's will in the joy of discipleship. For that reason,
general ethics as I describe it follows the Trinity in the part on canon, the
former context making clear the vertical dimension, the latter context
underscoring the horizontal dimension. Theological ethics is grounded
in the sovereign reality of the triune God; its content is to be sought with
eagerness and anticipation in the pages of Holy Scripture, where that
very God addresses his people in each new generation afresh.

Theological ethics of the divine command rejects any form of absolute
morality—that is, any attempt at constructing a rational system of values
or virtues in abstraction from the living person of God. God's commands
cannot be treated as self-grounded and self-sustaining moral principles
subject to human manipulation, especially pious manipulation. Every
such attempt inevitably brings evasion of the genuine claim of God, usually without any self-awareness of what has been lost. Only God opens
human eyes to a true understanding of his living will; every moralistic
attempt at wresting the divine command from the living God by moral
calculation leads only to moral blindness. As Jesus says after healing
the blind man: "I came into this world for judgment so that those who
do not see may see, and those who do see may become blind" (John
9:39). The command of God can never rightly be turned into an ethic
of moral values without losing the only thing that truly matters, which
is the living God himself.

Similarly, theological ethics of the divine command rejects any form
of casuistic or rationalistic application of the biblical text, as if true illumination of God's will were achieved by passing the witness of scripture
through a technique of rational human construction. Application of the
biblical text to the living moment is a gift of God through the presence
of the Spirit; it is not a human achievement based on any purported
capacity of spiritual insight or rational discernment. Micah exposes

the folly of an ever-ascending attempt to find God through moral self-transcendence: "With what shall I come before the LORD, and bow myself before God on high? Shall I come before him with burnt offerings, with calves a year old? Will the LORD be pleased with thousands of rams, with ten thousands of rivers of oil? Shall I give my firstborn for my transgression, the fruit of my body for the sin of my soul?" (Micah 6:6–7). God's will cannot be found through rational moral effort nor through pious self-affirmation; the gift of moral clarity comes through the Word of God, who declares without ambiguity the true content of his eternal will in the given moment.

Unfortunately the ethical confusion that appeals to "principles" and "values" and "virtues" in abstraction from the living God himself—who gives the knowledge of his will through concrete commands, not through moral principles—is endemic and early in the theological tradition. The confusion appears already in Augustine and spreads far afield. In his *Faith, Hope, and Charity* Augustine offers a profound and convincing theological ethic of the divine command, though without much detail. He describes true liberty as the "joy experienced in doing what is right."[2] Then he expands his point by referring to the self-declaration of the divine will in the command: "At the same time it [liberty] is a holy servitude arising from obedience to precept."[3] Here is contained the marvelous paradox of all Christian ethics: genuine freedom comes from service to God's revealed will, which rescues the sinner from compulsion to self-love and gives the freedom to live in authentic goodness before God. Later in the same volume he adds the well-known Augustinian dialectic that the love of God and neighbor is the true measure of the commandment, while the commandment is the true expression of all charity: "Accordingly, all the divine commandments hark back to charity."[4] Charity is a gift of the Holy Spirit; for that reason the law can only be fulfilled through the divine presence: "For without the Gift of God, that is, without the Holy Spirit, through whom charity is diffused in our hearts, the law can command, but cannot help."[5] So far so good, for here Augustine is operating within the basic stance of faith seeking understanding as it applies to theological ethics. Theological ethics demands careful rational reflection, but reflection is based on faith in the divine command and seeks to discern the divine purpose as it interprets the true content of the command. Reflection does not abandon the command nor seek in any way to correlate it with something else in an ethical version of natural theology.

2. Augustine, *Faith, Hope, and Charity*, 38.
3. Ibid., 38.
4. Ibid., 111.
5. Ibid., 109.

Things are very different, however, when one turns to Augustine's presentation in *Of the Morals of the Catholic Church*. Once again there is the concerted attempt to hold to a genuine theological ethic. Thus God himself is the ultimate measure of the good: "The perfection of all our good things and our perfect good is God. We must neither come short of this nor go beyond it: the one is dangerous, the other impossible."[6] If only Augustine had stopped here at this fine statement of the unbreakable bond between God and his command! Unfortunately, he does not but goes on to introduce the very alien language of virtues, clearly borrowed from the Neoplatonic philosophical inheritance: "As to virtue leading us to a happy life, I hold virtue to be nothing else than perfect love of God."[7] The four virtues (from Greek philosophical tradition) are in fact identical to four different forms of love. Each of the primary virtues, temperance, fortitude, justice, and prudence, is then defined by Augustine in reference to the modification of love that it manifests. Theological ethics proceeds in the form of analysis of the four virtues, of which scripture provides the primary examples.

Now, it is clear that Augustine has no intention whatsoever of introducing into theological ethics principles of interpretation—based on the philosophy of virtue—side by side with the reality of God. Quite the contrary, for Augustine continues to assert the basic logic of faith seeking understanding. For example, he makes the following clear affirmation of God's authority as the sole norm of appeal for all theological ethics: "Hence arises that principle on which we have all along insisted, that there is nothing more wholesome in the Catholic Church than using authority before judgment."[8] The authority of God is the only ground for the good, not human rational testing. Furthermore, he clearly intends not to sell out the gospel to Greek morality but to infuse the Greek virtues with the new meaning of agapic love. Nevertheless, despite his good intention, his introduction of the language of virtue in fact compromises the form of the divine command in favor of a rival ethic of self-analytical application. God's command is subsumed under the manipulable quantities of human moral virtue. An unfortunate impediment to genuine command ethics is introduced into the very heart of church tradition.

Given the authority of Augustine, it is no surprise to find the same confusion in Thomas, who goes even further by expressly correlating virtue with human reason: "Whatever accords with reason is humanly good, whatever goes against reason humanly bad."[9] Theological ethics of the divine command has been put into the alien theological context

6. Augustine, *On the Morals*, 45.
7. Ibid., 48.
8. Ibid., 55.
9. Aquinas, 249.

of human rational calculation, a position radically alien to the witness of scripture. Thomas only makes matters worse by his introduction of natural law, the ethical corollary of natural theology: "The light of natural reason, whereby we discern what is good and what is evil, which is the function of the natural law, is nothing else than an imprint on us of the Divine light."[10] Suddenly Augustine's adherence to divine authority has been expanded to include a correlation of divine authority and the authority of human reason, which somehow knows the content of God's eternal law. The same ethic of virtues is found in Bonaventure,[11] making it clear that the problem is not a narrowly Thomistic one.

The confusion is not cleared up in the contemporary *Catechism of the Catholic Church*. A beginning is made in the right direction by a clear and forceful confession of the christological basis of theological ethics: "The first and last point of reference of this catechesis will always be Jesus Christ himself."[12] Yet almost immediately the christological reference is left behind by appeal to human reason: "By his reason, man recognizes the voice of God which urges him 'to do what is good and avoid what is evil.'"[13] One is surely left to ask: what happened to the clear christological orientation of theological ethics, which is now suddenly beholden to human reason alongside of Christ himself? Moreover, freedom, which in Augustine is defined as service of God, is now defined in reference to innate human capacity for moral reflection: "Freedom is the power, rooted in reason and will, to act or not to act, to do this or that, and so to perform deliberate actions on one's own responsibility."[14] Again one must ask: where in all of scripture is there the slightest indication of an ethic grounded in "one's own responsibility"? On the contrary, for Christian life "living is Christ" (cf. Phil. 1:21). Again, moral acts are subject to the rational calculation of object, intention, and circumstances.[15] Where is the crystal-clear call of discipleship, which comes without any reference whatsoever to object, intention, and circumstances: "Come and see" (John 1:39)? Finally, conscience is defined as the voice of God in the depths of the rational structure of the person, having the role of connecting general principles of morality to concrete circumstances.[16] Yet such an understanding stems from the Greek philosophical tradition and contradicts at the most basic level the biblical witness to the sovereignty of God alone in laying claim to the moral life of humankind: "Thus says

10. *ST*, 2.997.
11. See Bonaventure, 193.
12. *Cat*, 423.
13. Ibid., 425.
14. Ibid., 430.
15. Ibid., 434.
16. Ibid., 438–9.

the Lord: Do not let the wise boast in their wisdom, do not let the mighty boast in their might, do not let the wealthy boast in their wealth; but let those who boast boast in this, that they understand and know me, that I am the Lord; I act with steadfast love, justice, and righteousness in the earth, for in these things I delight, says the Lord" (Jer. 9:23–24).

Several issues are at stake in rejecting the introduction of virtues, principles, or values side by side with the divine command, together with the natural theology that undergirds such language. First and most important is the self-grounded authority of Jesus Christ the risen Lord. There can be no absolute morality centered in rational moral consistency, for Jesus Christ alone is Head of the church. He and he alone defines what is good and right for his disciples. Through the witness of scripture, Christ calls his followers to radical obedience based solely and only upon his inherent authority to command. The commands of Jesus Christ create their own ethical space, and every human effort to provide additional rational backing only corrupts and distorts the very commands being sought. Of course there is no intention in those who speak on Christian grounds of moral "values" to undercut the authority of Christ; indeed, the endeavor is precisely to make that authority count. However, any appeal to values severs the living connection between Christ and his command. The command of Christ is falsely turned into a human moral value, whereas the role of the gospel is never to confirm human moral values but solely and completely to overturn them.

Second, Jesus Christ exercises his living authority over the church because he is risen and present. Grounded solely in his divine prerogative as Lord of all creation, Christ actively communicates his command to each new generation of the church through the witness of scripture. Christ sends his Spirit into the church to guide each new generation to a living understanding of his will for all dimensions of life in the world. The role of the church is one of service to Christ, not partnership. We make no ethical claim whatsoever, instead gladly conceding all authority to Christ alone: "So you also, when you have done all that you were ordered to do, say, 'We are worthless slaves; we have done only what we ought to have done!'" (Luke 17:10).

Third, the doing of God's revealed will is in no way whatsoever an exercise of natural human capacity. On the contrary, the source of the new life of Christian obedience is the energy of the Holy Spirit, who pervades the whole life of the human person and comes only as a miraculous gift. Freedom is a gift of the Spirit, not a human capacity, and is exercised not as self-grounded rational responsibility but as eager and joyful obedience to Christ: "For the law of the Spirit of life in Christ Jesus has set you free from the law of sin and of death" (Rom. 8:2). Despite its best intentions, the ethic of value—whether liberal or conservative—undercuts the work of the Spirit in the church, who fashions all things anew according to the sovereign purpose of God. The work of the Spirit is an ultimate mystery and is not coordinated by human definition of moral need or moral justification. What is at stake is a new creation, a new birth: "What is born of the flesh is flesh, and what is born of the Spirit is Spirit. . . . The wind blows where it chooses, and you hear the sound of it, but you do not know where it comes from or where it goes. So it is with everyone who is born of the Spirit" (John 3:6, 8).

Fourth, theological ethics of the divine command must everywhere reckon with the frailty of the human condition, which, far from the inherent quality of virtues and values, is sinful to the core: "The heart is devious above all else; it is perverse—who can understand it?" (Jer. 17:9). We need God's command for all guidance, for apart from his active revelation of his will we are all prone to human schemes ending only in moral failure of the worst kind. The role of God's command is not to serve as the basis for a correlation with human moral value. The role of God's command is radical transformation of our entire being through concrete obedience: "I appeal to you therefore, brothers and sisters, by the mercies of God, to present your bodies as a living sacrifice, holy and acceptable to God, which is your spiritual worship. Do not be conformed to this world, but be transformed by the renewing of your minds, so that you may discern what is the will of God—what is good and acceptable and perfect" (Rom. 12:1–2).

And finally, dogmatic theology, of which theological ethics is a part, must find its fundamental relationship to scripture through the help provided by biblical theology. Biblical theology has roundly rejected all appeals to absolute morality in abstraction from God himself.[17] How then can dogmatic theology simply turn to another mode of discourse altogether, despite the distinguished lineage of Augustine? Instead, dogmatic theology must return to scripture itself seeking a fresh vision of the majesty of God's sovereign will, in which alone is contained the well-being of all humanity. As in all other parts of dogmatic theology, so also in theological ethics we are not here limited to biblical theology. Theological ethics of the divine command has a different responsibility from biblical theology, for here too we are reading scripture as a whole in the light of God's will, striving to understand and reflect upon that will in the context of our contemporary world, seeking to express the divine command in words appropriate to our era. Nevertheless, while dogmatic theology undertakes a different labor with a different set of responsibilities, it begins its task by finding its way to scripture through the guidance of biblical theology. Since biblical theology has excluded

17. *BTONT,* 713.

such common appeals to ethical values and rational calculation, we today must search for a new form of theological ethics.

Two brief examples will illustrate the scope of the problem. The standard approach among conservative evangelicals is to merge the Ten Commandments into a rhetoric of "traditional values." Usually the tone is apologetic, as if striving to "defend" or even to "return" to such values. Efforts are often made in the legal realm to introduce the Ten Commandments into the public sector, disguised in the form of cherished communal values. Of course the intentions are noble; there is no doubt, as we shall see, that the Ten Commandments are at the heart of theological ethics. That is not where the dispute occurs. The dispute occurs rather when conservative evangelicalism seeks to place the law of God attested in scripture in the profoundly alien context of human moral values. The Ten Commandments are to be cherished because they are the revealed will of the living God, not because they are traditional moral norms of the community. Jesus attacks the Pharisees on just this point of confusing the divine will with moral custom (Matt. 15:1–9). The divine law is wrenched from the hand of God when it is made subject to moral value and becomes subject to human moral manipulation—always a prescription for disaster. For in human hands, moral values are easily twisted to serve self-interest in a way that directly contravenes the divine will. Jesus quotes Isaiah (from the LXX) to seal his point: "This people honors me with their lips, but their hearts are far from me; in vain do they worship me, teaching human precepts as doctrines" (Matt. 15:8–9). Despite good intentions, folding the law of God into an ethic of moral values is in fact an affront to the living God himself, who will not hand over to human beings the moral authority that is his alone. "Traditional values" underwrite the status quo in society; "traditional values" are unable to respond in moments when God himself brings change, as in the Emancipation Proclamation, or the civil rights struggle, or the struggle against apartheid. "Traditional values" lead to a cultural Christianity that undercuts the radical call of discipleship and in the end renders null and void the very obedience that is sought.

What is particularly ironic is that the language of "values" in fact stems from none other than Ritschlian liberalism. It was Albrecht Ritschl who argued in his *Theology and Metaphsics* for a post-Kantian ethic of value: "In all of its forms, the religious world view is established on the principle that the human spirit differentiates itself to some degree in value from the phenomena within its environment and from the workings of nature that press in upon it."[18] Based on this insight, Ritschl developed an ethic of values (see his *Instruction in the Christian Religion*) that he

18. Ritschl, 156.

then passed on, for example, to his disciple Adolf von Harnack: "The man who can say 'My Father' to the Being who rules heaven and earth, is thereby raised above heaven and earth, and himself has a value which is higher than all the fabric of this world. . . . It is here, truly, that the highest significance of great men lies: to have enhanced, that is, to have progressively given effect to human value, to the value of that race of men which has risen up out of the dull ground of Nature."[19] Without knowing it, the religious right is in fact defending a profoundly modern ethical concept, completely without any foundation in scripture or the confessing faith. The Bible knows nothing of "values"; it knows only the sovereign commands of God that undercut entirely every human value for the sake of God's living will.

One such "traditional value" was the segregation of the races in North American life. In the face of such evil racism, Dr. Martin Luther King Jr. attacked the system of racism in the name of the gospel. He acted as a witness of Jesus Christ throughout his ministry and died as a martyr of Christ. There is no doubt whatsoever that King spoke the living command of Christ confronting the situation in church and society. He did not pit black against white; on the contrary, he attacked the *system* of racism, which had in fact destroyed the humanity of both oppressed and oppressor: "We do not seek to remove this unjust system for ourselves alone but for our white brothers as well. The festering sore of segregation debilitates the white man as well as the Negro."[20] He struggled not for a triumph of one race over another but for the emergence of a new community of racial harmony: "It must be made palpably clear that resistance and nonviolence are not in themselves good. There is another element that must be present in our struggle that then makes our resistance and nonviolence truly meaningful. That element is reconciliation. Our ultimate end must be the creation of the beloved community."[21] He carefully avoided the means of violence, on the grounds that whatever means are employed already determine what will come as the end to be achieved.

King called upon the universal church to support civil rights and clearly had every reason and right to do so; his cause was just and should have been fully and actively supported by everyone, black and white. When it was not, King rightly chided the white church, including the white clergy, for their lukewarm inaction. In his *Letter from Birmingham Prison* to his fellow clergy, he laid out clear grounds for the transforming claim of the gospel upon all who serve Christ: "Injustice anywhere is a threat

19. Harnack, *What Is Christianity?* 67.
20. King, 145.
21. Ibid., 140.

to justice everywhere."[22] He expressed his frustration and exasperation at the white Christian community that ignored civil rights in the name of "moral values": "I have almost reached the regrettable conclusion that the Negro's great stumbling block in his stride toward freedom is not the White Citizen's Counciler or the Ku Klux Klanner, but the white moderate, who is more devoted to 'order' than to justice; who prefers a negative peace which is the absence of tension to a positive peace which is the presence of justice . . . who paternalistically believes that he can set a timetable for another man's freedom. . . . Lukewarm acceptance is much more bewildering than outright rejection."[23] King carefully avoided the black nationalism of the left yet also the complacency of the right: "I have tried to stand between these two forces, saying that we need emulate neither the 'do-nothingism' of the complacent nor the hatred and despair of the black nationalist. For there is the more excellent way of love and nonviolent protest."[24] Despite the clear and absolute claim that the civil rights struggle had on all Christians, many resisted or at best remained silent. King was therefore fully justified and right to express disappointment at the failure of those who, in the name of Christianity, clung to "traditional values" and denied the gospel: "I must honestly reiterate that I have been disappointed with the Church. I do not say this as one of those negative critics who can always find something wrong with the Church. I say this as a minister of the gospel, who loves the Church; who was nurtured in its bosom; who has been sustained by its spiritual blessings and who will remain true to it as long as the cord of life shall lengthen."[25] The gospel brings radical transformation of the whole world; those who cling to "traditional values" remove themselves from the presence of Christ.

"Injustice anywhere is a threat to justice everywhere." Even so, we in the Christian church today cannot stand idly by when injustice is allowed to flourish anywhere in the world. In particular, we fully support the just rights of the Palestinian people to a homeland. Of course, at the same time we embrace the right of Israel to secure existence within secure borders, free from the threat of terror. We join with the whole civilized world in denouncing acts of terror, including Palestinian terror. Nevertheless, now is the time for a just settlement of the conflict. Now is the time for compromise. Now is the time for oppression to end and justice to prevail. Now is the time for ancient hatreds to give way to a new era of peace. Now is the time for former enemies to become new friends in a new era of mutual respect. One more life wasted is one life

22. Ibid., 189.
23. Ibid., 195.
24. Ibid., 197.
25. Ibid., 199.

too many. In the eloquent words of Yitzhak Rabin, himself a martyr to peace: "We say to you today in a loud and clear voice: Enough of blood and tears. Enough. We harbor no hatred towards you. We have no desire for revenge. We, like you, are people who want to build a home, plant a tree, love, live side by side with you—in dignity, in empathy, as human beings, as free people. We are today giving peace a chance and saying to you: Enough. Let us pray that a day will come when we all will say: Farewell to arms."[26] It is time for the so-called security wall to be torn down; it is time for the Palestinian people to enjoy a meaningful state with contiguous territory. In the end, the only answer is forgiveness.

"Injustice anywhere is a threat to justice everywhere." As Christians, we renounce every form of imperialism in the name of Jesus Christ. Our renunciation of imperialism is not new; already Augustine in his magnum opus *The City of God* explained the fall of the Roman Empire in terms of the Romans' insatiable lust for power. There is, according to Augustine, in all persons and societies a will to dominate the other; the effort of one state to dominate another state is another expression of that terrifying impulse. In our world today, hidden behind every form of imperial aggression, even in the name of advancing the cause of "freedom," are the hidden perversions of national self-interest, the avarice of multinational corporations, the hideous abuse of the weak by the strong. We join with Christians everywhere in condemning the war in Iraq as a misguided application of just war theory in the name of the "moral value" of freedom. We wholeheartedly affirm freedom, and we are glad to see the end of a brutal tyrant; we cannot, however, accept that true freedom is the authentic horizon of military action in Iraq. Good intentions do not make war good. It is to be hoped that a genuinely free Iraq will emerge in the years ahead. However, if it does so, it will be because the sovereign God is able to bring good out of evil; it will not be because the war is morally justifiable. The advent of Jesus Christ is the end of all empire.

On the religious left, "reconciliation" is the oft-chosen moral principle by which to organize a systematic theological ethic. Once again, biblical texts, contrary to both the profound variety of biblical ethical concern and the theocentric grounding of all biblical ethics, are forced into a value-based conceptual mold that completely seizes ethical control away from God and places it in human hands. Every problem in human life is approached in terms of possible "reconciliation" between opposing parties. Now liberalism is certainly right: reconciliation is a clear sign of God's mysterious rule breaking into historical reality. When genuine reconciliation occurs, it is to be celebrated with deep gratitude. The clear

26. Gilbert, 632.

problem, however, is this: What about those horrific occasions in human history when radical evil shows its ugly face in the world? Are there not moments in human experience—thankfully rare—when reconciliation is impossible without compromising the true freedom and dignity of human life? Clearly, in the twentieth century, both fascism and communism proved to be radically evil forms of tyranny that offered nothing but oppression and despair to humanity as a whole. An abstract ethic of "reconciliation" can say nothing when the time of reckoning comes, when the absolute need arises for resistance to evil.

One such example occurred during the Peasants' War at the height of the Reformation. The peasants in Germany were in revolt against the landed classes for the injustice and tyranny that they exercised. Martin Luther was called upon by the peasants to address their grievances, for they understood their activities as an extension of his preaching of the gospel in a new way. Luther first voiced his concerns in the *Admonition to Peace* of 1525. Without any question, Luther blamed the rulers for what was occurring. Their efforts to squeeze the poor in order to support their own profligate lifestyle was the direct cause of unrest among the poor: "We have no one on earth to thank for this disastrous rebellion, except you princes and lords, and especially you blind bishops and mad priests and monks, whose hearts are hardened even to this present day. . . . You do nothing but cheat and rob the people so that you may lead a life of luxury and extravagance."[27] Luther points to the wrath of God against their cruel tyranny as the source of present woes. Rulers are appointed by God to care for the welfare of their subjects, but these rulers have abandoned justice for the sake of sheer greed. Nevertheless, while siding fully with the just claims of the peasants against the rulers, Luther likewise admonishes the peasants at all costs to avoid armed struggle as a means to achieve their aims. Citing Matthew 26:52 (all who take the sword will perish by the sword), Luther urges them to choose peaceful means to gain their just demands: "No one by his own violence, shall arrogate authority to himself."[28] Their situation, however unjust, is no excuse for pursuing lawful ends by unlawful means: "We do not have the right to use the sword simply because someone has done us an injustice and because the law and justice are on our side."[29] Having addressed first rulers, then peasants, Luther concludes by calling both to cordial reconciliation. Both sides need to learn the true meaning of justice. Luther recommends a course of binding arbitration carried out by representatives from both groups in dialogue.

27. *LW,* 46:19.
28. Ibid., 46:24.
29. Ibid., 46:30.

Luther's initial moderation is commendable and surely accords with the spirit of the gospel. However, the course of events had already overtaken his call to reconciliation. The peasants, egged on by Thomas Müntzer and others, went on a violent rampage. Luther then published his more famous treatise *Against the Robbing and Murdering Hordes of Peasants*, in which he calls upon the rulers to hunt down the peasants like dogs in the streets. By cloaking their murder and robbery under the guise of the gospel, they were committing blasphemy and therefore merited death.

Thus Luther began by pursuing the path of peace and reconciliation. He was surely right to do so, and one can only applaud his sympathy for the plight of the peasants. However, reconciliation became impossible once violence was embraced. The chaos of violence could be stopped only by the power of the sword. Of course this is not to endorse the unbridled exercise of force by the state, as later Lutheranism tended to do. Luther himself was horrified by the butchery of the peasants by the princes. Calvin in particular clearly saw that even duly constituted states can oppress their people and under certain conditions violent revolution by the people is sometimes the only option. The point rather is that while reconciliation between opposing parties is the highest good and the surest course, there are at least some circumstances in which it becomes impossible short of war, despite its frightful cost.

A second example will amplify the point. The North American church pursued an ethically vacuous course in the early 1930s. Confronted by the growing threat of German fascism, the Christian community tended to embrace a liberal gospel of love that held out the hope of ultimate acceptance of the new German movement. Support for war was considered unchristian on any grounds, for the love ethic of Jesus surely forbids taking up arms against anyone, including one's enemy. Once again, one can only agree with the fundamental instincts: Do we not as Christians believe in peace? Do we not desire peace on earth above all things? Nevertheless, it is one thing to desire peace above all; it is quite another to declare war unjust under any circumstances. It was in the context of such ethical paralysis in the face of radical evil that Reinhold Niebuhr wrote his brilliant essay "Why the Christian Church Is Not Pacifist." Only then was the church shaken out of its moralistically pure principle to confront the true complexity of life under the living command of God. According to Niebuhr, the living will of God must be lived out within the realities of this world; a pietistic withdrawal from that world will have the paradoxical effect of ensuring the ultimate triumph of evil within it. Even war is sometimes necessary for the sake of peace. Moreover, against the rising tide of Nazi terror, the confessing church in Germany did not in the slightest degree pursue an ethic of "reconciliation." In the Barmen

Declaration it called rather for resistance: "If you find that we are speaking contrary to Scripture, then do not listen to us! But if you find that we are taking our stand upon Scripture, then let no fear or temptation keep you from treading with us the path of faith and obedience to the Word of God, in order that God's people be of one mind upon earth."[30] Similarly, Niebuhr both exposes and attacks the "noxious demonry" of communism in his essay "Why Is Communism So Evil?" He declaims communism as an ideology "more dangerous than Nazism," which brings nothing but "nightmare" to millions of the world.[31] Thus despite the genuine desire for reconciliation, the church of the twentieth century was forced to draw firm lines against two equally demonic ideologies, even to the point of armed conflict when absolutely necessary.

An ethic of "reconciliation" cannot say no, even when the gospel says no, for the sake of human welfare. But as with both fascism and communism, there are times when the church must join with the world in saying no, even to the point of supporting armed conflict in a just war against radical evil. Of course not all war is just; however, as a last resort, support for war is a necessary dimension of Christian witness under certain conditions. Who can now deny that the same is true of the war against terrorism, which likewise presents to the world nothing but unredeemable evil? Christians have no desire for a war against followers of Islam; God's redeeming love embraces the entire cosmos, including the whole of humankind. We believe in equal rights for all people, regardless of religion, and we renounce the crusading mentality. We support an open and tolerant society in which all people, whatever their religious convictions, are embraced with equal rights under the law. We denounce the idea that Christians have any special privileges or prerogatives, any special status or superior vantage point. We denounce the notion of an established Christian religion as contrary to the gospel of Christ. What controls all our actions in relation to our neighbor, including our Muslim neighbor, is the sovereign command of Christ: "Do not judge, so that you may not be judged. For with the judgment you make you will be judged, and the measure you give will be the measure you get" (Matt. 7:1–2). Moreover, we vigorously support the rights of the Palestinian people to a homeland of their own. We deplore the Israelis' excessive use of force against innocent civilians and firmly believe not in a "greater Israel" but in a two-state solution. The Palestinian people must be given a viable state, and the Christian church must stand with the full weight of its ministry with them in their quest, even if that means direct and open criticism of Israeli policy. However, we also support

---

30. *Conf*, 256.
31. Niebuhr, "Why Is Communism So Evil?" 54, 60.

just war against those who would use religious language as a cover for fanatical and barbaric acts of cruel murder.

God's will is God's command, actively communicated by God to his children through the instrument of scripture. In making himself known in Jesus Christ, God lays a total claim upon the whole person, calling for an active and eager embrace of obedience through faith in his Word. Yet here we must make a clear distinction: while God's will for human life is clear and certain, the mystery of God's gracious purpose is reserved for God's own free majesty. God declares his will, yet God retains for himself the gracious purpose of his acts in human life and history. In scripture, whenever God reveals, he also at the same time conceals. According to Exodus 33:11, "The LORD used to speak to Moses face to face, as one speaks to a friend." God reveals himself to Moses with astonishing intimacy. God clearly makes his will known. Indeed God makes known to Moses his very identity and declares his name (Exod. 33:19). Yet Moses catches a glimpse only of God's retreating back, while God shields Moses from seeing his form directly (Exod. 33:23). Not even Moses can see God's face.

God's living will is made known for all the world in Jesus Christ. Through his command, God guides the whole of life according to his gracious purpose for human welfare. Our greatest joy on this earth is to give pleasure to God by the enjoyment of life under his pleasant ordering. Nevertheless, obedience to the command is one thing, and complete knowledge of God's purpose is quite another. We are not called upon to act because we fully understand God's purpose, for we do not. We are called upon to act because God has commanded us to act; only God knows fully his purpose in his commands. Clearly, there are times when faith is challenged by a seeming contradiction between God's clear command and God's hidden purpose. Abraham is commanded by God to sacrifice Isaac in direct contradiction to God's promise (Genesis 22). Here faith can only obey God's command and leave the accomplishment of God's purpose to God alone. "Once God has spoken; twice have I heard this: that power belongs to God" (Ps. 62:11). To obey is to do the will of God, leaving in God's hands the accomplishment of his wondrous purpose for all humanity. The one criterion that applies is faithfulness; success is not relevant to the serious ethic of discipleship.

12

The Law of Christ

God's self-revelation in Jesus Christ brings with it a claim of obedience for all humanity. That claim comes in the form of God's command, which cannot be abstracted from the living person of God himself. Jesus Christ the risen Lord is the one ultimate measure of God's will for all humanity. Scripture is the instrument through which the living call to discipleship comes upon every new generation of the church. In respect to all of these statements I am in full agreement with the command ethic of Barth and Bonhoeffer, which in every respect provides the church with sure guidance in a new direction for Christian obedience. But here we must take one step further. Instructed by biblical theology, the theological ethics of dogmatic theology must be open to a fresh proposal for handling the biblical text. Where do we look in scripture for our fundamental bearings on the life that pleases God?

Certainly every part of the canon can and does provide profound insight for the church's ongoing task of wrestling with the ultimate ethical question: what does Jesus Christ command the church in our contemporary world? Barth himself spoke of ethical summaries contained in the Bible, and Bonhoeffer filled out the divine claim by exposition of the Sermon on the Mount. In doing so, neither theologian compromised in any way the vertical dimension of the divine will. God's living will is an event in which human beings encounter the absolute reality of God that undercuts every ethical system or ideology. Nevertheless, to speak of God's will is to speak of the light of truth that Christ the living Lord shines upon human life. What is the content of that truth?

Dogmatic theology must get its bearings from biblical theology as it searches the scriptures. It must engage in critical discernment of the inner logic of divine truth, including the truth of God's living command. God's command is God's law. In binding himself to a people, God does not leave his claim upon that people unknown or uncertain; on the contrary, God himself declares his sovereign will in the majesty of his freedom. Because of his gracious redemption of his people, God has the right to announce his just requirement for their life of obedience. The Old Testament speaks of a new covenant in which God will write his law on the very hearts of his people: "But this is the covenant that I will make with the house of Israel after those days, says the LORD: I will put my law within them, and I will write it on their hearts; and I will be their God, and they shall be my people" (Jer. 31:33–34). Jesus Christ is the fulfillment of the promise of God; Jesus Christ is the new covenant; Jesus Christ is the law of God written on the hearts of his disciples.

The law of God is God's word of command for his people. Now, before we take a single step further, it is necessary to consider the dialectical shape of the law of God. Instructed by scripture as a whole, we must first of all recognize that the law is the realm of death. No human being can find God through the law. Moral effort will in no way put a human being right with God. It is through the gospel, not through the law, that God's redemptive love comes to all humanity. We know this to be true not because of a pessimistic view of human nature; instead, it is in God's act of salvation through Jesus Christ that the power of the law is exposed as impotent. The atoning death of Christ, not moral striving of any kind, reconciles humanity to God. "Christ is the end of the law" (Rom. 10:4). Here there can be no compromise with the legalistic moralism that time and again threatens the health and vitality of the church. If we today in the church are to rediscover the law of Christ in the search for active discipleship, we must constantly be on our guard not to fall back into the slavery of legalism. A rigid legalism has nothing to do with genuine obedience to God's revealed will: "For freedom Christ has set us free. Stand firm, therefore, and do not submit again to a yoke of slavery" (Gal. 5:1).

On the other hand, through faith in Jesus Christ, which is a gift of the Holy Spirit, we are set free from the realm of death to newness of life in obedience to Christ. Through the presence of the Spirit, we walk by faith in the service of Christ. And where does the living Lord make known his will to the church? It is through the commandments of the law that Jesus Christ continues to guide his church to genuine discipleship, and indeed Christ sends them out into the world to teach those same commandments. The role of the Spirit is to lead the church of every new generation to a fresh encounter with the risen Lord through the commandments. Through the presence of the Spirit the law is a faithful guide to new life in service to Christ. Here we must protest just as sharply against all forms of libertinism, as if the Christian life were without the discipline of divine instruction. We must wholeheartedly affirm the law of Christ as the fundamental basis for Christian living in everyday life: "I am not free from God's law but am under Christ's law" (1 Cor. 9:21).

More specifically, the Decalogue continues to retain its role as the normative guide for Christian ethics. This is not an ethical "choice" I am making, grounded in some higher criterion of truth. Rather, my affirmation of the role of the Decalogue is a recognition of the divine decision to make known God's will in this form. God has the right to make this decision because God is God. The authority to rule his universe and to guide his church belongs to Jesus Christ alone, the sovereign Lord of all creation. Moreover, it is a gracious decision, indeed the sum of all divine mercy and kindness. It is through God's love for humankind that he gives the gift of the Decalogue as the clear expression of his eternal will. The law of Christ is not a burden to be shouldered with morbid moral severity; on the contrary, the Ten Commandments are for the joyous embrace of eager service. Upon one's hearing the Ten Commandments, the response of faith is overwhelming gratitude: "I delight in the way of your decrees as much as in all riches" (Ps. 119:14). They serve not to crush humanity but to lighten the path of life: "Come to me, all you that are weary and carrying heavy burdens, and I will give you rest. Take my yoke upon you, and learn from me; for I am gentle and humble in heart, and you will find rest for your souls. For my yoke is easy, and my burden is light" (Matt. 11:28–30). If the church is to find a rebirth of proclamation and a renewed confession of the stunning truths that constitute our message to the world, we must at the same time gather with energy and imagination around the Decalogue.

We live in a time of moral nihilism. Where human beings reject relationship with God as the heart of human life, human reason and experience become the only norm by which the moral life is judged. Human beings are thus held captive to their own confusion and weakness. The result is not the personal self-enhancement that is always expected from self-affirmation. The result rather is the self-destruction that follows in the wake of rejection of God's living claim upon his creatures. God grants life in abundance through his will; human beings turn away and lose the very life they seek. Here the church must respond to the needs of our time with a clear voice. God's revelation of his will is not a destruction of the freedom of human life. On the contrary, it is only through the service of

God that we find true freedom. Only through obedience to God's command do we find the true meaning of life for which we search. Only God's will shows us the true form of outer service to others which constitutes our authentic humanity. Only obedience to Christ delivers us from the final tyranny, which is tyranny to self. It is not only for the sake of the church but also for the sake of the world that the church must recover in its proclamation and in its very existence the true understanding of God's living will made known in the Ten Commandments.

That we are well within the parameters of canon is clear to see. The Decalogue occurs twice in scripture itself, the former time at Mt. Sinai (Exod. 20:1–17), the latter in the speech that Moses gives to the new generation of God's people as they are poised to enter the Promised Land (Deut. 5:1–21). The content is the same, yet the application varies at different times and situations. There is no set of rules that govern the movement from one situation to the next. Rather, it is God himself who illumines his people afresh in a new generation, the generation that has grown up since the exodus from Egypt and therefore needs fresh instruction for the journey that lies ahead. Thus God establishes an eternal rule by which the life of his people is governed. Yet God himself applies that same rule in a new way when the new situation of his people requires it. Indeed, the Decalogue has had exactly that role in the life of the church. There is virtually unanimous consent in all branches of the historic church—Catholic, Orthodox, and Protestant—that the Ten Commandments contain an eternal rule of faith for the life of obedience. To them the church has returned time and again in every conceivable circumstance of its life. Yet in each era of the church new insights have been discovered in the light of the ongoing encounter of Christ the risen Lord with his people. That dynamic is the essence of canon: a rule of faith by which the church is guided in every new generation in a fresh way through encounter with the living Lord of all reality.

Thus our aim cannot be simply to understand the Ten Commandments within the limits of biblical theology. Theological ethics is certainly based on biblical theology and dare not stray from the limits and flexibility that it delineates. Nevertheless, theological ethics, as a dimension of dogmatic theology, has the responsibility to address the living ethical questions of our contemporary world. We turn to the Bible instructed by the needs and concerns of our present-day generation of disciples, especially the living concerns of ordinary Christians as we face the struggle of faith in our society. True faithfulness is always lived out in relevant speech and action. Our aim must be thus to seek the living God himself as we strive to interpret these central passages of our faith.

A brief description of the Reformers' handling of the Decalogue is helpful; it is also instructive, indeed troubling, to see how quickly their approach degenerated within a very short period. There is no doubt whatsoever that the Ten Commandments are at the heart of the moral vision of the Reformers. What is the will of God? According to Luther and Calvin, the answer is to be found in the Decalogue. The stress on the Decalogue was no less characteristic of Luther than of Calvin, despite the popular impression to the contrary. Luther argued for a firm distinction between command and promise: "Here we must point out that the entire Scripture of God is divided into two parts: commandments and promises. Although the commandments teach things that are good, the things taught are not done as soon as they are taught, for the commandments show us what we ought to do but do not give us the power to do it."[1] That is the first side of the dialectic, which is indeed essential in church proclamation: no human being is justified by any form of moral effort. Here there can be no compromise with any form of works-righteousness, which certainly continues to appear in our day in the widespread appeal to values.

However, what is stressed by Luther with equal force is the other side of the dialectic (which is of course ultimately Pauline): the Decalogue continues to provide the basic form of Christian obedience under the guidance of the Spirit. There are, according to Luther, two kinds of righteousness: the alien righteousness that comes from Christ alone apart from all moral accomplishment, and our own proper righteousness that consists of the new life that is engendered in all who believe. The one is never separated from the other. Rather, the alien righteousness of Christ is the basis for our own proper righteousness, which is transformed into the image of Christ. Luther eloquently seals the twofold movement: "Through the first righteousness the bridegroom says to the soul I am yours; through the second the bride says—I am yours."[2] Luther therefore speaks of the good works that necessarily accompany the life of faith. The point is not thus that the law is useless as a guide for Christian life. The point of Luther rather is that faith in Christ is the necessary starting point for a true understanding of the law, which is otherwise profoundly misconstrued in the form of pious custom. Real good works spring from faith and correspond to the true intent of God's commandments, not human custom or virtue. Only arid legalism grows wherever faith is absent, even if such legalism makes a vain appeal to the divine law. Luther's basic criticism is of a false understanding of works, not of the reality of new life in the believer: "Our faith in Christ does not free us from works but from false opinions concerning works,

1. Luther, *Christian Liberty*, 11.
2. *LW*, 31:89.

that is, from the foolish presumption that justification is acquired by works."[3]

It is therefore entirely consistent theologically for Luther, the adamant opponent of all works-righteousness, to expound the Decalogue as the basis for Christian ethics, as he does for example in his *Treatise on Good Works* and in his *Large Catechism*. Luther is unambiguous: "Anyone who knows the Ten Commandments perfectly knows the entire Scriptures. In all affairs and circumstances he can counsel, help, comfort, judge, and make decisions in both spiritual and temporal matters. He is qualified to sit in judgment upon all doctrines, estates, persons, laws, and everything else in the world."[4] As summarized by Bernhard Lohse: "Alongside its accusing function [the law] remains in effect as commandment, as admonition, as announcement of the divine will. Luther actually assumed a persistence of the law into eternity. . . . The law is and remains God's word. . . . As God's word it has abiding significance."[5] Any rebirth of theological reflection on the Decalogue today will find in Luther an excellent example, and no claim should be made to the legacy of Lutheran ethics that is not based squarely in the Decalogue. It is worth remembering that neither pietism nor rationalism, still less neo-Protestantism, ever came even close to the profound reading of the Ten Commandments one finds in Luther.

Luther's basic insight is carried over into the *Formula of Concord* in its fine section on the Third Function of the Law. There are three basic uses of the divine Law: "1) to maintain external discipline against unruly and disobedient men, 2) to lead men to a knowledge of their sin, 3) after they are reborn, and although the flesh still inheres in them, to give them on that account a definite rule according to which they should pattern and regulate their entire life."[6] Through faith in Christ the law is faithfully kept in the form of spontaneous obedience, not inner compulsion. The Spirit brings rebirth and renewal, in such a way that the law of Christ is a guide to a new obedience out of sheer unbounded joy. It is not as though one began with faith and then moved on to something different; rather, genuine faith is always expressed in the form of active obedience. The law contains the "immutable will of God according to which man is to conduct himself in this life."[7] It is understood wrongly where faith is absent; it is understood rightly where the Spirit leads faith to newness of life. The same broad affirmation of the law of Christ is found in the *Augsburg Confession*, indeed precisely in the article on justifica-

3. Luther, *Christian Liberty*, 35–36.
4. *BC*, 361.
5. Lohse, *Martin Luther's Theology*, 275–26.
6. *BC*, 479–80.
7. Ibid., 566.

tion, where the truth of the gospel is at stake: "When faith takes hold of Christ, the mediator, the heart is at peace and begins to love God and to keep the law."[8]

Unfortunately, later Lutheran scholasticism introduced a systematic use of the notion of natural law as a complement to the moral law. Thus, according to Johann Andreas Quenstedt: "in original, uncorrupted nature the natural and moral Laws were entirely the same, but in corrupted nature a great part of the Natural Law has been obscured by sin, and only a very small part of it has remained in the mind of man; and so a new promulgation of Law was instituted upon Mount Sinai, which Sinaitic law is particularly called the Moral Law, and does not in kind differ from the Natural Law."[9] The sharp dialectical affirmation of Luther yields to a rationalistic system in which the very meaning of the moral law is in terms of reproduction of natural law. The Decalogue is thus locked into a moral system whose ultimate basis is anthropological, not christological, for the function of the Ten Commandments is to publish in written form what is in fact written on human consciousness. Of course Luther too occasionally referred to the natural law; however, his estimation of it was very different. Luther stressed the insufficiency of the natural law: "Still, awareness of natural law is not sufficient, due not so much to the fact that humans would not have known enough of the law as to the fact that they draw no conclusions from what they know."[10] By contrast, the later Lutheran scholastic David Hollaz draws a more positive conclusion: "There nevertheless remain certain vestiges of it, namely, universal principles, from which the difference between right and wrong is naturally apparent."[11] In the former case natural law serves to expose the weakness of the human moral condition; in the latter case natural law becomes the hermeneutical basis for understanding the moral law. One is immediately struck by the overwhelming loss of verve and clarity in the shift from the early Lutheran vision of ethics to the later Lutheran rationalism, with its center of gravity located in a decidedly different nexus of issues—far removed from the Pauline dialectic.

Despite the later conflicts between Lutheran and Reformed, John Calvin differs in matters of presentation and emphasis from Martin Luther on the question of the law, not in theological substance. Their primary concerns are identical. In his presentation of the law of God, Calvin begins by stressing the need to discern the genuine purpose of the law, for without such understanding the impious miss the entire point: "That is, they do not pay attention to the purpose of the law; if the forms

8. Ibid., 147.
9. *Theologia didactico-polemica* IV, 1, in Schmid, 513.
10. Lohse, *Martin Luther's Theology*, 274.
11. *Examen Theologicum Acroamaticum*, ed. Teller, 1750, 999, in Schmid, 513–14.

of the law be separated from its end, one must condemn it as vanity."[12] In fact, the moral law has a threefold function or use (Calvin here takes up the theme of *tertius usus legis*, first developed by Philipp Melanchthon). First, the law acts as a "mirror" in which human beings are able to contemplate the frailty of their own condition. Second, through fear of punishment it acts as a deterrent against the cruelty and violence of unjust people in society. Third, its primary and proper use is to serve as the instrument for learning God's will through the presence of the Spirit in the believer. Unquestionably for Calvin the role of the law as an eternal expression of the divine will is inviolable: "There are not many rules, but one everlasting and unchangeable rule to live by."[13] The law constitutes a "perfect pattern of righteousness" by which to discern the divine command.

Calvin refers to the natural law, but only in order to show its complete impotence due to the depth of human depravity: "But man is so shrouded in the darkness of errors that he hardly begins to grasp through this natural law what worship is acceptable to God. Surely he is very far removed from a true estimate of it."[14] Indeed, the errors run so deep that the human person is unable even to discern his or her own failure: "He is so puffed up with haughtiness and ambition, and so blinded by self-love, that he is as yet unable to look upon himself, and, as it were, to descend within himself, that he may humble and abase himself and confess his own miserable condition."[15] Thus human moral blindness eliminates the efficacy of natural law and makes revealed law essential. God wills what he wills not by caprice but according to the divine purpose; the role of human obedience is to concede to God the right to will whatever he pleases. One cannot measure the divine will by human ability; the proper response is total obedience to whatever God requires. Human beings are in fact powerless to do God's will apart from his mercy; genuine obedience springs not from human moral virtue but from humility. The law drives humanity to despair, and only then to the gospel. God's self-revelation is opposed to all piety, which is the effort to attain God's favor by human religiosity. Calvin refers to the "irreligious affectation of religion" which in fact contradicts God's Word, however spiritual it may sound.[16]

The law of God makes a total claim upon human life in every dimension, inner and outer. Christ himself is the true interpreter of the law: "When we say that this is the meaning of the law, we are not thrusting

12. Calvin, 1.349.
13. Ibid., 1.362.
14. Ibid., 1.368.
15. Ibid.
16. Ibid., 1.371.

forward a new interpretation of our own, but we are following Christ, its best interpreter."[17] Christ is not the giver of a new law, a "law of the gospel," as if the Decalogue were deficient; rather, Christ restores the Decalogue to it true moral integrity. While the verbal sense of the commandments is essential, it is necessary to be led from the words to the divine meaning. Calvin thus eschews a narrow biblicism and while ardently anchored in the literal sense insists that the true subject matter of scripture—God's living will—is the ultimate goal of all authentic interpretation: "We must if possible, therefore, find some way to lead us with straight, firm steps to the will of God."[18] Such steps include considering the theological purpose of each command and converting each prohibition into its opposite positive, though such rules are really clear only in the actual doing of interpretation. The two tables of the law apply to love of God and love of neighbor, but the inner order insists that the former is the basis for the latter.

One is amazed at the skillful simplicity with which both Luther and Calvin could lay out for their readers a profound moral vision, yet without compromising the genuine complexity of biblical truth. The early Reformed confessional theology certainly continues the major thrust of Calvin's approach and appears to be in full accord with the similar statements of the early Lutheran tradition. The Scots Confession emphasizes human incapacity and the need for divine grace: "The cause of good works, we confess, is not our free will, but the Spirit of the Lord Jesus, who dwells in our hearts by true faith."[19] The Heidelberg Catechism organizes the human response of obedience around the central theme of gratitude and stresses the radical transformation from the old to the new life in complete joy in God. The Second Helvetic Confession stresses that the entire divine will is contained in God's revealed will, which must neither be added to nor subtracted from by human opinion: "We believe that the whole will of God and all necessary precepts for every sphere of life are taught in this law."[20] Human beings are not born to be idle but to be active in faith, pleasing God. (Compare Luther's statement in the *Preface to Romans*: "O when it comes to faith, what a living, creative, active, powerful thing it is. It cannot do other than good at all times."[21])

However, when one comes to the Westminster Confession, it is clear that the inroads of later Reformed scholasticism are surfacing. For it refers to a "covenant of works" into which the law of God was originally

17. Ibid., 1.373.
18. Ibid., 1.374.
19. *Conf*, 16.
20. Ibid., 75.
21. Luther, *Martin Luther: Selections*, 24.

inserted, whereby humanity could have earned the divine favor through obedience. Where does this idea of a "covenant of works" come from? It reflects in fact a development within later Continental Reformed theology, often associated with Johannes Cocceius (1603–69) but in fact shared by a variety of authors.[22] Early Reformed theology knew of course of God's one covenant with humanity, administered one way in the Old and another way in the New Testaments. But later Reformed scholasticism, hampered by a biblicistic reading of scripture, converted the complex dialectic of Calvin into a unilinear historical progression. There is thus a history of the covenant with different stages, including a covenant based on works. Furthermore, to the idea of a covenant of works is added the natural law view that human moral consciousness contains in itself the basic requirements of the covenant. In other words, human nature teaches that whoever does God's will earns God's favor: "Conscience attests to man that for him as a personal being in God's image God and communion with God is the supreme essential good which God Himself has granted him, which he must strive for according to God's will and appropriate to himself by obedience to Him."[23] With subtle but crucial alteration of the theological subject matter, through the notion of a "covenantal history" and the innate power of human self-consciousness, later Reformed scholasticism is teaching a perspective on the law that is profoundly different from Calvin's marvelous vision. The christological basis of ethics is removed; works-righteousness is reintroduced; the threat of Pelagianism reappears; a rigid rationalism is again prominent. The door is open to the narrow legalism and introspective severity of Puritanism, which Calvin everywhere guarded against.

Now, my point of this brief rehearsal of the Reformation and post-Reformation debate is not to argue that there are no differences between Luther and Calvin when it comes to the issue of law and gospel. There are; clearly Luther sought above all to ward off works-righteousness, while Calvin focused on sanctification as the proper goal of justification. Why should there not be different emphases, since an entire generation separated these two Reformers, not to speak of differing personalities and theological resources? My point rather is that, despite important differences, they shared a moral vision that centered on the continuing role of the Ten Commandments as the instrument by which Christ guides his disciples to know and do the living will of God. What characterizes their shared vision is the astonishing range of imagination with which they articulated the true content of the commandments as living instruction for the problems of the day. Both their vision and their imagination

22. See the discussion in Pelikan, 4:362–74.
23. Heppe, 286.

seem quickly to have been lost among their followers, despite concerted attempts to be faithful to their fundamental thrust.

On one issue, my canonical proposal for theological ethics in fact differs from the that of the Reformers. There are at least some texts in the major Reformers that suggest that the role of the state is to protect and preserve Christian orthodoxy. Other texts point in another direction, but the very presence of ambiguity on this issue should now be replaced with moral clarity. As Christians we affirm the separation of church and state. We denounce every effort to establish the Christian religion as the law of the land. The role of the state is to protect religious freedom, not to ensure Christian truth. Thus, the widespread effort to enshrine the Ten Commandments in the public sphere—however well intended—does not spring from the confessing church but from a misguided conservative ideology. My critique has nothing to do with secularism; it is based rather on the heart of biblical faith. Saul is anointed king by Samuel the prophet. Saul musters the Israelite army to fight the Philistines (1 Samuel 13). The people gather at Gilgal, awaiting the signal to attack. Saul must wait for Samuel the prophet to come and offer sacrifices before battle can begin. But Samuel does not appear; the Israelite soldiers begin to melt away. Saul in desperation offers the burnt offering in place of Samuel; the king makes himself into a prophet. Then Samuel arrives and discovers to his horror what has happened: "You have done foolishly; you have not kept the commandment of the LORD your God" (1 Sam. 13:13). At that very moment Saul loses the divine blessing and eventually the kingdom itself. Scripture itself thus protests the politicization of the sacred.

Instructed by the example of the Reformers and chastened by the failure of their near successors, let us ask what concerns must be met by any viable theological ethics of the divine command today. I am not seeking a return to the Reformation; our time is in numerous ways very different from theirs. I am seeking rather to embrace their imaginative moral vision in our world today, for I believe that it is the vision that scripture itself evokes. Still, we cannot simply move backward; we must seek to move forward in the church of Jesus Christ. And indeed, while I highlight the fine exposition of the Decalogue by the Reformers, there is no doubt that all Christians in the mainstream of Christian tradition share the same commitment. We all gather around the Ten Commandments as we search for God's will in our world today. For example, the *Catechism of the Catholic Church* states: "In fidelity to Scripture and in conformity with Jesus' example the tradition of the Church has always acknowledged the primordial importance and significance of the Decalogue."[24] Similarly, the Eastern Orthodox tradition affirms the same conclusion: "If a man asks 'How can I become god?' the answer is very simple: go to church, receive the sacraments regularly, pray to God 'in spirit and in truth,' read the Gospels, follow the commandments. The last of these items—'follow the commandments'—must never be forgotten. Orthodoxy, no less than Western Christianity, firmly rejects the kind of mysticism that seeks to dispense with moral rules."[25] We therefore join together with the universal church, Eastern and Western, under the authority of Christ and ask: How are we to interpret the law of Christ today?

1. *Jesus Christ and he alone, is the true interpreter of the law.* He is the Son of God, who alone declares the true intent of God's living will for all humanity. He is not only greater than Moses; he is greater than the Old Testament itself, whose teaching he is free to correct (cf. Mark 7:19). Jesus Christ is the sole manifestation of God's true claim upon humanity. He alone is the true measure of Christian speech and conduct. His command is the highest priority and radically undercuts every tie of culture and custom, including religious custom. He possesses his authority in and from himself and declares his command in the free sovereignty of his eternal rule over all reality. He is the one standard by which all claims to ethical truth are judged; his authority is the one truth in reference to which the entire scriptures are rightly understood.

2. *The Ten Commandments forever remain the one eternal expression of God's living will for all humankind in every time and place.* The Decalogue circumscribes the essential requirements of God given to his covenant people. The Ten Commandments come as gift, grounded in the freely given promise of the gospel through the forgiveness of sins. The divine claim upon human life is above all gracious, for in it God gives himself to humanity. The commandments of God guide human life to the true joy that fulfills all human desire: "I long for your salvation, O LORD, and your law is my delight" (Ps. 119:174). Yet the Ten Commandments also come as demand, requiring the radical response of obedience in the whole person, without evasion and without restraint: "The sum of your word is truth; and every one of your righteous ordinances endures forever" (Ps. 119:160). Obedience to God comprises mind, will, emotion, and body. The error of all moralism is not that it is too strict in the interpretation of God's commands; the error of the moralist is precisely the failure to obey fully and radically with one's whole being, by misunderstanding the purpose for which God gives his commands: "Do not think that I have come to abolish the law or the prophets; I have come not to abolish but

24. *Cat*, 504.
25. Ware, 241.

to fulfill. . . . For I tell you, unless your righteousness exceeds that of the scribes and Pharisees, you will never enter the kingdom of heaven" (Matt. 5:17, 20). Genuine obedience without hypocrisy is complete adherence by the whole person to the divine command in word and deed in the gratitude and joy of life.

3. *The role of the Holy Spirit is to guide the church through the living experience of its ongoing life to a fresh encounter with Christ the risen Lord through the witness of scripture.* Without the Spirit, scripture is a dead letter that is taken captive by a new legalism. Through the gift of the Spirit, scripture serves as a sure and reliable medium through which Christ is present with his disciples in all times and places. Appeals to the Spirit in neglect or distortion of scripture are false appeals; appeals to the Spirit as a symbolic reference to human modes of consciousness are likewise vain and deceitful. The work of the Spirit is to falsify all human ideology, left or right, in order that the living voice of Christ alone may be heard in his church. The Spirit leads the church in its application of scripture to every new problem of life, shaping the ethical imagination of every new generation in the image of Christ.

4. *Perfect freedom is found only in the service of God; while true service of God is perfect freedom.* The church recognizes the ever-present threat of self-righteousness and moral self-enhancement. The true entry into ethical reflection is not moral self-worth nor the human capacity of reason and experience. We need ethical guidance because we are human, not divine, and because we are sinners who have forsaken our humanity at the very core of our being. We are not partners in relation to God, but servants. True freedom comes from service to God, not through the illusion of inner self-fulfillment, which only brings a new tyranny. Human personhood is not destroyed by the divine will but indeed upheld and fulfilled. Nor is God's will the capricious declaration of a willful tyrant but the righteous claim of a wise and loving Lord. Nevertheless, true personhood is discovered only in recognition of God's inherent right to command.

5. *Knowing God's will is possible only by doing it; doing God's will is accomplished only where God is truly known.* There can be no advance by the church in a true understanding of God's command without active obedience. Hearing God's will proclaimed is nothing without doing it. Wherever God's will is done, God's rule is present as event. Yet the human response is secondary, the divine command is primary. God commands his church on his own initiative, and according to his own gracious design. We are freely given the clear direction of God's command; it remains for us only to do it. However, we are not given the hidden mystery of God's eternal purpose, which he retains in the sovereign freedom of

his majesty. God's purpose in Jesus Christ is good, beyond all goodness; but its full reality is known ultimately only to himself.

6. *The twofold command of love is the one divine purpose for human life.* The Ten Commandments are not a list of virtues and vices or a handbook of moral values. The commands of God cannot be manipulated by human calculation as a system of rules awaiting moral rational application. The will of God is summarized by Christ himself in the twofold command of love. To love God with one's heart, soul, and mind is the whole point of God's command. To love neighbor with radical affirmation is necessarily joined to the love of God. There can be no love of God without love of neighbor; nor can there be true love of neighbor without love of God. However, there is an inner order that must be preserved, for love of God comes first as the basis without which love for neighbor is impossible. The twofold command of love claims the whole person in every dimension of intellect, will, emotion. Love of God and neighbor is not different from obedience to God's commands; rather, it is through obedience to God's commands that authentic love of God and neighbor is realized.

7. *The will of God is always practical and concrete, a summons to active service of Christ in everyday life for ordinary people.* God's will is never a higher righteousness for a professional Christian elite; it is the light of life for common people in the struggle to be faithful in practical existence. On some issues it sets boundaries that can never be crossed under any circumstances. On other issues it leaves plenty of room for thoughtful variation in the freedom of the gospel. Conscience is not a divine voice in human experience but a human capacity for critical self-awareness. Radical obedience is not blind or reactionary; it necessarily involves reasoned judgment in making the hard decisions that life sometimes presents. Yet through the presence of Christ the Christian retains the confidence to act, never looking back, relying only on the forgiveness of sins through the electing love of God: "We know that all things work together for good for those who love God, who are called according to his purpose" (Rom. 8:28).

8. *God is a righteous God; he calls his people to live before him in righteousness as an earthly reflection of his eternal being.* There is no absolute morality in abstraction from God himself, nor can the commandments be merged into higher ethical principles. Our goal of obedience is to become like God in passionate justice and mercy. It is not a goal that is set too high for human capacity, nor is it a a burden too difficult to bear. On the contrary, true freedom and spontaneous joy in life are found only in service to God, whereby we are daily transformed into his image. The righteousness of God's rule is found in solidarity with the

outcast and the sinful. "Be perfect, therefore, as your heavenly Father is perfect" (Matt. 5:48).

9. *The Ten Commandments are received in the church not as a dead letter but as a living witness.* They constitute an invitation to search for God's will in our world today. Affirmation of their authoritative role is not the end of ethical reflection but the beginning. A response of faith is required by the church as we seek God in our world. Our understanding of God's will is expanded first of all by the larger narrative context of scripture. In the stories of scripture, the complexity, energy, and vivacity of God's will is portrayed in endlessly fruitful variation. Theological study of the commandments today means theological exegesis of biblical narrative. Furthermore, our understanding is developed through imaginative connection between the biblical world and our own. Guided by the theological shape of scripture itself, our moral vision can be completed only through disciplined use of the imagination in confronting the ethical dilemmas of contemporary life.

10. *The Ten Commandments are the true guide to genuine enjoyment of life.* They are not given by God to suppress what is truly human; indeed, they are given precisely to show what constitutes genuine humanity. They are like markers to show where the true treasure of human joy is found: not there, not there, but here! God's revealed will shows where human integrity flourishes in preservation of the common good, where mutual respect and affection enhance all that is good in human society, where priorities are ordered in such a way as to liberate human fulfillment from every self-destructive habit, where the goodness and kindness of God are properly reflected in the good ordering of human life. The Ten Commandments show forth the light of authentic life.

When he was confronted by the rich young man's question concerning the true way to eternal life, Jesus repeated the Ten Commandments (Matt. 19:16–30; Mark 10:17–31; Luke 18:18–30). Jesus does not bring a new law or law of the gospel (*lex evangelii*); rather, by the authority of Christ himself the Decalogue remains the eternally valid revelation of God's will. In obedience to Christ, the church of all times and places has returned again and again to the Decalogue in every era of crisis and confusion. Yet Christ brings home the full thrust of God's will by his concrete summons to sell all, give to the poor, and follow him. His summons is not an additional command, nor is it a higher ethical plateau or an alternative avenue to obedience. His concrete summons engenders the true perspective on God's command as a whole, which is love for God above all things and love for neighbor. The church must today turn to the Ten Commandments, seeking the will of God; it must learn from Christ himself the practical words and deeds that are their true application in our world. We have no desire whatsoever to enforce the Ten Commandments upon society; the moral life of the Christian cannot be legislated. We believe in the strict separation of church and state. Nevertheless, the Ten Commandments remain for the community of faith the light of God's will for the whole world.

13

Transformation

Why did God in Jesus Christ enter the world of human space and time? We do not inquire here concerning the inner motive of God, which is hidden in the mystery of God's sovereign freedom. Of God's motive we can only record in astonished wonder that it so pleased God to draw the world into the communion of love that he himself is in all eternity. God's love for his creation is grounded in his own passionate desire to be with humankind: "For God so loved the world that he gave his only Son, so that everyone who believes in him may not perish but may have eternal life" (John 3:16). God was moved by love in the freedom of his eternal being. More cannot be said; we must hold fast rather to the joyful silence of awe.

We ask instead concerning the aim, or goal, of God's self-disclosure in Christ. Of that goal both Testaments of scripture bear abundant witness. God revealed himself in order that the glory of his eternal being might be known and enjoyed among humankind:

> I am the LORD, and there is no other;
>> besides me there is no god.
>> I arm you, though you do not know me,
> so that they may know, from the rising of the sun
>> and from the west, that there is no one besides me;
>> I am the LORD, and there is no other.
> I form light and create darkness,
>> I make weal and create woe;
>> I the LORD do all these things. (Isa. 45:5–7)

> So if anyone is in Christ, there is a new creation: everything old has passed
> away; see, everything has become new! All this is from God, who reconciled
> us to himself through Christ, and has given us the ministry of reconciliation;
> that is, in Christ God was reconciling the world to himself, not counting
> their trespasses against them, and entrusting the message of reconciliation
> to us. (2 Cor. 5:17–19)

In Christ, God reconciled the entire cosmos to himself. Through Christ,
God fashioned a new creation. By drawing near in Jesus Christ, God
has restored the whole creation. Jesus Christ is the one ruler of all reality; Jesus Christ is Lord of all creation. All things in existence serve his
sovereign purpose of love. Nothing whatsoever is outside the scope of
his absolute control of the entire cosmos. Even evil, which the eternal
God abhors and struggles to overcome—even evil, despite its force for
harm, in the end serves the rule of Christ for the good of his universe. The
message of the gospel is the one call to all humanity to be reconciled to
God through the forgiveness of sins. Calvin was certainly right: all right
knowledge of God begins in obedience. But we must also reverse his
point with equal truth: all genuine obedience flows from right knowledge
of God. Theological ethics of the divine command is thus a response,
based on the divine initiative.

What kind of response? To know God rightly is to be transformed into
his image in every dimension of life. The goal of Christian ethics is that
we might be like God: "Be perfect, therefore, as your heavenly Father is
perfect" (Matt. 5:48). John Henry Newman eloquently summarizes the
essence of the matter in his beautiful epigram "To live is to change; to
be perfect, is to have changed often." Martin Luther, in his commentary
on Romans, echoes the same theological insight: "To change our mind
is the purpose of every word of scripture and every action of God."[1]
Christian life is transformation into the image of Jesus Christ through
the joy of discipleship. Change means radical obedience to God's living
will with one's whole being: the way we think, the way we act, the way
we feel, the way we make decisions. To know Christ is to follow him;
to follow him is to be conformed to his likeness. It is to move from the
old to the new under the guidance of the Spirit. Transformation comes
through embracing the joyous freedom of the gospel with the whole
person. Radical obedience involves using all our gifts, talents, and resources with eagerness and spontaneous delight in the service of Christ.
It means learning to see the world as God sees it, learning to cherish
the things that God values, learning to pursue the goals that reflect the
glory of God.

1. LCC, 15:83.

God's initiative in no way cancels out human personhood; on the contrary, according to the Christian confession of faith only God's initiative brings ultimate fulfillment to human personhood. Human imagination is enraptured by the vision of God's eternal will for the good of humanity; human resourcefulness and initiative are challenged by the call to give our best in the service of Christ in all things; human desire is enriched and elevated through the treasure of truth made known in the gospel; human resilience is drawn to the undying claim of Christ in every circumstance. Transformation comes only through radical obedience to Christ with the whole person. Earthly attachments are interrupted and transcended; cultural and family ties are intersected from above and decentered; the various cultural and personal agendas that hold us captive are rendered obsolete by the sheer newness of life in God's realm. Through Christian faith there is a radical break with the past; the old is gone, a new life has begun. The service of God is now the highest priority of life; other priorities recede into the shadowy past, long forgotten in the bright hope of Christian discipleship. To serve Christ is to be seized by the claim of single-minded obedience to the living command.

Change comes only from hearing the proclaimed Word, the one source of all Christian ethics; yet true hearing is realized only in practical doing. God in Christ transforms the whole church; yet real change always involves the practical life of the solitary disciple. Christ calls each individual by name. There is no greater satisfaction on this earth than Christian obedience, for it alone fulfills the human person beyond words; yet the goal is not human actualization but the celebration of God's radiant splendor. Through faith our lives become transparent to Christ. The change is not a growing old; the change of life is growing young in the childlike wonder of faith. The transformation of life under the rule of Christ never ends in this life. We all need to grow in every season of life, and that growth ends only with our death; only then is liberation from the struggle of faith graciously received in the free gift of eternal life.

Radical transformation means an end to all theology of correlation, whether on the religious right or on the religious left. Every attempt to interpret the will of God in correlation with the self-authenticating claims of human reason and experience seriously distorts the call of discipleship and perverts the true content of God's living command. The same error is made with equally disastrous consequences in both the conservative and liberal camps and is unfortunately endemic in both. Among conservative evangelicals the error is clearly seen already in the natural theology of Charles Hodge, who asserts of the divine law: "This law is revealed in the constitution of our nature, and more fully and clearly in the written word of God."[2] There is thus a correlation to be established in Christian ethics between human moral nature and the will of God revealed in scripture. That principle of correlation is carried through to the present among evangelicals, as can be seen in the work of Richard Mouw, *The God Who Commands*. The principle of correlation clearly governs his ethics, as his explicit affirmation of Paul Tillich suggests.[3] Against what he considers a Barthian "kerygmatic" approach, Mouw presents a Tillichian "method of correlation" in which the various concerns and themes of the non-Christian world are correlated with the content of scripture. The overall aim of theological ethics falls into this basic pattern of correlation: "The secular quest finds its fulfillment in the moral perspective contained in the Christian scheme of things."[4] Theological ethics thus becomes another branch of apologetics, "moral apologetics."[5] The proper theological effort is to find a way to "appeal to divine commands in a reasonable fashion."[6] Indeed, Mouw is not so much interested in theological ethics as he is in "philosophical moral theology,"[7] in which the basic questions of all life are considered: "Who am I? Where am I? What's wrong? What is the remedy?"[8] He seeks to render God's will in a way that "satisfies requirements for moral justification."[9] Much like Hodge, and indeed the entire evangelical tradition, Mouw attempts to blend the Reformed theology of John Calvin with the pietism of the eighteenth and nineteenth centuries. In his reference to God, he points to various attempts to do an ethic of the Father and an ethic of the Son; he now wants to offer an ethic of the Holy Spirit.

Mouw of course is to be commended for a serious effort to offer a theological ethics of the divine command. In this we are in full agreement. Nevertheless, the differences between his work and that of Karl Barth and Dietrich Bonhoeffer, not to speak of Calvin and Luther, are profound and comprehensive. One is particularly disturbed to see his self-advertisement as a student of Calvin, for in fact the ethics of Mouw are heavily indebted to the tedious rationalism and moralism of later scholastic Calvinism, especially the nineteenth-century Dutch theologian Abraham Kuyper, whose cultural Christianity is little more than a pale shadow of the brilliant light of the Reformer. Kuyper too speaks of

2. Hodge, 3:266.
3. Mouw, 283.
4. Ibid., 185.
5. Ibid., 2.
6. Ibid., 20.
7. Ibid., 22.
8. Ibid., 26.
9. Ibid., 27.

a "mutual relation" between natural theology and special revelation.[10] Without natural theology based on the "natural principium," there is no valid understanding of God's revelation; indeed such a revelation is strictly "inconceivable."[11] The reason is that grace never truly creates what is radically new: "grace never creates one single new reality."[12] No new reality originates in heaven; rather, the new creation is simply a matter of rearrangement of existing reality, involving "new relations, new methods of existence, new forms."[13] Natural and special theology thus possess a "higher unity."[14] One can only shudder at this straightforward denial of the sheer eschatological horizon of the gospel. For the gospel is nothing but what is radically new: the resurrection of Jesus Christ from the dead.

> You have heard; now see all this;
>   and will you not declare it?
> From this time forward I make you hear new things,
>   hidden things that you have not known.
> They are created now, not long ago;
>   before today you have never heard of them,
>   so that you could not say, "I already knew them."
> You have never heard, you have never known,
>   from of old your ear has not been opened. (Isa. 48:6–8)

Kuyper's entire system founders on the glorious newness of Easter faith.

The Dutch tradition is far better served by the humane and expansive approach of Herman Bavinck, whose grasp of the biblical rule of faith far outshines that of his antirevolutionary contemporary Kuyper. Bavinck, in sharp contrast to Kuyper, fully agrees with Calvin's very negative evaluation of the role of natural theology:

> Despite all this, the truth remains, as St. Paul put it, that the world by wisdom has not known God in His wisdom (1 Cor. 1:21). When Paul ascribes wisdom to the world, he means what he says in full seriousness. In the light of general revelation the world has gathered together a treasure of wisdom, of wisdom, that is, concerning the things of this earthly life. But this wisdom of the world constitutes the world the less excusable, for it proves that mankind did not lack such gifts of God as mind and reason, rational and moral ability. The wisdom of man demonstrates that man

10. Kuyper, 155.
11. Ibid., 156.
12. Ibid., 156.
13. Ibid., 156.
14. Ibid., 157.

because of the darkness of his mind and the hardening of his heart has not used the gifts which were given him aright.[15]

There is no method of correlation; indeed, the proper evaluation of general revelation is possible only on the basis of special revelation, which reverses the hermeneutical relation of Kuyper: "The special revelation of God, consequently, is necessary also for right understanding of His general revelation in nature and history."[16] Consequently, again in sharpest contrast to Kuyper, Bavinck is able to affirm forthrightly the fully eschatological reality of the gospel: "The reality of special revelation can be demonstrated only by its own existence. It is only by its own light that it can be seen and acknowledged."[17] Bavinck is infinitely closer to Calvin, and to the Bible, than is Kuyper.

At any rate, several serious criticisms must be made of Mouw's attempt, criticisms that apply *mutatis mutandis* to the conservative evangelical group as a whole. First, according to Mouw, "obedience to divine commands derives its significance from a particular kind of world-view."[18] This is simply false; obedience to divine commands derives its significance from the absolute authority of Jesus Christ. Scripture has no "worldview"; the Christian confession knows no "worldview"; scripture bears witness to the truth of the gospel, and it is that same truth that the church confesses in our world today. Christology, not rational philosophical debate, is the basis for Christian ethics; how can it possibly be otherwise? We follow a risen Lord in every issue of life and death, not a "worldview"; we owe our very being to One who gave his life on the cross for our sins, not to a "worldview"; my only comfort in life and in death is, not my affirmation of a worldview but "that I belong—body and soul, in life and in death—not to myself but to my faithful Savior, Jesus Christ, who at the cost of his own blood has fully paid for all my sins and has completely freed me from the dominion of the devil."[19] Faithful Christians are martyred not for a "worldview" but for a blessed Savior, to whom they would gladly give a thousand lives if they but had them to give.

Second, God's will requires no moral justification whatsoever. God's will is to be obeyed because it is God's will. There are times for every Christian when God's will seems to contradict all that we hold precious and dear in this world, including our reason and experience. The answer is not to seek to adjust the divine will to our self-grounded conceptions

15. Bavinck, 59–60.
16. Ibid., 62.
17. Ibid., 63.
18. Mouw, 26.
19. Heidelberg Catechism, in *Conf*, 29.

and concerns by a method of ethical correlation; the answer is to live through the challenge of faith in radical obedience to Christ, in order that we might grow in our understanding of God. Obedience is not blind; it comes from a firm grasp of the divine call. Nevertheless, obedience to Christ changes our understanding of God's purpose. We move, in the phrase of Paul (Rom. 1:17), from faith to faith (εκ πιστεως εισ πιστιν).

Third, Christian faith is not at all an attempt to address the identity crisis of the old humanity, as formulated by Mouw's questions. Indeed, Jesus seldom, if ever, answers directly the questions that the merely curious bring to him. On the contrary, he seizes the initiative and questions the questioner, thus creating the only real possibility for the new humanity, which is repentance in order to follow Christ in newness of life. Genuine transformation does not come as a confirmation of the concerns of the old; it comes from repentance of the old and free and joyful embrace of the radically new world of God. Christian ethics of the divine command is not an argument with the old world; it is joyful proclamation of the new world of the gospel, together with the compassionate summons "Be reconciled to God!"

Fourth, in keeping with the needs of his method of correlation, Mouw dismisses concrete commands in favor of a broader pattern of divine address. In fact, the essence of the divine command is found only in the concrete, not in broader patterns. To Abram, God says, "Go from your country and your kindred and your father's house to the land that I will show you" (Gen. 12:1). To Moses, God says, "Come no closer! Remove the sandals from your feet, for the place on which you are standing is holy ground" (Exod. 3:5). To Samuel, God says, "Fill your horn with oil and set out; I will send you to Jesse the Bethlehemite, for I have provided for myself a king among his sons" (1 Sam. 16:1). To Zacchaeus, Jesus says, "Hurry and come down; for I must stay at your house today" (Luke 19:5). One is struck by the sheer lack of any knowledge of the direction of contemporary biblical theology in Mouw's work, for the search for philosophical principles is now thoroughly discredited no matter how useful it may appear to a defensive "apologetics."

Fifth, Mouw's attempt to chart an ethics of the Spirit, side by side with an ethics of the Father and an ethics of the Son, falls far short of the grandeur of trinitarian doctrine. According to Mouw, Christian theology has been dominated by ethical principles derived from the first and second persons of the Trinity. He, by contrast, now offers the church a theological ethic derived from the third person, the Spirit. In response, I do not see how Mouw can escape the threat of tritheism. Christian faith knows of no separation of the persons into distinct ethical concerns; on the contrary, the triune God has one will, one purpose, one concern. "The Father is eternal, the Son is eternal, the Holy Spirit

is eternal; and yet they are not three eternals but one eternal."[20] There
are of course significant differences among the major branches of the
confessing church, Roman Catholic, Eastern Orthodox, and Protestant.
Yet no branch, and no confession, suggests that the triune God yields
three different ethics. There are not three commands but only one command of the triune God. Indeed, Mouw's search for an ethic of the Spirit
sounds very close to Joachim of Fiore, whose similar attempt to inau-
gurate a "third age" of the Spirit was condemned as antitrinitarian by
the Lateran Council of 1215.

Finally, Mouw's approach yields not true transformation but an easy
cultural Christianity of cheap grace. He wants, for example, to convert
Calvinism into an "ethical style"[21]; he wants to coordinate "proper"
self-fulfillment with conformity to God in Christ[22]; he wants a mature
Christianity free from all fear of eternal punishment; he desires to
affirm the "worth of the individual"[23]; he applauds the "cultural attractiveness" of narrative theology.[24] In all these ways, Mouw's work
stumbles on the stumbling block of the gospel: "Then Jesus told his
disciples, 'If any want to become my followers, let them deny themselves and take up their cross and follow me. For those who want to
save their life will lose it, and those who lose their life for my sake
will find it'" (Matt. 16:24–25). The call of the gospel brings a radical
break with the old order and a total transferal to a new order of life.
The call is received in the serious decision of faith, in which the ultimate fear of God is never lost, even while it yields to undying love.
"Do not fear those who kill the body but cannot kill the soul; rather
fear him who can destroy both soul and body in hell" (Matt. 10:28).
It is precisely the true fear of God that purges human weakness of all
other fears, giving rise to the courage of discipleship. To lose the fear
of God would mean to allow in all lesser fears and thus lose what is
essential to humanity: the courage to act. In the words of Luther's
famous hymn "A Mighty Fortress,"

> And though this world, with devils filled, should threaten to undo us,
> We will not fear, for God hath willed his truth to triumph through us.
> Let goods and kindred go, this mortal life also;
> The body they may kill, God's truth abideth still;
> His kingdom is forever.

20. Athanasian Creed, in *BC*, 19.
21. Mouw, 3.
22. Ibid., 37.
23. Ibid., 46.
24. Ibid., 120.

Theology of correlation is of course equally prominent on the religious left, with the same deleterious effects. It is clearly seen in the basic principle of ethics found in Tillich's *Systematic Theology*: "Morality is the function of life in which the centered self constitutes itself as a person; it is the totality of those acts in which a potentially personal life process becomes an actual person."[25] Three separate functions of life are embraced in the process of self-actualization: self-integration, self-creation, and self-transcendence. Thus the human existential quest, philosophically determined and defined, constitutes one pole of a critical correlation. The other pole is the "Spiritual Presence" in the spirit of humankind. The divine Spirit, present in the media of sacrament and word, is manifest wherever the New Being overcomes the fragmentation of life in its ambiguities. The spiritual presence is manifest in threefold form: "in mankind as a whole in preparation for the central manifestation of the divine Spirit, in the divine Spirit's central manifestation itself, and in the manifestation of the Spiritual Community under the creative impact of the central event,"[26] in which the central event is the Spiritual Presence in Jesus as the Christ. The element of correlation is essential for Christology itself, for the identity of Jesus is a function of his relation to the disciples: "As we have emphasized in the Christological part of the system, the Christ would not be the Christ without those who receive him as the Christ."[27] The picture is completed only by observing the principle of correlation at work in uniting the various spheres of human historical life: "The transcendent union of unambiguous life in which the Spiritual Community participates includes the unity of the three functions of life under the dimensions of the spirit—religion, culture, and morality."[28] The lines of division between morality, religion, and culture are eliminated by the transcendent unity of the divine Spirit. Despite the shifts of conceptuality provided by existentialism, Tillich without doubt continues the Protestant liberal tradition going back to Schleiermacher and honors the post-Kantian turn-to-the-subject.

Nor is the matter any different when one takes account of the late-twentieth-century turn-to-the-community, which is in every respect merely an extension of the same tradition into new territory. This is seen, for example, in the ethics of liberation theology as present in the widely popular *God of the Oppressed* by James H. Cone. Cone dismisses the Christology of the ancient church, and in particular the *homoousion*, on racial grounds: "The *homoousia* question is not a black question."[29]

25. Tillich, 3:38.
26. Ibid., 3:149.
27. Ibid.
28. Ibid., 3:157.
29. Cone, 14.

Rather than a confessing christological basis for theology, Cone introduces the principle of correlation, corrected by the idea of community: "My point is that one's social and historical context decides not only the questions we address to God but also the mode or form of the answers given to the questions. That is the central thesis of this book."[30] Black theology necessarily arises out of black experience: "The categories of interpretation must arise out of the thought forms of the black experience itself."[31] The identity of Jesus Christ is to be discovered through correlation with the black experience: "Indeed it can be said that to know Jesus is to know him as revealed in the struggle of the oppressed for freedom. Their struggle is Jesus' struggle, and he is thus revealed in the particularity of their cultural history—their hopes and dreams of freedom."[32] This yields the central theological affirmation of correlation between race and divinity: "Blackness and divinity are dialectically bound together as one reality."[33]

For the interpretation of scripture this yields the following comprehensive rule of reading, in which the gospel is defined in terms of the struggle of the oppressed: "The hermeneutical principle for an exegesis of the Scriptures is the revelation of God in Jesus Christ as the Liberator of the oppressed from social oppression and to political struggle, wherein the poor recognize that their fight against poverty and injustice is not only consistent with the gospel but is the gospel of Jesus Christ."[34] According to Cone, the determination of truth is strictly correlated with consciousness: "Truth does not destroy consciousness; truth affirms consciousness in the struggle to be through an affirmation of its right to be. This is what I mean by the Word of God in the lives of black people."[35] Correlation defines Christology, for just as Jesus was once a Jew in Nazareth, now he is black: "It is on the basis of the soteriological meaning of the particularity of his Jewishness that theology must affirm the Christological significance of Jesus' present blackness."[36]

The basic principle of theology is liberation, which is defined in terms of human self-actualization: "Liberation is knowledge of self; it is a vocation to affirm who I am created to be."[37] In the cross of Christ, Jesus identified with the pain of the oppressed, defeating the power of suffering over their lives. Cone's theology of liberation includes a Christian

30. Ibid., 15.
31. Ibid., 18.
32. Ibid., 34.
33. Ibid., 35.
34. Ibid., 81–82.
35. Ibid., 105.
36. Ibid., 134.
37. Ibid., 146.

ethic of liberation that is profoundly critical of such figures as Luther: "Luther could not hear God's liberating Word for the oppressed because he was not a victim."[38] Similar statements abound with respect to Calvin, Wesley, and others.

The primary directive of God is for the self-fulfillment of the oppressed: "God enters the social context of oppression and liberates the people into a new existence. At the precise moment that divine liberation happens, a divine claim is laid upon the oppressed to be what God has made them."[39] In the light of this basic definition, the hope for a new humanity is located among the oppressed: "Oppressed blacks and other people of color are the only signs of hope for the creation of a new humanity in America."[40] Like virtually all liberation theologians, Cone appeals to Karl Marx for his basic orientation: "Marx's chief concern was to uncover the ideological distortion of bourgeois thought which he believed could be overcome through the revolutionary praxis of the proletariat."[41] Cone's conclusion concerning the basic political shape of all theological thought is again universally shared among liberation theologians: "This means that theology is political language."[42] One avenue for the achievement of the political struggle is the use of violence by the oppressed against the oppressor, an issue on which Cone disagrees with Martin Luther King Jr.: "His [King's] dependence on the analysis of love found in liberal theology and his confidence that 'the universe is on the side of justice' seem not to take seriously white violence."[43] Despite his many protestations against "white theology," the basic correlation structure of Cone's theology is thoroughly Tillichian, with the difference being the shift from the individual subject to the community—a variation within a single lineage of nineteenth- and twentieth-century theological liberalism going back to Schleiermacher.

Our rejection of the ethics of correlation theology on the religious left must be just as decisive as our rejection of the religious right. First, Jesus Christ and he alone is the true measure of the absolute claim of God upon all human life. The church is not over Christ; the church is not in partnership with Christ in an easy correlation; we in the church are disciples of Christ, followers, who are below, not above, our Master. We know no definition of true humanity apart from him; we desire no future apart from him; we listen to no voice but his voice. All that we have and all that we are we have received freely as a gracious gift from

38. Ibid., 200.
39. Ibid., 207.
40. Ibid., 221.
41. Ibid., 44.
42. Ibid., 45.
43. Ibid., 221.

him, for he and he alone is the one source of our life. We are radically dependent upon him, and he exercises direct, absolute, active, and self-grounded authority over the church, whose one Head he is. We have no aims, no cultural or personal agenda, no political schemes to follow; our one purpose on this earth is to know Jesus Christ, as we have been known by him. Our life together as the church of Jesus Christ has the one role of bearing witness to his love in every word and deed: "I pray that you may have the power to comprehend, with all the saints, what is the breadth and length and height and depth, and to know the love of Christ that surpasses knowledge, so that you may be filled with all the fullness of God" (Eph. 3:18).

Tillich operates with a fatal reversal of the relation of Christ to his church, a reversal that Cone adopts and adapts to the black consciousness agenda. Cone's Christology is a radical departure from the catholic faith, which does indeed insist on the *homoousion* and which continues to confess that Jesus the Jew of Nazareth is even today Lord of all creation: "Jesus Christ is the same yesterday and today and forever" (Heb. 13:8). Jesus Christ is not a religious symbol of human aspiration, malleable according to changing mode; he is the sovereign Lord of all reality, to whom we owe our very being: "Long ago God spoke to our ancestors in many and various ways by the prophets, but in these last days he has spoken to us by a Son, whom he appointed heir of all things, through whom he also created the worlds. He is the reflection of God's glory and the exact imprint of God's very being, and he sustains all things by his powerful word" (Heb. 1:1–3). The theology of correlation founders on the sheer majesty of Christ the risen Lord.

Second, both Tillich and Cone shatter the unity and universality of the church. For Tillich, the church is simply merged into the broader realms of morality and culture; the church is just one instance of a broader historical-cultural spirituality. We can only ask, of whose spirit does Tillich speak? The church of Jesus Christ, filled with his indwelling Spirit, is not one instance of a broader force but "the household of God, which is the church of the living God, the pillar and bulwark of the truth" (1 Tim. 3:15). For Cone, the black church rejects its connection to historic Christianity and constitutes itself a self-grounded community without heritage and without living connection to the church universal. Its connection is with the "oppressed of the earth," not the communion of the saints (who in fact were all too often severely oppressed, Luther included). Yet scripture teaches, and the church confesses, one universal church, based on the unity of the one Lord: "There is one body and one Spirit, just as you were called to the one hope of your calling, one Lord, one faith, one baptism, one God and Father of all, who is above all and through all and in all" (Eph. 4:4–6). Correlation theology of the religious left walks away from the unity of the church.

Third, the reality of God is self-contained and stands in radical judgment over all human pretensions to self-righteousness. Both Tillich and Cone evince a moral arrogance based on a basic misunderstanding of human sin. Sin is not estrangement from one's true self (Tillich), and sin is not the oppression of the oppressed (Cone), though certainly sin distorts the integrity of the human self and manifests itself in social inequality. Sin is a willful affront of the living God, who stands in condemnation of all humanity for their foolish pride: "All have sinned and fall short of the glory of God" (Rom. 3:23). Christ did not act merely to heal the estrangement of the self; Christ did not act only to rescue the innocent oppressed from guilty oppressors. Christ gave his life on the cross as an atoning sacrifice for the sins of all humanity, bearing on his shoulders the just condemnation of us all in our place and for our sakes: "All we like sheep have gone astray; we have all turned to our own way, and the LORD has laid on him the iniquity of us all" (Isa. 53:6). The cross of Jesus Christ is the end of all correlation theology, for it exposes the sheer folly of all human pretense to be in the right before God. Reconciliation with God is the heart of the gospel, not healing of the estranged self nor liberation of the oppressed. We are certainly made whole through faith in Christ; the poor are certainly delivered through the compassionate presence of Christ; the gospel is not indifferent to but addresses the real frailties of human existence and the political realities of unjust tyranny. It is Christ alone who makes humankind whole; it is Christ alone who visits the poor in their distress, bringing relief from suffering, including political liberation of the oppressed. But the rule of faith has always and everywhere seen these as fruits of reconciliation with God, not the very form of salvation itself. Like the ancient Gnostics attacked by Irenaeus, correlation theology takes biblical themes and places them in an alien context, with the result that the true content of scripture is warped beyond recognition. Where the religious right leads to an easy cultural Christianity, the religious left leads to an easy countercultural Christianity; both eliminate the offense of the gospel.

Fourth, the "hermeneutical suspicion" of liberation theology is not radical enough. Certainly it is true that white Western experience is no avenue to the divine. On that I am in full agreement with Cone. But it was only modern theological liberalism and fundamentalism that have made such a perverse claim; the historic faith of the church never based itself on "white Western experience" but on the self-revelation of God in Jesus Christ. Indeed, feminist theologians are right in this: not even the experience of the biblical writers, mostly male, is an avenue to God. The authority of scripture has nothing to do with the self-grounded experience of the biblical authors, who are everywhere presented in the Bible itself as frail and confused. There is no pure core to biblical experience; at the moment it was receiving the Ten Commandments from God on Mt. Sinai, Israel built the golden calf in rebellion against that very God (Exodus 32). The authority of scripture is grounded in the authority of Christ the exalted Lord, and its message is understood only in relation to his sovereign rule, through the presence of his Spirit. But here is the issue: In their criticism of others, why do liberation theologians not include themselves? Is there not in their self-exception a remarkable hubris, equally as self-deluded as the theological liberalism that gave rise to it? Is not liberation theology the cul-de-sac of the religious left in which the fury of moralistic self-righteousness is ultimately turned in upon itself? Granted that African-American Christians need a voice of their own in the theological community, especially in light of the rich heritage that stands behind them, why can't that voice be the voice of the gospel, joining in a common confession that includes Luther, Calvin, Wesley, and Athanasius, even though the African-American voice should be uniquely its own? Would not the universal church only be uplifted by such a genuinely new voice? Once again, the image of Dr. Martin Luther King Jr. stands brilliantly in the foreground, for somehow the genuine unity of Christians of all races that he taught and fostered is surely the only way forward for all theology, black and white.

And finally, the correlation theology of the religious left has saddled the church with the moral arrogance of good causes, which in a steady stream have distracted the church for several decades, one after the other. Has not the sheer collapse of Marxism, upon which virtually all liberation theologians placed their hopes, been a sure indication of the theological vacuity of such an approach? In his *Prophesy Deliverance!* Cornel West clearly and forthrightly rests the whole truth of the gospel on a correlation with Marxism: "Revolutionary Christian perspective and praxis must remain anchored in the prophetic Christian tradition in the Afro-American experience . . . and informed by the social theory and political praxis of progressive Marxism."[44] Surely West has seriously compromised the radical newness of the gospel by wrongly joining it to a totalitarian ideology of violence and oppression now rightly despised throughout the earth.

Moreover, liberation theology has openly espoused the use of violence as a tool for achieving those good causes. In the light of September 11, appeals to violence in support of good causes now seem highly suspicious. For on that day a "good cause" was carried through with murderous barbarism. Nearly three thousand human beings perished at the hands

44. West, 146.

of those who claimed to merge the will of God and the destruction of human life in the name of their righteous cause. Here I can only sharply disagree with Cone's rejection of the nonviolence of King, whose efforts on behalf of civil rights for blacks and all human beings shine like a light in the darkness. Violence for a "good cause" is now clear for what it is: it is terrorism, and it should be universally condemned by the church. As Moses himself discovered after killing the Egyptian, revolutionary violence is not the true way to social transformation (Exod. 1:11–14).

To be sure, the legacy of September 11 likewise condemns the "good causes" of the religious right, whose effort to eliminate the distinction between church and state equally contradicts the gospel. All correlation theology, left and right, gives rise to ideology; all ideology spawns "good causes" that quickly displace the gospel of Christ. The true God made known in Jesus Christ has nothing to do with the idols of ideology:

> Our God is in the heavens;
>   he does whatever he pleases.
> Their idols are silver and gold,
>   the work of human hands.
> They have mouths, but do not speak;
>   eyes, but do not see.
> They have ears, but do not hear;
>   noses, but do not smell.
> They have hands, but do not feel;
>   feet, but do not walk;
>   they make no sound in their throats.
> Those who make them are like them;
>   so are all who trust in them.
>
> O Israel, trust in the LORD!
>   He is their help and their shield. (Ps. 115:3–9)

The cross of Jesus Christ shatters all correlation theology. The cross condemns and bears away all moral arrogance, including every human claim to enter into partnership with God concerning his gracious purpose for human life. We do not live by triumphant ideology, whether conservative or liberal; we live by faith in Jesus Christ, and conformity to him is the one goal we seek. Not in the boastful pride of self-actualization but in humility is the true path of discipleship to be found. Only on this path is lasting joy; only on this path is genuine contentment; only on this path is the radical call of obedience to Christ with the whole person. Only through humility is there the transformation that results when the new world of God draws near, seizing human life for the joyful service of Christ in the world. At the end of the day our only word is humility: "But many who are first will be last, and the last will be first" (Mark 10:31).

Jesus Christ the crucified Lord is risen and now rules all reality. The gospel is not limited to private, interior life; the gospel has already transformed the whole of creation, including the common social life of humanity. How are we to obey Jesus Christ in the contemporary world? In my judgment, this is the burning issue of theological ethics of the divine command in our time and central to the very mission of the church in the world. My aim now is to give some initial bearings toward moving in a fresh direction.

As Christians, we share a common life with our fellow human beings. We share institutions of government, family, culture, economics, and law; we share the task of education; we share the joy of play. It is easy to discern where the church falls short in relation to the world. The role of the church is not to support the status quo as in the various versions of conservative evangelicalism. Nor is the role of the church to tear down the structures of society for the sake of human self-liberation, as in the various versions of liberation theology. Nor is withdrawal into the interior spaces of human piety the appropriate response; for that door is forever closed by the stunning challenge of Christ: "You are the light of the world. A city built on a hill cannot be hid. No one after lighting a lamp puts it under the bushel basket, but on the lampstand, and it gives light to all in the house. In the same way, let your works shine before others, so that they may see your good works and give glory to your Father in heaven" (Matt. 5:14–16). It is far more difficult to discern the path of faithful involvement in the common life of culture and society. There is no program for change in scripture, nor is there any room for the tyranny of good causes in the theological confession of the church. Nevertheless, the fact remains that faith is an explosive force for change in human society.

Faith is always active through real change in human society, not by eliminating every form of social structure but by a gradual humanizing of all dimensions of common life. Faith is the channel through which the explosive transformation of life is engendered in the world, for faith is the living unity of the church with Christ the risen Lord. The church of Jesus Christ must always engage the world through active involvement in social life, for its mission to do so is grounded in the claim of Christ himself. It does not happen by adopting principles or platforms of change, nor does it ever fall into the trap of endorsing change for its own sake. Not all change is good, and at times the best remedy is to hold the course. Nevertheless, the mainstream of the Christian church has never turned away from passionate concern for justice in society, nor has it tried to eliminate the distinction between the church and the world; it has tried rather to reshape the common life according to the energy and insight of faith. The great challenge to the church today is to engage the world free from the illusions of conservative and liberal ideology. We can do so with confidence in the future because we trust that God himself governs the social life of humankind. We cannot always see his hand at work, and at times the better part of wisdom is to remain silent or at least open-minded about the range of possibilities. We are weary of hasty solutions and pat answers, from both extremes of the theological spectrum. Moreover, the church does not know the right answer to every question, and on some issues there is plenty of room for tolerant disagreement within the church itself. Still, the exciting frontier of mission to the world is practical involvement within the limits of human understanding.

Indeed, the new world of God brings a new society, and those who belong to Jesus Christ are obliged to him to discern the shape of that new society in the struggle of faith. We believe in good government; we believe in a civil society; we believe in human rights for every human being on the earth, regardless of their religion; we believe in freedom for all peoples; we believe in the rule of law, not persons; we believe in the role of liberal education for the welfare of humanity; we believe in compassion for the poor; we believe in sharing the goodness of life with our neighbors on this planet; we believe in sharing concern for the health of the planet itself; we believe in democracy and despise all forms of human tyranny; we believe in the enjoyment of human creativity. Not by legislating morality nor by an ideology of good causes, but by the powerful role of example, we affirm the role of the church in the practical shaping of a new society, a challenge that even now awaits us.

The relationship between Christ and culture is best described as dialectical. The Christian church is in a give-and-take relationship to the surrounding world. On the one hand, we are the beneficiaries of our participation in the common life of human society. We are blessed by government that secures freedom of religion and protects citizens from radical evil; we are blessed by liberal education and freedom of speech; we are blessed by free exchange of ideas in a tolerant and open society. In all these ways, we see the hand of God at work in the gifts of human culture, and we are grateful for his bounty. On the other hand, Christian faith is called by Christ himself to act for transformation in society. Our role as Christians is to help reshape our common life more closely to the norm of divine justice and mercy. We engage in that role within the limits of human wisdom and ability and with open-minded flexibility concerning the range of possibilities. Still, we are not merely passive in relation to society but active, and our activity flows freely from our living faith in Jesus Christ as Lord of all reality. The history of the church confirms, despite regrettable mistakes, that Christians have played exactly that role wherever the gospel has gone in the earth. To be sure, we cannot build the kingdom of God; we are not given that ability, or that prerogative, for we are sinners. God alone builds his kingdom. Real transformation of human society is not a human possibility, but a gracious divine act transcending all moral effort. Nevertheless, we are called by Christ himself to critical engagement with society in mission to the world. We are not here as the conscience of the world; we are not here to win influence; we are not here to succeed in an agenda; we are here only to be faithful. Our mission is not a decision that we make but the definitive declaration of Christ himself that we cannot evade: "You are the salt of the earth" (Matt. 5:13). Ultimately, our confidence to be so engaged comes not from the moral arrogance of ideology but from our assurance of God's electing love in Jesus Christ. We live by prayer: "God give us the grace to accept with serenity the things that cannot be changed, courage to change the things that should be changed, and the wisdom to distinguish the one from the other."[45]

Transformation comes through wisdom. What is wisdom? In the church of Jesus Christ, we learn wisdom from the Bible, for Jesus Christ himself is the wisdom of God.[46] Wisdom unfolds in the basic tension of Christian existence. In Jesus Christ, God has restored the whole of creation; God has reconciled the whole world; God has already entered human life in order to transform it from the inside. God in Christ has already fashioned a new world: "For I am about to create new heavens and a new earth; the former things shall not be remembered or come to mind. . . . They shall build houses and inhabit them; they shall plant vineyards and eat their fruit" (Isa. 65:17, 21). "Then I saw a new heaven and a new earth . . . Then he said to me, 'It is done! I am the Alpha and the Omega, the beginning and the end'" (Rev. 21:1, 6). God's new world is utterly new; it cannot in any sense whatsoever be converted into the categories of the old. The new is not in any fashion a critical perspective from which to change the old. The new is irreducibly new, for the new is Jesus Christ the risen Lord. God's new world is received by faith, in which the Christian participates through the Spirit in the infinite blessings of the gospel. The gospel is greater than all creation, which is as nothing in comparison with the treasure of truth that it contains.

Yet the Christian lives in the midst of the old; we continue to share life with our fellow human beings on this planet. We continue to share with them in the structures of society and continue to feel the sorrows and enjoy the challenges of life in our world. Human life as a whole

45. Attributed to Reinhold Niebuhr.
46. In what follows, I have learned much from Davis, *Proverbs, Ecclesiastes*.

continues to flourish only in connection to the ecological health of the surrounding biosphere. The new world of God is not an "alternative community" to the old world, as if tearing down the old structures will automatically bring new being. Nor is the new world of God simply a pious affirmation of society's status quo coupled with a withdrawal into the interior space of private spirituality. Jesus Christ is the new world of God, for in him God's realm enters directly into human life in the mystery of God's gracious rule. The new world of God enters the old only as a gift, never as a human achievement. The presence of the new in the midst of the old is discerned through wisdom.

Wisdom affirms the goodness of God's creation as a gracious divine gift. The world is fallen, but it is not abandoned by God. There remain in it abundant signs of God's kindness in all things. Our search for the new humanity encompasses all peoples on earth; our celebration of the new society surrounds the whole of humankind. Wisdom exercises critical discernment in reflecting on the ways of God in human life. God's will is perfectly made known in Jesus Christ; to turn away from the clarity of his self-manifestation is always the way of folly. Nevertheless, we are not robots; we are called by God himself to use every power of our intellect and imagination in seeking the will of God in our world. We are, according to Paul, to discern (δοκιμαζειν) God's living will through critical examination and testing (cf. Rom. 12:2). Genuine obedience requires seasoned reflection. Wisdom is a divine gift and in no sense a human achievement; to look for wisdom in the human ability to find God is the ultimate folly, for only an idol can be found that way. Nevertheless, the gift of God brings with it the requirement for a disciplined human search. The paradox of divine wisdom is both gift and challenge: coming to us freely from God's mysterious grace, yet challenging us always to search eagerly for fresh understanding.

Wisdom searches for the right word at the right time and recognizes the abysmal failure of moral absolutes in abstraction from the living will of God. Wisdom recognizes the need for structures of authority in the world; it also recognizes the strong temptation to abuse power for the sake of self-enrichment. Wisdom sees the world in all its mysterious interconnection and defines excellence in terms of the ability to play a necessary role to the best of one's ability, not in terms of the defeat of one's neighbor. Wisdom sides with humility and despises moral arrogance and intransigence in all forms. Wisdom affirms the profound good of human friendship in a world where genuine connection is the rarest of gifts. Wisdom abhors a culture of consumption, in which the goods of the earth are hoarded and displayed for the sake of show; wisdom embraces a culture of shared life, in which the divine provision for human welfare is freely used for generous support of those in need. Wisdom is skeptical of any claim to speak the last word on a subject; there is always room for growth in learning, for the individual as well as for the community. Wisdom always avoids peer pressure and sticks to what is right no matter what social ostracism it may bring; yet wisdom also recognizes the temptations of isolation and receives with joy the sheer gift of common life. Wisdom never runs from the need to choose between relative goods, knowing that a desire for perfection in the things that matter most in life is usually a moral blind spot.

Wisdom admits the need for mystery and silence in the face of the unanswerable questions of life, questions that linger not to defeat human life but to enrich it. Wisdom always avoids the empty platitudes of the naive, but neither is it attracted to the self-confirming nihilism of the cynic. Wisdom celebrates the divine gift of human sexuality and exposes all forms of prudery as a rejection of God; yet wisdom also carefully discerns the limits of sexual expression in the unrestrained and binding commitment of love. Wisdom never views the acquisition of knowledge as an end in itself but always as a means to the art of living well in the world. Wisdom insists on accuracy in detail, yet it always takes in a broad perspective of the whole. Wisdom perceives the shape of authentic human happiness, which is that wisdom is itself the ultimate goal of life and contains in itself the true horizon of joy encompassing all experience.

Wisdom loves children and nourishes the free individuality of youth, but it also insists on the need for self-discipline, without which the marvelous gifts of God only go to waste. Wisdom loves diligence and foresight; for the sake of long-term gain it carefully eschews the lure of transient pleasure. Wisdom enjoins the care of the poor and needy, who are made in God's image. Wisdom withholds criticism that only demeans and destroys, yet it is willing to risk plain speaking when the good of the community will be served by frank and open exchange. Wisdom is conducive to self-reliance yet knows the irreplaceable value of companionship; it knows the joy of solitude yet reaches for the pleasure that comes only in human company. Wisdom receives the joyful delights of life as gracious divine gifts, yet it refuses to be enslaved by the sad inhumanity of addiction. Wisdom gets along and turns aside the power of anger and envy. Wisdom looks for peaceful balance in human relationship and abhors injustice. Wisdom rightly perceives the astonishing enjoyment to be found in the simplest pleasures of life: hard work, time spent with family and friends, the varied harmony of unfolding time. Wisdom loves fitting words yet never speaks more than is necessary in the given moment. Wisdom values the equal contribution of women in human society and insists on the just treatment of women throughout the global community.

Where does wisdom come from? Our answer can only be a paradox. On the one hand, wisdom is a gracious divine gift that can never be transformed into a self-grounded rational perspective. On the other hand, wisdom requires the devotion of one's whole life based upon the fear of God, which is the proper acknowledgment that God's unlimited power controls all things far beyond human insight and ability and that we are accountable to him for the use of our gifts and resources. Wisdom is sought and proclaimed in the Christian community; yet wisdom is declared in the heart of human society, at the intersection of the problems and challenges of life in our world. Jesus Christ alone is the wisdom of God; yet the light of Christ illumines the entire cosmos and surrounds the daily experience of all humankind.

May God grant a rebirth of wisdom in his church and world in the extraordinary times in which we live.

Abbreviations

ACW   *Ancient Christian Writers*, edited by Johannes Quasten and Joseph C. Plumpe. New York: Newman.

ANF   *Ante-Nicene Fathers*, edited by Alexander Roberts and James Donaldson. Reprint Grand Rapids: Eerdmans, 1996.

BC   *The Book of Concord*, translated and edited by Theodore G. Tappert. Philadelphia: Fortress, 1959.

BTONT   Brevard S. Childs. *Biblical Theology of the Old and New Testaments*. Minneapolis: Fortress, 1992.

Cat   *Catechism of the Catholic Church*. Liguori, MO: Liguori, 1994.

CD   Karl Barth. *Church Dogmatics*, edited by G. W. Bromiley and T. F. Torrance. 13 vols. Edinburgh: T & T Clark, 1936–1969.

Conf   Office of the General Assembly, Presbyterian Church (USA). *The Book of Confessions*. Louisville, KY: OGA, 1994.

LCC   *Library of Christian Classics*, ed. John Baillie, John T. McNeill, and Henry P. Van Dusen. Philadelphia: Westminster Press, 1953–.

Leith   *The Creeds of the Churches*, rev. ed., edited by John Leith. Atlanta: John Knox, 1973.

LW   *Luther's Works*, American ed., edited by Jaroslav Pelikan and Helmut T. Lehmann. St. Louis: Concordia; Philadelphia: Fortress, 1955–.

NPNF 1   *Nicene and Post-Nicene Fathers*, 1st ser., edited by Philip Schaff. Reprint Grand Rapids: Eerdmans, 1996.

NPNF 2   *Nicene and Post-Nicene Fathers*, 2nd ser., edited by Philip Schaff and Henry Mace. Reprint Grand Rapids: Eerdmans, 1996.

ST   Thomas Aquinas. *Summa Theologica*, translated by Fathers of the English Dominican Province. 5 vols. Reprint Allen, TX: Christian Classics, 1981.

Works Cited

Abraham, William J. *Canon and Criterion in Christian Theology.* Oxford: Oxford University Press, 1998.

Aquinas, Thomas. *Summa Theologiae: A Concise Translation.* Edited by Timothy McDermott. Westminster, MD: Christian Classics, 1989.

Augustine. *The Catechising of the Uninstructed.* In NPNF 1.3.283–314.

———. *Faith, Hope, and Charity.* In ACW 3.

———. *On Christian Doctrine.* Translated by D. W. Robertson Jr. Indianapolis: Bobbs-Merrill, 1958.

———. *On the Morals of the Catholic Church.* In NPNF 1.4.41–63.

———. *On the Trinity.* In NPNF 1.3.1–228.

Barr, James. *The Concept of Biblical Theology.* London: SCM Press, 1999.

Barth, Karl. *Dogmatics in Outline.* Translated by G. T. Thompson. New York: Harper and Row, 1959.

———. "The Strange New World within the Bible." In *The Word of God and the Word of Man,* translated by Douglas Horton. New York: Harper and Row, 1956.

Bavinck, Herman. *Our Reasonable Faith.* Translated by Henry Zylstra. Reissued Grand Rapids: Baker Book House, 1977.

Bonaventure. *The Breviloquium.* In *The Works of St. Bonaventure,* vol. 2, translated by Jose de Vinck. Paterson, NJ: St. Anthony Guild, 1963.

Bonhoeffer, Dietrich. *The Cost of Discipleship.* Translated by R. H. Fuller. New York: Simon and Schuster, 1959.

Brueggemann, Walter. *The Prophetic Imagination.* Philadelphia: Fortress, 1978.

Calvin, John. *Institutes of the Christian Religion,* 2 vols. LCC 20–21.

Childs, Brevard S. *Biblical Theology in Crisis.* Philadelphia: Westminster, 1970.

————. *Introduction to the Old Testament as Scripture.* Philadelphia: Fortress, 1979.

————. *The New Testament as Canon.* Philadelphia: Fortress, 1984.

Chrysostom, John. *Six Books on the Priesthood.* In NPNF 1.9.33–83.

Cone, James. *God of the Oppressed.* Minneapolis: Seabury, 1975.

Cyril of Alexandria. *On the Unity of Christ.* Translated by John Anthony McGuckin. Crestwood, NY: St. Vladimir's Seminary Press, 2000.

Davis, Ellen F. *Imagination Shaped.* Valley Forge, PA: Trinity Press International, 1995.

————. *Proverbs, Ecclesiastes, and the Song of Songs.* Louisville, KY: Westminster John Knox, 2000.

Donne, John. *Sermons on the Psalms and Gospels.* Edited by Evelyn M. Simpson. Berkeley: University of California Press, 1967.

Frei, Hans. *The Eclipse of Biblical Narrative.* New Haven, CT: Yale University Press, 1974.

————. *The Identity of Jesus Christ.* Philadelphia: Fortress Press, 1975.

Gagnon, Paul. *The Bible and Homosexual Practice.* Nashville: Abingdon, 2001.

Gilbert, Martin. *History of the Twentieth Century.* New York: William Morrow, 2001.

Gilson, Étienne. *Reason and Revelation in the Middle Ages.* New York: Charles Scribner's Sons, 1938.

Haegglund, Bengt. *History of Theology.* Translated by Gene J. Lund. St. Louis: Concordia Publishing House, 1968.

Hall, Joseph. *The Works of the Right Reverend Joseph Hall, D.D.* 10 vols. Reprint New York: AMS Press, 1969.

Harnack, Adolf von. *Outlines of the History of Dogma.* Translated by Edwin Knox Mitchell. Boston: Beacon, 1957.

————. *What Is Christianity?* Translated by Thomas Bailey Saunders. New York: Harper and Row, 1957.

Henry, Carl F. H. *God, Revelation, and Authority,* vol. 2. Waco, TX: Word, 1976.

Heppe, Heinrich. *Reformed Dogmatics.* Revised and edited by Ernst Bizer, translated by G. T. Thomson. Reprint Grand Rapids: Baker Book House, 1978.

Hodge, Charles. *Systematic Theology.* 3 vols. Reprint Grand Rapids: Eerdmans, 1973.

Hodgson, Peter C., and Robert H. King. *Christian Theology.* 2nd ed. Philadelphia: Fortress, [1982] 1985.

Irenaeus. *Against Heresies.* In ANF 1:315–567.

Jenkins, Philip. "The Next Christianity." *Atlantic Monthly* 290, no. 3 (October 2002): 53–68.

John of Damascus. *Exposition of the Orthodox Faith.* In NPNF 2.9.1–101.

Kelly, J. N. D. *Early Christian Doctrines*. Rev. ed. San Francisco: Harper and Row, 1978.

Kelsey, David. "The Bible and Christian Theology." *Journal of the American Academy of Religion* 48 (September 1980): 385–402.

———. *The Uses of Scripture in Recent Theology*. Philadelphia: Fortress, 1975.

King, Martin Luther Jr. *The Autobiography of Martin Luther King Jr.* Edited by Clayborne Carson. New York: Warner, 1998.

Kuyper, Abraham. *Sacred Theology*. Translated by Rev. J. Henrik de Vries. Wilmington, DE: Associated Publishers and Authors, n.d.

Lessing, Gotthold Ephraim. *Lessing's Theological Writings*. Translated by Henry Chadwick. Stanford, CA: Stanford University Press, 1956.

Lindbeck, George. *The Nature of Doctrine*. Philadelphia: Westminster Press, 1984.

Locke, John. *The Reasonableness of Christianity*. Edited and abridged by I. T. Ramsey. Stanford, CA: Stanford University Press, 1958.

Lohse, Bernhard. *A Short History of Christian Doctrine*. Translated by Ernest Stoeffler. Philadelphia: Fortress, 1966.

———. *Martin Luther's Theology*. Translated and edited by Roy A. Harrisville. Minneapolis: Fortress, 1999.

Luther, Martin. *Christian Liberty*. Translated by Harold J. Grimm. Rev. ed. Philadelphia: Fortress, 1957.

———. *Lectures on Romans*. In LCC 15.

———. *Martin Luther: Selections From His Writings*. Edited by John Dillenberger. Garden City, NY: Anchor, 1961.

MacDonald, Neil B. *Karl Barth and the Strange New World within the Bible*. Carlisle, UK: Paternoster, 2000.

Machen, J. Gresham. *Christianity and Liberalism*. Grand Rapids: Eerdmans, 1923.

Melanchthon, Philipp. *Loci Communes Theologici*. In LCC 19.18–152.

———. *On Christian Doctrine: Loci Communes 1555*. Translated and edited by Clyde L. Manschreck. New York: Oxford University Press, 1965.

Mouw, Richard. *The God Who Commands*. Notre Dame, IN: University of Notre Dame Press, 1990.

Niebuhr, H. Richard. *Christ and Culture*. New York: Harper and Row, 1951.

Niebuhr, Reinhold. "Why Is Communism So Evil?" In *The World Crisis and American Responsibility*. New York: Association Press, 1958.

———. "Why the Christian Church Is Not Pacifist." In *The Essential Reinhold Niebuhr*, edited by Robert McAfee Brown, 102–119. New Haven, CT: Yale University Press, 1986.

Oberman, Heiko. *Forerunners of the Reformation*. Philadelphia: Fortress Press, 1966 and 1981.

Old, Hughes Oliphant. *The Reading and Preaching of the Scriptures*. Grand Rapids: Eerdmans, 1998–.

Origen. *De Principiis*. In ANF 4, 239–382.

Parker, T. H. L. *Calvin's Preaching*. Louisville, KY: Westminster John Knox, 1992.

Packer, J. I. *"Fundamentalism" and the Word of God*. Grand Rapids: Eerdmans, 1958.

Pelikan, Jaroslav. *The Christian Tradition: A History of the Development of Doctrine*. 5 vols. Chicago: University of Chicago Press, 1971–1989.

Preus, James Samuel. *From Shadow to Promise*. Cambridge, MA: Harvard University Press, 1964.

Quasten, Johannes. *Patrology*. 4 vols. Utrecht: Spectrum, 1975–1986.

Ritschl, Albrecht. *Three Essays*. Translated by Philip Hefner. Philadelphia: Fortress, 1972.

Ruether, Rosemary Radford. *Sexism and God-Talk*. Boston: Beacon, 1983.

Ryrie, Charles Caldwell. *Dispensationalism Today*. Chicago: Moody Press, 1965.

Schaff, Philip. *Creeds of Christendom*. 3 vols. Reprint Grand Rapids: Baker Book House, 1977.

Schleiermacher, Friedrich. *The Christian Faith*. Edited by H. R. Mackintosh and J. S. Stewart. Philadelphia: Fortress, 1976.

Schmid, Heinrich. *Doctrinal Theology of the Evangelical Lutheran Church*. Translated by Charles A. Hay and Henry E. Jacobs. Third edition, revised. Minneapolis: Augsburg Publishing House, 1961.

The Teaching of the Twelve Apostles. In ANF 6:377–82.

Tertullian. *On Prescription against Heretics*. In ANF 3:243–65.

Tillich, Paul. *Systematic Theology*. 3 vols. Chicago: University of Chicago Press, 1951–1963.

Turner, H. E. W. *The Pattern of Christian Truth*. London: Mowbray, 1954.

Vincent of Lerins. *The Commonitory*. In NPNF 2.11.131–56.

Ware, Timothy. *The Orthodox Church*. Middlesex, UK: Penguin, 1963.

Warfield, Benjamin Breckenridge. *The Inspiration and Authority of the Bible*. Philadelphia: Presbyterian and Reformed, 1948.

Webster, John. *Holy Scripture: A Dogmatic Sketch*. Cambridge: Cambridge University Press, 2003.

West, Cornel. *Prophesy Deliverance!* Philadelphia: Westminster Press, 1982.

Wolterstorff, Nicholas. "The Migration of the Theistic Arguments: From Natural Theology to Evidentialist Apologetics." In *Rationality, Religious Belief, and Moral Commitment*, edited by Robert Audi and William J. Wainwright, 38–81. Ithaca, NY: Cornell University Press, 1986.